The All-American Aquatic Handbook: Your Passport to Lifetime Fitness

Jane Katz

City University of New York:
John Jay Community College
of Criminal Justice

Allyn and Bacon

Boston London Toronto Sydney Tokyo Singapore

To my parents, Dorothea and Leon,
who brought the gospel of swimming to their children,
family, friends, and the community at large.
Through their love and devotion for more than one-half century,
they have introduced and taught the benefits of water
for physical fitness and good health.
Aquatics is for everyone—for lifetime wellness
into the 21st century!

Senior Editor: Suzy Spivey
Editorial Assistant: Lisa Davidson
Marketing Manager: Anne Harvey
Editorial-Production Administrator: Deborah Brown
Text Design and Composition: Denise Hoffman, Glenview Studios
Composition Buyer: Linda Cox
Manufacturing Buyer: Aloka Rathnam
Cover Design: Suzanne Harbison
Illustrator: Ethan Berry

A Simon & Schuster Company
Needham Heights, MA 02194

Library of Congress Cataloging-in-Publication Data

Katz, Jane.
The aquatic handbook for lifetime fitness / Jane Katz.
p. cm.
Includes index.
ISBN 0-205-19990-9 (pbk. : alk. paper)
1. Aquatic exercises—Handbooks, manuals, etc. 2. Swimming—Handbooks, manuals, etc. 3. Physical fitness—Handbooks, manuals, etc. I. Title.
GV838.53.E94K38 1996
613.7'16—dc20 95-39144
CIP

Printed in the United States of America

10 9 8 7 6 5 4 3 2 1 00 99 98 97 96 95

Contents

Preface

When I began swimming as a young girl, recreation and competition were my personal goals. But from the very beginning I had the total support of my parents. In our house, swimming was a family affair.

Regardless of the season, Papa Katz, Mama Katz, and the four Katz children trooped off to one of the New York City Parks Department pools for their free dip in the neighborhood watering hole. The outdoor pool was our country club in the summer, and in the winter the indoor pool at the facility was our health club. We learned our strokes, lapped, practiced, played water games, and had a great time. My father, a swimming buff from the age of 14 when he was saved from drowning, led his family on a course of lifetime fitness through swimming. In the 1950s when he started the regimen, rigorous training was understood to mean sports competition; it now means, as *The All-American Aquatic Handbook: Your Passport to Lifetime Fitness* shows, both good mental and good physical health.

Good health as a result of swimming does not mean you have to be in training for a triathlon. Today physical fitness through swimming is for everyone; programs ranging from mild to vigorous exercise are available to everyone. Across the country, schools, health clubs, community recreation centers, spas, Ys, and aquatic facilities offer a variety of aquatic fitness activities.

For over 30 years I have taught swimming in the City University of New York system, and am presently at John Jay College of Criminal Justice. These colleges represent a varied student body from all over New York and all over the country with a large range of ability and experience and with ages ranging from eighteen to eighty. In my years of teaching, I have developed a very effective group of water exercise techniques which I call WETs. What I have done is to translate what has worked on land for general physical and aerobic workouts to water. In addition, I have created the WETs to relate directly to learning and improving swim strokes.

These water exercises and drills are spelled out, step by step, in the handbook. In addition, there are prescribed workouts that reinforce the drills and techniques; a beginning swimmer, an infrequent swimmer, or an advanced swimmer can set up a program of laps for improving their strokes and health. An aquatic fitness program can be individually tailored from this handbook and carried out at any pool or open water setting.

The handbook is arranged in a modular format and covers aquatics—its history, preparation for entering the water, and building blocks—stroke techniques; lap fitness training; water exercises for deep and shallow water; additional water fitness activities, such as diving, synchronized swimming, cross training, and pool games. Also covered are ancillary topics which work toward setting the framework of a lifetime fitness activity, such as safety regulations for pool and open-water swimming, swimming tips at various stages of the lifespan, nutrition, and how to swim with physical and medical disabilities. Appendixes at the end of the handbook list resources for classes, training, umbrella associations, gear, competitions, and more. There are illustrations and photos throughout the handbook. A companion video is also available to use with the handbook.

The All-American Aquatic Handbook: Your Passport to Lifetime Fitness came about as a result of many people to whom I offer a collective thank you. They include: Pat Berland; Ethan Berry; Peter Blume; Ted Bolen; Deborah Brown; Pat Collins; Herbert Erlanger, M.D.; Donald Farber; Donal Farley; Elaine Fincham; Anton Fig; Delia Goldberg; the Guzman family; Anne Goldstein; Fran Hare; Anne Harvey; Denise Hoffman; the aquatic students and staff of John Jay College; Austen, Arden, and Paul Katz; Douglas Kirkland; Elaine Kuperberg; Stephen Kuperberg; Susan Larkin, Ph.D.; Shane Newmark; Carlet Oberley; Speedo®; and Suzy Spivey.

See you poolside.

Jane Katz

MEDICAL DISCLAIMER

Swimming and other physical activities are often strenuous and require good health for participation. Do not engage in this or any other exercise program without first consulting your physician.

Unit I

Introduction to Aquatics

Aquatics has its own unique progression of skills, as does any academic subject. Unit I provides the information needed to master the fundamental components and techniques of movement in the water. Chapter 1 introduces the history and benefits of water fitness. It also covers the properties of water, and the scientific principles which apply to aquatics. Chapter 2 provides information on practical matters such as swim gear and equipment, workout and training principles, as well as swimming pool health and safety guidelines. Chapter 3 presents the building blocks of aquatics: warm-ups, the elements of breathing, floating, and treading water. These basic skills are the foundation of successful progression in learning any swimming and/or water exercise activity.

This introductory unit provides an overview for acquiring a lifelong recreational and health activity which can enhance many areas of daily living. Whether in a class for personal fitness, or to increase swimming skills, or to help meet a physical education requirement, swimming and aquatic fitness will open new horizons in health and enjoyment.

Chapter 1

History and Hydrodynamics of Aquatics

Water Fitness

Webster's dictionary defines **water** as the colorless, transparent liquid occurring on earth as rivers, lakes, oceans, and so on, and falling from the clouds as rain. Approximately two-thirds of the earth is composed of water. Webster's defines **fitness** as the condition of being fit; suitability, appropriateness, and healthiness. When you combine these two into **water fitness,** you create an enjoyable, low-impact, affordable component of better health.

The Romans did it. . . . The English did it. . . . An American statesman did it. And some have written about it as well. For centuries, people have swum and engaged in water sports, and from all written accounts, they were quite expert at it. Englishman Christopher Middleton wrote the first swimming instruction book, *A Short Introduction to Learne to Swimme* in 1595. In 1726, Benjamin Franklin published *The Art of Swimming Made Safe, Easy, Pleasant and Healthful by the Instruction Set Forth Herein*. The educator Frank Eugene Dalton in his 1912 book, *Swimming Scientifically Taught*, wrote that swimming "reduces corpulency (obesity), improves the figure, expands the lungs, improves the circulation of the blood, builds up general health," in addition to having special benefits for "nervous people."

Aquatics is the umbrella term for an activity or physical exercise done in the water. Aquatic activities fall into many categories, such as swimming, water exercise, synchronized swimming, diving, open water swimming, water polo, as well as water therapy. Each of these can be achieved by anyone, from a novice to an advanced competitor.

Water exercise, now considered a standard in aquatics, has roots in the elegant "water cure" spas popular in Europe in the nineteenth century. In North America, hydropathy, the taking of hot and/or cold baths, was prescribed for a number of ailments. In the United States, the most ardent proponent of water therapy was President Franklin Delano Roosevelt, who was struck with polio in early adulthood and lost the use of his legs. During his presidency he was a frequent visitor to Warm Springs, Georgia, for exercise and relaxation, where he especially enjoyed the swimming pool. Newspapers and newsreels often photographed him while swimming.

Today, water activities are used as part of sports medicine and physical therapy programs and often in rehabilitation of sports injuries. Recent developments in rehabilitation and sports medicine include deep-water running and adaptive aquatics. Water activities, as a therapeutic medium, are also used by people with physical, mental, and emotional disabilities.

Synchronized swimming, now an Olympic sport, is the elite form of water exercise. Its figures and movements require strength, stamina, and timing. Called *water ballet* in the 1940s, it was popularized by swim champions and motion picture stars Esther Williams, who appeared in lavish Hollywood aquatic extravaganzas, and by Buster Crabbe and Johnny Weismuller, who starred as Tarzan.

The connection between health and exercise is not a new idea. Hippocrates and Galen, medical men of ancient Greece, were aware of the relationship between physical fitness and well-being. In the late 1960s, Dr. Kenneth H. Cooper popularized a name for this interaction. He called it **aerobics,** which he defined as the positive correlation between sustained physical activity and cardiovascular health. Medical studies since have indicated the positive effect that exercise has on general health and psychological well-being. This research confirms that physical fitness should be a way of life.

As the exercise boom of the 1970s and 1980s peaked and the baby boom generation matured, a growing need for moderation in fitness choices became evident, due in part to injuries from high-impact exercise. What was missing was a fitness activity that combined stretching, aerobic conditioning, strength training, and flexibility. Exercising in water was the answer. Lap and fitness swimmers have increased in numbers, and as many as 30 million Americans are swimming laps as their exercise of choice.

However, approximately 50 percent of the population stays on the sidelines. These people do not swim well enough to get an aerobic workout. Many do not know how to swim or have had a bad experience in the water and are afraid to learn how to swim or even be in the water.

Becoming familiar with water exercise bridges the gap between being reluctant to go near the water and eventually learning to swim. Not only is aerobic benefit derived from water exercise, but comfort and self-confidence in the water can grow. These lead, in turn, to the skills and techniques that develop into efficient swimming.

Fitness Benefits of Aquatic Exercise

According to the President's Council on Physical Fitness and Sports, people who are physically fit generally enjoy a happier, healthier, and more productive life. Medical research has confirmed that a consistent and enjoyable fitness program can prolong and enhance the quality of one's life.

A fitness workout produces a physiological and psychological exhilaration. As the workout proceeds, **endorphins**—natural opiate-like hormones manufactured by the body—are released into the system. The result is a feeling of well-being, and lots of energy. Some experts believe that these natural mood boosters are effective in helping to combat depression, and produce a natural "high" that may extend throughout the day.

The components of physical fitness include strength, muscular endurance, flexibility, body composition (muscle/fat ratio), motor coordination, and cardiovascular efficiency. They can all be improved through swimming and exercising in water.

Swimming in warm water or warm weather helps restore the body. Water is buoyant. It is resistant. It is aerobic. It is soothing. It is refreshing. It is sensuous. It is mentally restorative. It is relaxing. And, it is fun.

A body's range of motion, energy expenditure, and coordination may be enhanced in water. Swimming and water exercise utilize large muscle groups: the upper body muscles including the triceps, the biceps, the deltoids, and the trapezius; the middle body muscles including the abdominals, the intercostal, and the latissmus dorsi; and the lower body muscles including the gluteal, the quadriceps, the hamstrings, and the gastrocemius muscles.

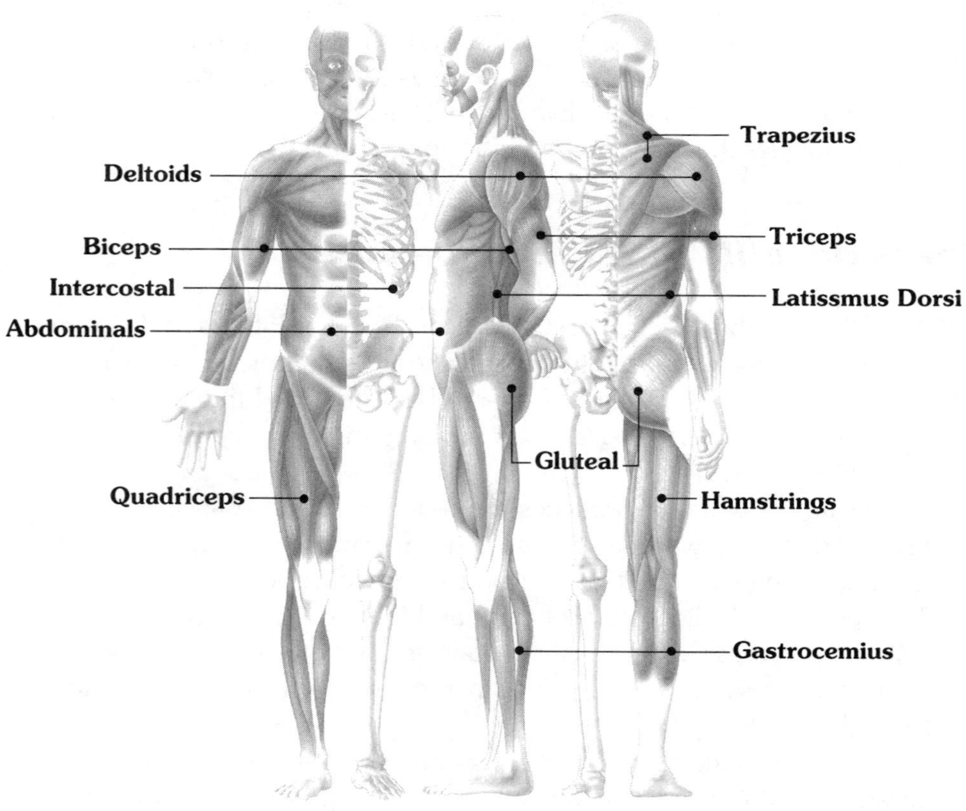

Muscle Groups

The cardiovascular system has to work hard to provide these large muscles with oxygen-rich blood. The condition of the heart and lungs improves with consistent use, and the body adapts by using oxygen more efficiently. This is the aerobic conditioning effect. Being in water makes a person keenly aware of his or her anatomy and what water can do for a body's total physical development.

Exercising in water burns approximately 500 calories per hour. However, many variables can alter this figure. They include: weight, height, position in the water (horizontal or vertical), water temperature, water depth, use of resistance equipment, as well as the physical condition of the person exercising, and the intensity of the workout. Each of these factors affects the amount of energy the exerciser expends during his or her workout. The bottom line is that a water fitness program done consistently, three times a week on alternate days, helps to promote general fitness and can be, as well, an important part of the weight loss process if that is a goal.

What Is Water to the Swimmer?

As mentioned earlier, water is buoyant and resistant. When swimming, the resistance or force of water must be overcome if forward movement is to be accomplished. The resistant forces include: drag resistance, frictional resistance, and turbulence resistance.

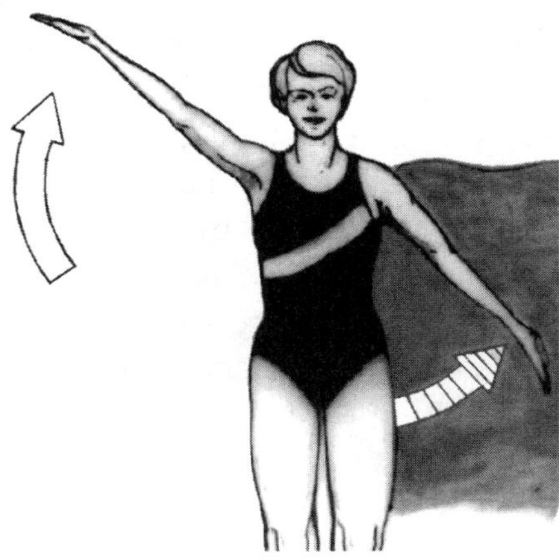

Resistance

Movement in water has twelve times greater resistance than movement in air. Molecules in air are relatively few and randomly spaced, whereas, in water, molecules are more closely structured. In order to move through water, one must displace the water or move it—either vertically, horizontally, or circularly. This multi-directional movement requires considerable effort which over time strengthens the heart and muscles in their ability to utilize oxygen.

When swimming, either in a pool or in an open body of water, the medium of water provides a superior environment for exercise. The buoyant support of the water allows a person to move without jarring joints, muscles, and organs. The buoyant effect also improves circulation because the water is applying constant pressure, a kind of massage, on every part of the body. The water also enables the body to be more flexible. In neck-deep water, a body weighs one-tenth what it weighs on land. For people who are overweight, out of shape, pregnant, or have back or joint problems, water is an accommodating and beneficial environment.

In addition exercising in water produces an "air conditioning" effect on the body because of water's evaporation. The body keeps cool. This permits a person to sustain longer exercise periods, which, in turn, helps to work toward cardiovascular fitness.

Hydrodynamics: The Physics of Water and Swimming

Perhaps, your reaction to the above heading is, "I thought this was fitness swimming, not science!" Remember, if you were studying ship design, you would certainly expect to study the properties of water and its interaction with the structure, surface material, and power plant of a ship. In swimming, the swimmer is traveling in the same medium (water), and the body is both the vessel and the power plant. Hydrodynamics is the branch of the physical sciences pertaining to the motion and action of water (and other liquids and gases).

Archimedes' Principle: Buoyancy

The Greek mathematician and inventor Archimedes (c. 287–212 BC) stated the main principle that applies to both cruise ships and swimmers: *An immersed object is buoyed up (lifted) by a force equal to the weight of the water displaced.* This principle is very plausible. Water originally occupied the region now occupied by the displacing object. That water was at rest, that is, was in equilibrium between the downward pull of the earth (its weight) and the pressure on it from the surrounding water. When the water is *replaced* by an object (a ship or a person) the water surrounding the replacing object cannot tell the difference and continues to push upward with the same force as it exerted on the displaced water. This upward force is called **buoyant force.**

Whether an object placed in water floats or sinks depends on both the shape of the object and the material of which it is made. A good example is a cargo ship carrying a load of heavy machinery. The shape of the ship is deliberately designed for considerable displacement of water in order to develop a large buoyant force, whereas if the cargo of heavy machinery were placed directly in the water, it would immediately sink.

Specific Gravity

The ability of a person to float (without the aid of a flotation device) is associated with the property known as **specific gravity.** This is defined as the ratio of the weight of a given volume of a material to the weight of the same volume of water. The specific gravity of water itself is 1.0. Our bodies are composed of bone, muscle, body fluids, and adipose tissue (that is, fat). Bone and muscle have a specific gravity slightly greater than 1.0, body fluids about 1.0, and adipose tissue less than 1.0. Therefore, the ability to float without sustaining motion is influenced by individual body build.

The ability to float is *not* essential in order to swim on the surface of the water! The ability to stay on the surface of the water is contingent on **dynamic forces,** that is, forces caused by motion.

The ability to float or to almost float depends on the specific gravity of each person and varies because of the different distribution of the four body constituents. Most people have a specific gravity either slightly less than 1.0 and therefore float, or slightly greater than 1.0 and therefore require either inflating the lungs to make the average specific gravity less than 1.0 or moving the hands and legs to produce upward dynamic forces.

When learning to swim, rather than just staying afloat, the details of the position assumed by the body either in the face down (prone) position or on the back (supine) position are important. This depends on the particular distribution of the four body constituents in a person and on the swimmer's **center of gravity** and **center of buoyancy.**

The center of gravity is the one point on which the total weight of an object is concentrated and the movement of this point will determine the general movement of the object as a whole or the **center of mass**

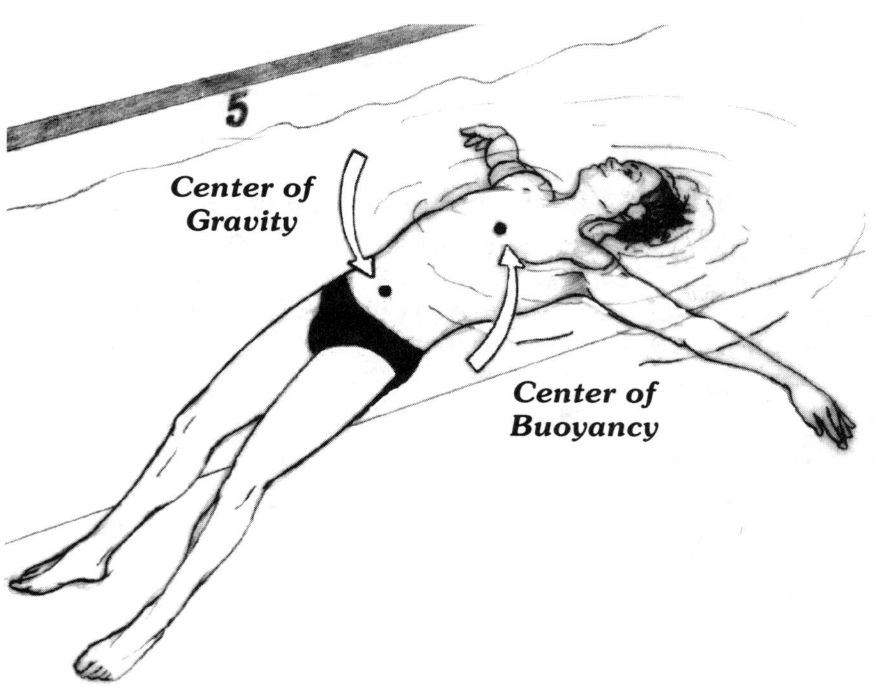

of an object. Physicists have an equation for calculating the location of the center of gravity. For our purposes, it is the location of the point where the object balances. For the human body it is *roughly* located at the navel. (A dancer will support another dancer overhead at this point.)

Another important point in dealing with either ship design or swimming is the center of buoyancy of a submerged object. This is the center of gravity of the water displaced by the object. Since water is of *uniform* density and the human body is not, this is *not* the same as the center of gravity of a submerged object. When these two centers do not coincide, the object tends to *rotate* about a point halfway between them. For the human body in the prone float position, the center of buoyancy is located *roughly* in the chest due to the low specific gravity of the air-filled lungs. The center of gravity is above the center of buoyancy, for instance, when someone stands up in a small rowboat or canoe and the boat becomes unstable and starts to capsize. In the case of a swimmer, controlling the position of the center of buoyancy and center of gravity by movement of the limbs and head is what is needed. This aquatic handbook focuses on learning to control the position of the centers of gravity and buoyancy by body movement.

Resistant Forces

Buoyant forces help the swimmer, but resistant forces in the water, defined as drag resistance, frictional resistance, and turbulence resistance, must be overcome.

- **Drag resistance** is caused by the mass of the body pushing water ahead of it. In swimming, drag resistance is overcome by assuming a streamlined body position.
- **Frictional resistance** is caused by the water washing over the body, the swimming suit, and the hair. Smoother materials for swimming suits and sleek swimming caps for both men and women help to reduce the force of friction. Top competitive swimmers even "shave down" for important competitions.

Wave Resistance

- **Turbulence** or **wave resistance** is usually caused by other swimmers splashing in the water. As swimming skills improve, smooth, elegant stroking and hand control keep wave resistance to a minimum. State-of-the-art lane lines in a pool are designed to absorb turbulence.

Newton's Laws: Three Laws of Motion

Isaac Newton (1642–1727) is considered the father of modern physics. Newton's Laws of Motion apply to a swimmer's motion as well as to all moving objects, from stars to electrons. Here is how Newton's laws apply to swimming.

- Newton's **First Law of Motion** states: *A body at rest tends to remain at rest; a body in motion tends to remain in motion unless compelled by force to change its state of rest or motion.*

  What this says for any swimmer is that when making a forward push-off in a streamlined body position from the wall of a pool or bottom of a pool, a swimmer will coast or glide without moving either arms or legs.

- Newton's **Second Law of Motion** (modified) states: *The acceleration of a body is proportional to the net force applied to it and inversely proportional to its mass.*

The requirement for swimmers is to maximize acceleration or forward motion, use muscle power, and learn to reduce the resistant forces.

- Newton's **Third Law of Motion** states: *For every action (force) there is an equal (and opposite) reaction force.*

  In swimming, this means that as hard as you push back on the water, the water will push you forward.

Bernoulli's Equation: The Lift Law

A final and subtle physical law, very applicable to swimming, is Bernoulli's equation (established by Bernoulli, 1700–1782). This equation, which is actually an application of Newton's laws to liquids and gases, is the basis of the design of airplane wings. The air flowing over the top of a curved wing will travel a longer path than the air traveling along the straighter lower section of the wing. According to Bernoulli's equation, when a fluid is moving faster, it exerts less pressure. All the molecules of air starting at the leading edge of the wing meet up again at the trailing edge of the wing. This causes the air to flow faster at the top of the wing because these molecules have a further distance to travel; this top air has lower pressure than at the bottom of the wing. The difference in pressure is the source of the *lift* force of the wing. In swimming, the faster one swims, the higher the swimmer rides in the water.

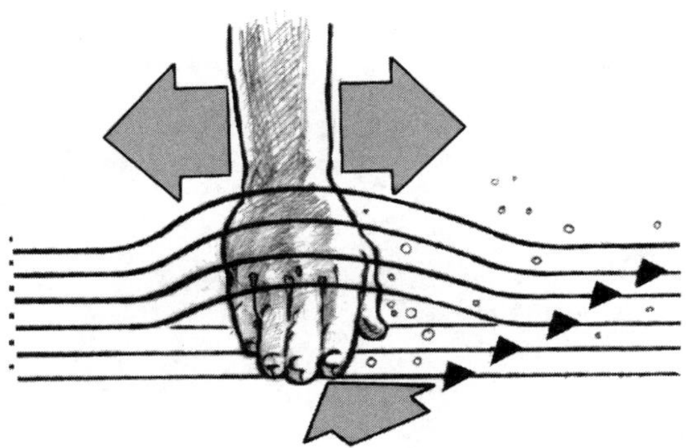

Bernoulli's Lift Law

Experience Bernoulli's Lift Law by standing in water with forearm and hand 6 inches below water, parallel to water's surface. Move hand back and forth in a steady rhythm, with hand cupped slightly, simulating the shape of an airplane wing. Feel carefully for a gentle *upward* lift exerted by the water on the palm of the hand.

TRY THIS: *Try blowing air across the top of a light piece of paper, 3 inches × 5 inches, held the long way. The paper should lift slightly if you maintain a steady, strong air stream.*

If swimming is thought of as an application of these laws of matter and motion in which energy is applied to obtain motion and the body is the energy source, you will enjoy and benefit from this handbook.

Chapter 2

Preparing for Aquatic Fitness

Preparation for an aquatic fitness workout means never having to say "I forgot my suit." This chapter delineates important swim gear and equipment, workout and training principles, and pool safety and courtesy.

Gearing Up

Swim Equipment

There is a vast array of aquatic fitness gear currently on the market. Many choices of style, color, and materials are available in several price ranges. See Appendix B for sources for major brands of all types of equipment.

A **swimsuit** should be comfortable, lightweight, and sleek. The most comfortable suits are made of Lycra; the most durable are nylon. New fabric blends are now on the market as well. Women's suits are usually sized by chest measurement and are designed to help streamline the body. There are many back and strap placement designs for a suitable fit. Men's swimsuit sizes correspond to waistline measurement. To prolong the life of a suit, rinse it thoroughly after each use.

A **bathing cap** protects the hair. To keep hair dry, choose a snug fitting bathing cap made of either latex rubber, Lycra, silicone, or a combination of materials that covers the ears. Lycra caps are not waterproof and can be worn to restrain long hair or give extra protection under another cap.

Goggles improve underwater vision (there's a whole new universe underwater!) and can enhance aquatic enjoyment. A well-fitting pair makes a big difference. A number of features should be considered: lens tint (light for indoor, dark for outdoor), nose piece and strap placement, anti-fog lenses, foam cushioning, and allowance for peripheral vision. The shape of one's face will influence the choice of goggles that fit. Goggles are necessary for people who wear contact lenses. Goggles with ready-made prescription lenses are available to accommodate nearsightedness. They can be obtained at most sporting goods stores.

A **waterproof watch** that indicates seconds as well as minutes is a smart investment. Choose either a digital or analog waterproof watch.

Standard Swim Training Equipment

Most aquatic facilities have the following equipment poolside whether the workout is water exercise or lap swimming.

A **kickboard** is a standard aquatic accessory for practicing kicking as well as for supporting the upper body in the water. Because kickboards are light and buoyant, they are excellent for water exercise and provide extra resistance to make upper body exercises more energetic.

A **pull-buoy** helps to develop upper body strength and technique by immobilizing one's legs during swimming and thus focusing on arm strokes. It is usually made of two connected styrofoam cylinders.

Fins are another popular piece of equipment and are worn like shoes. When fins are used, resistance has to be overcome by exerting the thigh, calf, and abdominal muscles. Fins improve cardiovascular capacity and leg flexibility. Fins enhance both a water exercise and a lap swim workout, and are lots of fun to use. A popular fin is the monofin, which looks like a fishtail with both feet inserted into one fin. Select fins according to purpose of exercise, their size, their shape, and material.

Hand paddles, usually made of plastic, are worn on the hands. They increase the amount of resistance needed to push against the water and develop arm power. Swim mitts or gloves can accomplish a similar purpose.

Water exercise gear help to maximize the effectiveness of water exercises by adding varying amounts of resistance against the water. In addition to hand-held paddles of various sizes, there are many types of flotation devices and gear, including deep-water jogging belts, vests, and rubber tubing. A recent trend in water fitness includes the aquatic exercise step, which should be used with aqua shoes. Specific water exercise equipment will be discussed in Unit IV.

Aquatic Fitness Workout Training Components

A water fitness workout should include these key elements for a typical class or session of 45 minutes.

1. the warm-up
2. the main set
3. the cool-down

The **warm-up** is a 5- to 10-minute period during which the swimmer prepares the body by using all the muscles in a series of short, routine exercises in the water, that slowly elevate the heart rate. The warm-up exercises are followed by a series of stretches. The warm-up allows the water exerciser to adjust mentally and physically from a land environment to a water environment.

The **main set** is the aerobic part of the workout, consisting of approximately 20 to 40 minutes of continuous movement in the water during which new skills can be added. The main set exercises all parts of the body, accelerating and then maintaining a target heart rate, which is described below.

The **cool-down** concludes the swim workout with approximately 10 minutes of review of skills and easy swimming and stretching exercises to gradually return the body to its warm-up state and heart rate.

Finding Your Target Heart Rate

Pump Up the Volume

The aerobic effectiveness of an aquatic workout is measured by checking pulse rate at the warm-up, the main set, and the cool-down phases. During the main set, the heart rate or pulse increases. During the warm-up and cool-down phases, the pulse or heart rate lowers and should be similar to each other.

To find the **target heart rate (THR),** the ideal rate your particular workout should be geared to, the American Heart and Medical Associations recommend the following formula which first calculates a person's **maximum heart rate (MHR).** The maximum heart rate is based on a person's age. The MHR equals 220 minus chronological age. If a person is 45, his or her MHR is 220 – 45 or 175. The target heart rate or THR for this person's workout should be between 60 to 85 percent of the MHR. In this case, the MHR was 175 and 60 to 85 percent of 175 equals a THR between 105–149. If a person is 20 years of age, his or her MHR is 220 – 20 or 200. This swimmer's THR range is 120–170, depending on their fitness level.

To calculate heart rate, take your pulse at either wrist or on either side of the neck at the carotid artery, by holding a finger on the pulse and counting the number of beats for 6 seconds. Multiply the number of beats by 10 by adding a 0. After calculating a target heart rate based on the MHR, take the pulse at the beginning of the warm-up, during the main set, and during the cool-down.

Carotid Artery Pulse

TABLE 2.1 *Aerobic Target Heart Rate (THR) Guide*

Age	Maximum Beats per Minute (220 – Age)	THR: 60–82% of MHR in Beats per Minute	THR Goal 75% of MHR in Beats per Minute
20	200	120–170	150
25	195	117–166	146
30	190	114–162	142
35	185	111–157	139
40	180	108–153	135
45	175	105–149	131
50	170	102–145	127
55	165	99–140	124
60	160	96–136	120
65	155	93–132	116
70	150	90–128	112
75	145	87–123	109
80	140	84–119	105

Note: This 75% THR is a general guide for monitoring the main set of a workout. If you count a beat more or less within the six-second pulse count, you're still within THR range (60–85%).

TABLE 2.2 *Target Zone Heart Rate Guide*

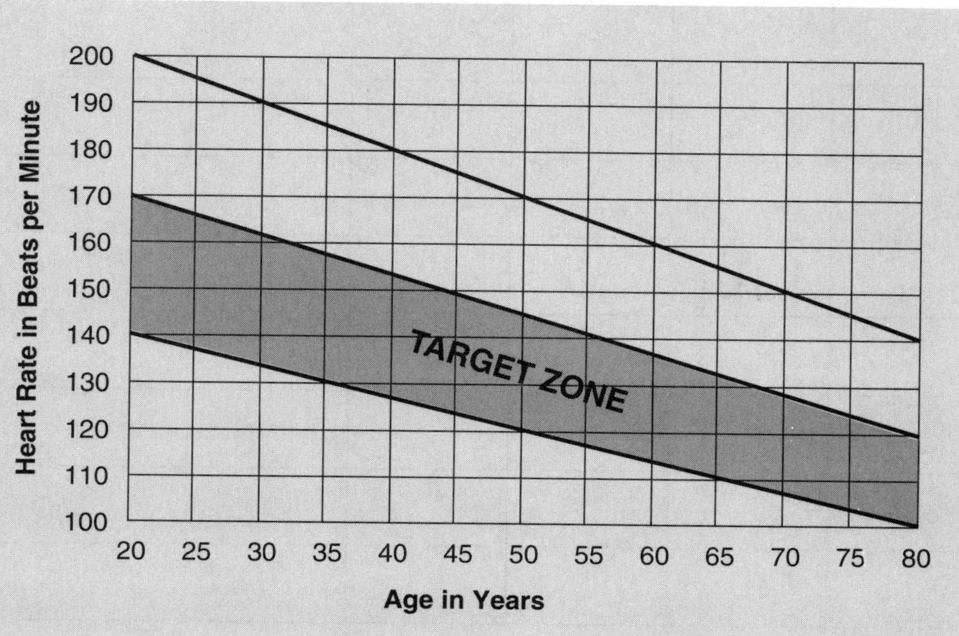

FIGURE 2.1 ***Anatomy of an Aquatic Workout***

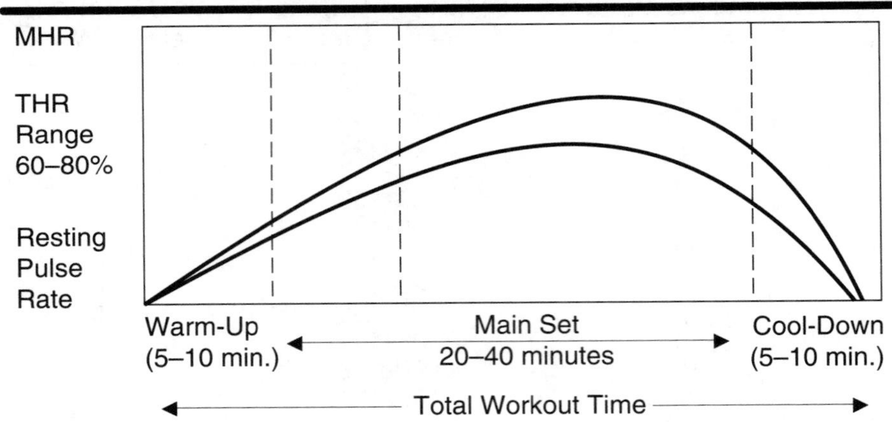

For each workout, mark the appropriate pulse counts in the spaces provided below to show improvement over time.

Day/ Date	Warm-Up	Aerobic Main Set	Cool Down	Aerobic Activity	Comments

How Are You Doing? Perceived Energy Exertion

Researchers in exercise physiology have found that exercisers themselves are best able to provide an accurate guide as to how hard they are really working.

As exercise increases in exertion, heart rates rise in proportion to the increase in effort. Exercisers working below their target heart rate perceive that their energy exertion is light to moderate. As exercisers approach maximum heart rate, their perceived energy exertion is that they are working very, very hard.

Use Table 2.3 as a guide for perceived energy exertion. Correlate perceived exertion with the number in the left column. Then compare perceived exertion to your target heart rate (THR) range.

With increased physical conditioning, the resting heart rate becomes lower than it was in the pre-fitness state because the heart is stronger and is working more efficiently.

TABLE 2.3 ***Perceived Energy Exertion***

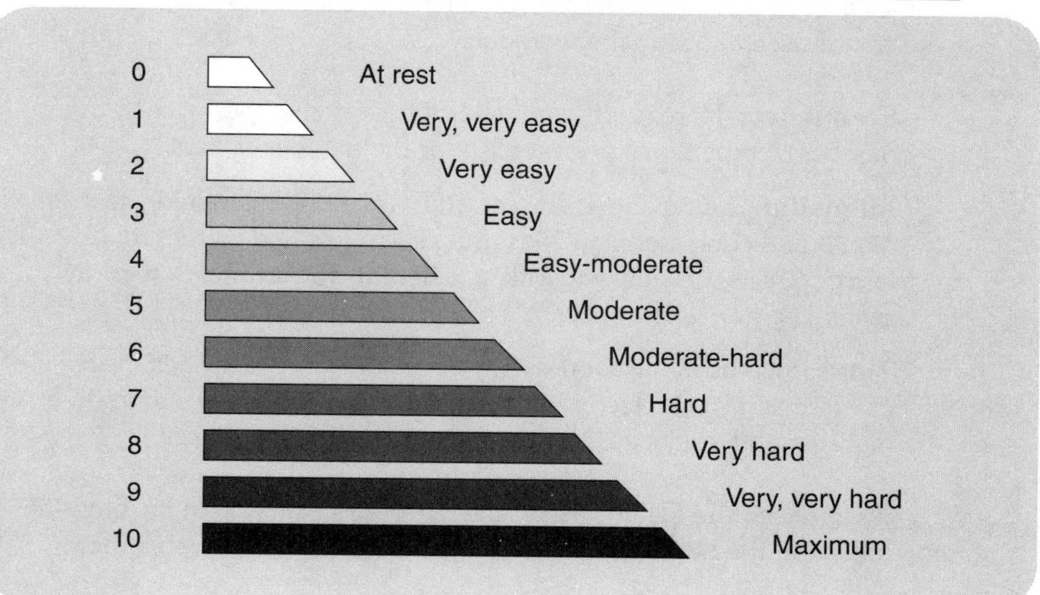

0	At rest
1	Very, very easy
2	Very easy
3	Easy
4	Easy-moderate
5	Moderate
6	Moderate-hard
7	Hard
8	Very hard
9	Very, very hard
10	Maximum

The FIT Principle

The word *aerobic* is part of our modern vocabulary. Aerobic literally means "with oxygen." Good aerobic conditioning results in efficient delivery of oxygen throughout the body. The **aerobic training effect** is an exercise program that strengthens the heart muscle, enabling it to pump more blood more efficiently (and therefore supply more oxygen).

Aerobic conditioning also increases the size and number of blood vessels to supply the blood (and oxygen) to the body tissue, as well as increases the amount of blood in the body. In short, it also means that as blood vessels and muscles are toned and strengthened, the whole body works more efficiently.

This aerobic training effect is achieved by progressively placing more demand on the body than it can comfortably handle. The body gradually adjusts to the increased workload; it becomes stronger and its capacity for endurance, flexibility, speed, and skill increases. The way to "overload" the body is to follow the **FIT principle.** Increase the frequency, intensity, and time of the aquatic workout. Research has shown that the most benefit comes from working out approximately 30–45 minutes at least three times a week on alternate days. There are several ways to enhance and vary the workout.

Frequency: Increase the number of workouts per week, the number of repetitions per exercise, or the number of laps.

Intensity: During the main set add variations in training techniques and equipment, such as using swim fins and increasing distance. Challenge yourself with a different environment, such as swimming at a lake or beach.

Time: Increase your workout by combining two activities (water exercise and laps). Decrease the number of rest periods during the main set and gradually increase the length of the main set.

By applying the FIT Principle, the cardiovascular system becomes more efficient, the heart pumps more blood, and the cells receive more

TABLE 2.4 *FIT Principle*

	Examples
FREQUENCY	Increase number of workouts per week.
INTENSITY	Increase and vary intensity with varying kinds of resistance equipment.
TIME	Increase length of main set.

oxygen, but with less effort from the heart. This is why being physically fit is so important from a medical and health standpoint and explains why a person feels so much better when in condition.

Pool Safety and Etiquette

All swimming and water fitness classes require that safety practices and pool courtesy be observed at all times. Guidelines for these standards of behavior are usually posted in the pool and locker room areas and explained by the instructor and lifeguards. Adhering to the rules at the pool ensures a safe and enjoyable class environment.

All aquatic classes are best enjoyed by following these basic guidelines for safety, health, and courtesy.

Personal Safety

- *Get a medical check-up before beginning an aquatic fitness program or any exercise program.*
- *Safety comes first.* Always swim with a lifeguard and/or instructor on deck.
- *Enter the pool in shallow water* if a less experienced swimmer. Note changing water depths and lifeline placement in the pool, and read posted signs.

- *Start slowly and listen to the body.* Pace yourself during a swim class workout, and rest when you need to.
- *Never hold breath!* Breathe rhythmically and continuously.
- *Be sure to hydrate (drink water)* both before and after swimming. You do sweat during a workout. (Find the nearest water fountain, or bring a water bottle poolside.)
- If swimming outdoors, *use waterproof sun protection.*
- *Never skip any part of the workout.* Always remember that the warm-up and cool-down are part of the total swim workout.
- *If any pain, shortness of breath, dizziness, or disorientation occurs* during a swim, *stop* immediately, leave the water, and seek help.
- *Exercise with a buddy.*

You may have seen health rules such as these at an aquatic facility.

HEALTH RULES

1. No one is allowed in the pool when a lifeguard is not on duty.
2. Persons with inflamed eyes, nasal or ear discharge, boils, open sores, cuts or other evident skin or bodily infections are not permitted in the pool. Persons with bandages are not permitted in the pool.
3. All persons must take a soap shower before entering the pool.
4. Children who are not toilet trained must wear rubber pants without diapers.
5. Urinating, discharging of fecal matter, expectorating, or blowing the nose in swimming pool is prohibited.
6. No pets allowed in pool area.

The following safety rules apply to most pools.

POOL SAFETY RULES

- Diving from the pool deck is not permitted in shallow water. Feet first entry only.
- Standing or hanging onto diving boards, starting blocks, or lane lines is prohibited.
- Walking, standing, hanging onto or swimming under the bulkheads is prohibited (where applicable).
- Use of starting blocks is prohibited except during instructional swim training or competitive swimmings activities, and under proper supervision only.
- Running, pushing, or rough play are not permitted.
- No food, beverages, gum chewing, or glass items are permitted in locker room or pool area, unless otherwise noted.
- No street shoes are permitted on pool deck. Deck shoes are permitted.
- Children must be accompanied by an adult.
- No jewelry, gym shorts, or cut-offs may be worn in pool. All swimmers must wear a suit.
- Leave the water immediately if there is an electrical storm.

General Swimming Pool Etiquette

- Most aquatic facilities have recreational time for adults, staff, families, children, and community. The hours are usually posted by the pool.
- When the pool is divided into lap lanes, choose the one that is most appropriate to your swimming speed or level (slow, medium, fast, beginner, intermediate, advanced).

- When circle swimming, always swim counter-clockwise and stay to the right of the lane. If you find yourself behind a slower swimmer, tap his/her foot two times, then pass the slower swimmer at the wall.
- When resting at poolside, whether in or out of the water, stay clear of swimmers who are making turns.
- In some pools it is common practice to "split" the lane. In this case, choose the side you will swim on and then abide by this choice.
- Place swim equipment on the deck in a courteous and safe manner.
- Shower before and after you swim. Bring amenities in plastic containers; avoid bringing glass to the aquatic facility.
- Be considerate of others in the locker room.
- Additional courtesy rules of your pool:

____

____

____

Circle Swim

Chapter 3

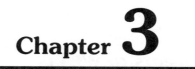

Building Blocks of Aquatics

Water fitness encompasses a variety of activities: recreational swimming, water exercise, lap swimming, water sports and fun at a favorite watering hole with friends and family. Learning to swim provides the basis of a positive activity that is both aerobic and enjoyable for mind, body, and soul for a lifetime.

*Adjustment to Water Through WETs**

This chapter and the unit that follows introduces swim skills, beginning with the building blocks of water fitness, **Water Exercise Techniques,** or **WETs.** Both basic and advanced stroke techniques can be practiced and perfected by using WETs, which are swim-skill specific. Use this progression of WET drills throughout the learning process.

WETs are exercises that are performed in the water in order to tone and strengthen muscles. These exercises isolate and refine swim skills as well as develop new ones.

*WET (Water Exercise Technique) is a registered trademark of the author, Jane Katz, Ed.D.

Sweats to WETs

Getting adjusted to the water's environment is part of taking the plunge—mentally and physically.

Sweats are familiar exercises used for warming up and stretching on land. WETs are exercises adapted for the water as a basis for building swim skills, as well as the elements of an aquatic fitness workout.

The following Sweats to WETs are ideal for the warm-up or the cool-down. Do 5 to 10 minutes of various combinations of WETs at the beginning and end of the swim workout.

Entering the Water

Sit on the edge of the shallow end of the pool with feet in the water. Enter the water by placing both hands at one side of the body on the deck and turn toward that side. Slowly lower the body into the water by supporting total weight with both arms until feet touch the bottom.

Entering the Water

Every aquatic environment has its own distinctive features. Many factors determine where the water level will be in relation to the swimmer; that is, swimmer's height, depth of pool, number of people in pool, configuration of pool, and so forth. Ideally, warm-ups in the water occur at chest to chin depth for maximum comfort, safety, and resistance, keeping arms underwater when appropriate.

Sweats to WETs Warm-Ups

- **Bobbing:** Bobbing is an initial warm-up for adjusting the body's temperature to the change from land to water. Standing in chest-deep water, holding on to the edge of the pool if necessary. Do a knee bend so that the chin touches the water's surface. Jump up and straighten legs. Repeat the knee-bend and jump in rapid succession.

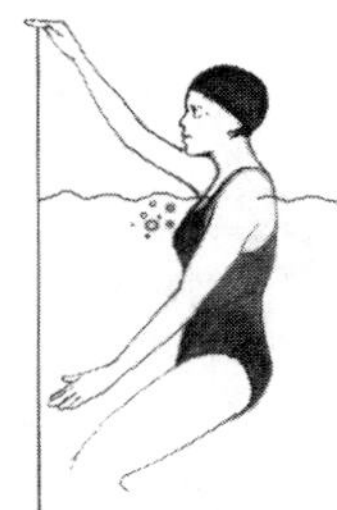

- **Water Walking/Water Jogging:** Water walking/water jogging immediately adjusts the body to the temperature of the water and its resistance, helping the body to warm up. Standing in chest-deep water, walk, then jog through the water forward, backward, diagonally, and/or in a circle. Move arms back and forth in a pumping action underwater, coordinating them with a walk or a jog, as if walking or jogging on land. Water walking can be expanded to be a workout by itself.

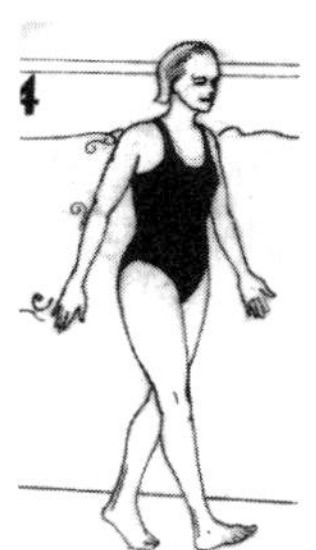

- **Head Turn:** For the head turn, tip the head from one side to the other, keeping the ear in line with the shoulder. Lower the chin to the chest and make a semicircle with the head by rolling it on the chest from one shoulder to the other. Looking straight ahead, pivot the head to the right over the right shoulder, and hold. Repeat to the left. This pivoting action is preparation for rhythmic breathing that is needed to swim the crawlstroke properly. All head turn motions should be done slowly and evenly.

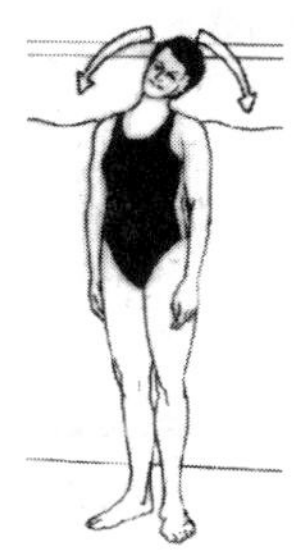

- **Shoulder Roll:** Shoulder rolls warm up and loosen the shoulder area and help increase the range of motion of the shoulder area. With arms relaxed at both sides, lift up both shoulders toward the ears. Roll the shoulders backward, then forward several times. Alternately lift and roll each shoulder separately, backward and forward.

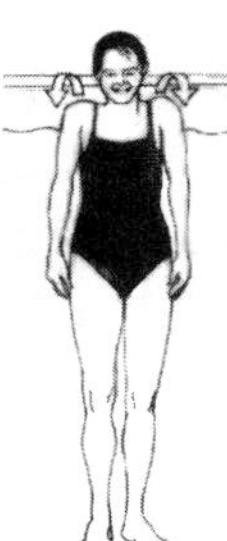

- **Trunk Turn:** The trunk turn warms up the midriff muscles and helps increase midbody flexibility. With hands on hips, twist the body to one side at the waist and inhale at the same time. Exhale and return to the center position at the same time. Inhale and turn to the opposite side.

- **Triceps and Shoulder Stretch:** The triceps stretch, a popular swimmer's stretch, helps to limber the upper arm and shoulder area. Extend the left arm over the head, palm facing in. Grasp the left elbow with the right hand, bending it and guiding the left arm to reach behind the head, resting the hand at the base of the neck. Gently pull on the left elbow for additional stretch. Release and reverse arms.

- **Cross-Chest Stretch:** The cross-chest stretch is also a common swimmer's stretch and helps to loosen the back, upper arm, and shoulder muscles. Extend the right arm in front of the body, with thumb pointing up. With the left hand, grasp the right arm underneath the elbow and bring the right arm across the chest under the chin. Repeat with the other arm.

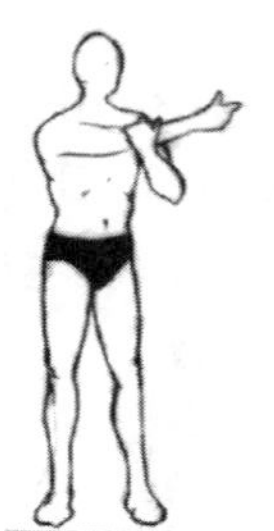

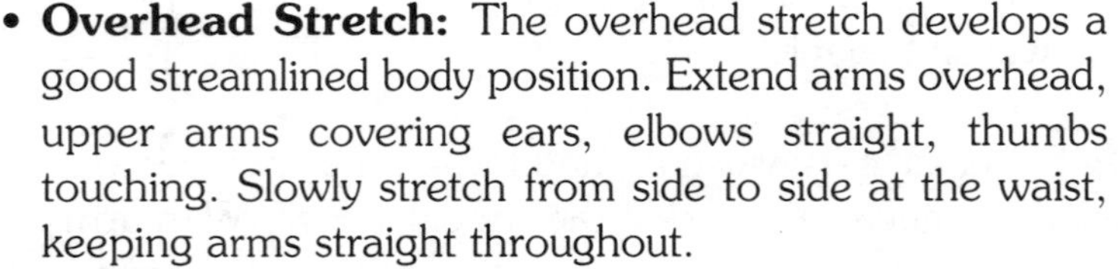

- **Overhead Stretch:** The overhead stretch develops a good streamlined body position. Extend arms overhead, upper arms covering ears, elbows straight, thumbs touching. Slowly stretch from side to side at the waist, keeping arms straight throughout.

- **Runner's Leg Stretch 1:** The runner's leg stretch stretches the large muscles of the legs—the back of the leg, the calf, and the front thigh muscles. These are the muscles most vulnerable to cramping. Standing waist-high in the water, hold the edge of the pool ledge with the left hand. Place

the right foot straight behind you, the heel touching the bottom of the pool. Bend the left knee and lean forward while stretching the extended leg. Change leg positions and repeat.

- **Runner's Leg Stretch 2:** Holding on to the pool edge for support, lift the right leg and bend it behind you as if folding it against the body. Grasp the right foot with your right hand, and pull the foot toward the right buttock. Release the foot to a standing position. Repeat on the left side.

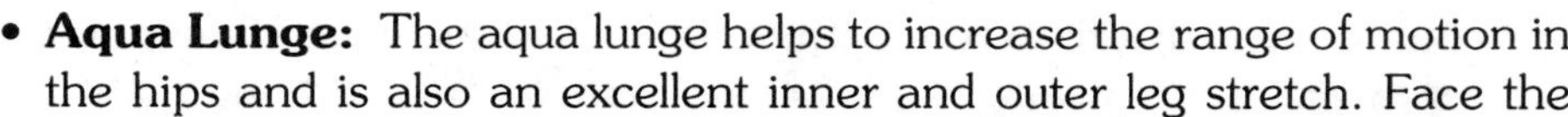

- **Aqua Lunge:** The aqua lunge helps to increase the range of motion in the hips and is also an excellent inner and outer leg stretch. Face the pool wall and hold the edge with both hands, shoulder-width apart. Place your feet against the wall in a straddle position, wider than shoulder width. Shift body weight to the right, bending the right knee, while the left leg is extended. Hold the stretch. Return to center and shift body weight to the left.

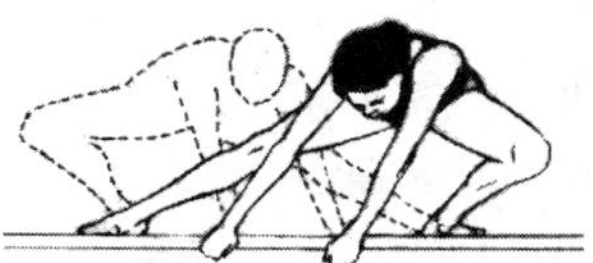

Additional warm-up/cool-down exercises

Breathing—Back to Basics

The secret to swimming efficiently is a proper breathing technique. The ability to control the position and movement of the head in order to inhale and exhale air will help control accurate body position and the coordination of the arms with the legs. Correctly developed, the skill of rhythmic breathing is the main factor that allows for efficient use of one's swimming energies, especially in the crawlstroke.

Many swimmers, including experienced fitness swimmers, have not developed good breathing techniques. This failure results in wasted energy and rapid exhaustion. Even a perfect armstroke and powerhouse kick will only go so far (or fast) if the body does not receive the oxygen it needs.

The objective of rhythmic breathing for swimmers is to make breathing as regular and as automatic as breathing is out of water. This is accomplished by mastering the following techniques:

1. *Breathe! Don't overlook the obvious*—inhale with face out of the water and exhale with face in the water (except for the backstroke). Few swimmers try to inhale with their faces in the water—but many forget to exhale with their faces in the water. The point is to breathe regularly and continuously. Never hold breath while swimming, and never inhale under the water.

2. *Breathe deeply.* Feel as if completely filling and emptying the lungs with each inhalation and exhalation of the breathing cycle. Practice "ripple breathing" by placing the chin on the water's surface, exhaling through nose and mouth, forming ripples on the water's surface.

3. *Use both nose and mouth.* When inhaling, suck air in through the mouth as if through a straw, and simultaneously in through the nose as if inhaling the fragrance of a flower. When exhaling, blow out through the mouth as if blowing dust off an object, and simultaneously expel air through the nose as if sneezing.

4. *Rhythmic breathing.* During the crawlstroke, turn the face to one side (whichever side you prefer) and barely clear the nose and mouth out of the water, inhaling continuously from the moment the face leaves the water to the moment it returns. As the face turns forward and the nose and mouth enter the water, exhale continuously until the next inhalation. This is called **rhythmic breathing.**

The following exercises will help to improve rhythmic breathing. Use the chart on page 34 to record rhythmic breathing progress. Practice breathing skills at home by using a sink, bowl, pot, or wok. Just five minutes of practice daily will enhance progress tremendously.

- **Ripple Breathing:** Practice exhaling in a steady and deliberate flow. It is similar to blowing out birthday candles. This simple exercise is preparation for breathing during swim strokes. Using the pool edge for support, with chin resting on water's surface, blow on the water, creating a rippling of the water in front of the mouth.

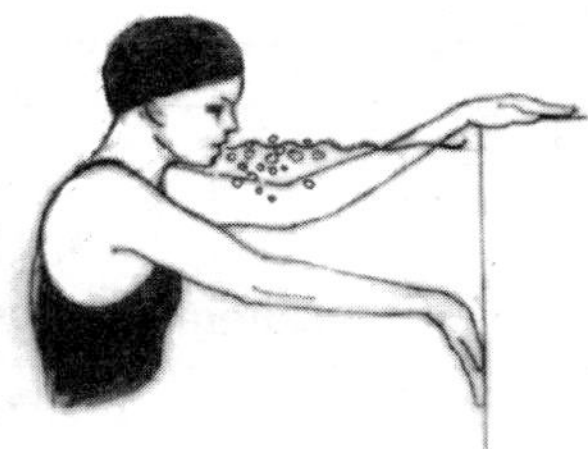

- **Bobbing with Breathing:** Practice breathing while bobbing at the pool wall. Inhale with face out of the water, and exhale with face submerged in water. This exercise not only accustoms the swimmer to continuous inhalation and exhalation as the face enters and leaves the water, but it is also a good way of warming up before a swim and of relaxing between sets in a workout. As a variation, practice bobbing with a buddy.

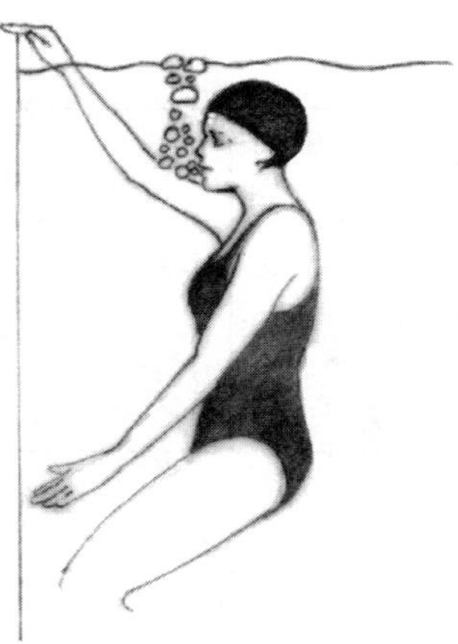

- **Controlled Breathing with Kickboard:** Practice controlled breathing while holding on to the pool wall or kicking with a kickboard. Consciously slow the rate of exhalations as a means to improving breathing efficiency. Inhale and exhale continuously, but slow the exhalation so that the face remains submerged for increasing lengths of time.

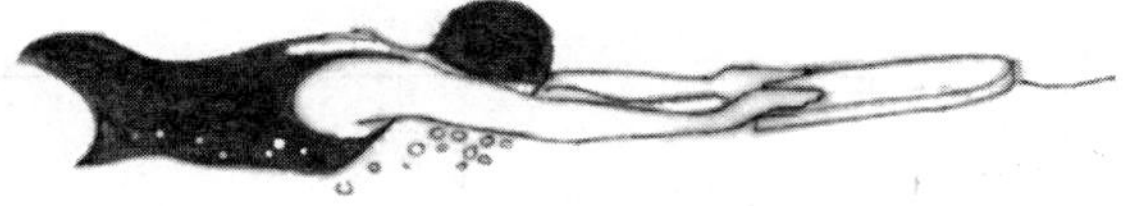

- **Rhythmic Breathing (for Crawlstroke):** Practice rhythmic breathing (turning head to one side only) while standing in chest-deep water, holding on to the pool wall.

BREATHING PROGRESS CHART

Name ______________________ Class ____________

Day/Date	Time in Min. or Number of Repetitions	Breathing Techniques	Comments

Floating and Streamlined Body Positions

Floating—both prone (face front) and supine (on back)—is basic to developing a sense of security in the water. It is also the foundation for **streamlining** the body, the foundation for swimming efficiently.

Face Front (Prone) Float and Recovery

The **recovery** to a stand from a prone floating position is an essential safety skill. The **face front (prone) float** is the first step to literally moving the feet off the bottom of the pool, particularly for a novice swimmer. To recover from a prone position to a stand, simultaneously bend the knees, press arms downward at the sides, lift the head, and place both feet on the bottom. If you are a novice floater, review the recovery to a stand before practicing the float. It is similar to rope jumping forward. (The jump rope WET drill highlights this effect.)

Face Front Float and Recovery

Gliding

After floating and recovering to a stand, the next step is to **glide.** The forward movement of the glide results from the momentum of pushing feet off the bottom of the pool or off the pool wall. This movement is similar to coasting on a bicycle or in a car. The energy of the initial push-off allows the body to coast, or glide, without any further effort.

To maximize the glide, minimize the resistance against the water by streamlining the body. To practice the glide, face away from the wall, extend arms overhead, covering the ears, thumbs together, and bend forward from the waist. Inhale and at the same time bend the knees and push off from the bottom of the pool with the balls of the feet. As face lowers into the water to forehead level, begin exhaling, straighten legs, and assume a face float streamlined body position.

WET Drills: *Prone Float and Recovery*

- **Jump Rope:** To practice front float recovery, simulate jumping rope. As arms bring "rope" forward, knees bend and legs lift to clear rope.

- **Push-Off Glide to the Wall:** Face the wall just beyond arm's length distance, one leg placed in front of the other. Push off the bottom by bending the knees, placing the face in the water, and extending the arms so that they are in line with the head and touching the ears. Straighten the legs to a streamlined body position.

- **Push-Off Glide from Wall:** Standing with one foot on the bottom and one foot against the wall, bend knees and push off, simultaneously extending arms and body forward with face in the water. As the glide loses momentum, recover to stand.

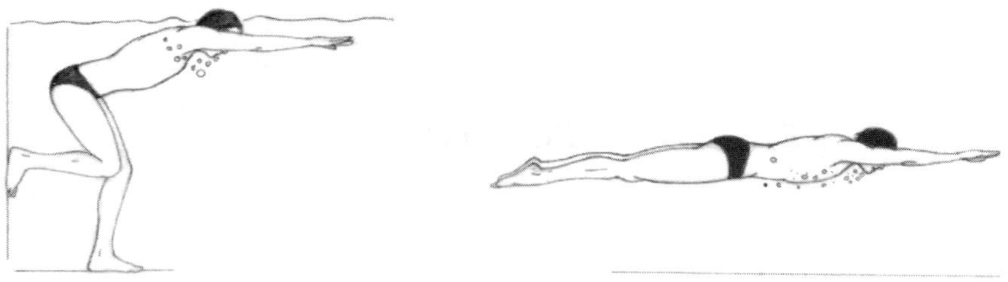

Prone Push-Off and Glide from Wall

Additional Drills

____

____

____

Back (Supine) Float and Recovery

Assume a back float position by tilting head back and leaning body backward, allowing feet to leave the pool bottom and rise to a back float position. Keep arms at sides or extended overhead.

Recover to a stand by bending at the waist, drawing knees up to chest, lifting head forward, and scooping arms downward and then upward (as if to wash your face). The head, arm, and leg movements are to be done simultaneously. It is as if the swimmer was being punched in the stomach and is bending or piking at the waist and jumping rope backwards.

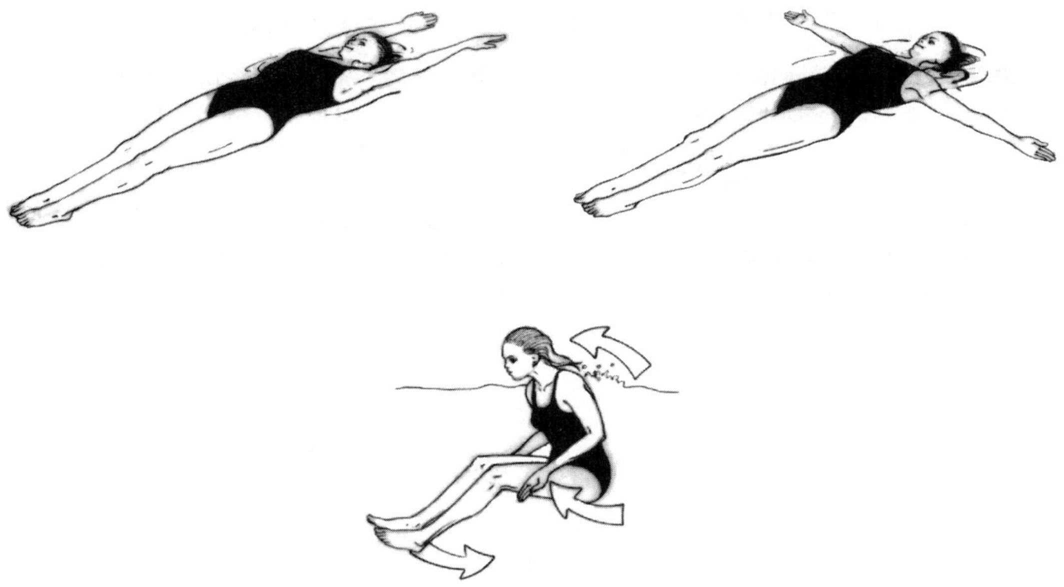

Back Float and Recovery

WET Drills: *Back Float and Recovery*

- **Back Jump Rope:** Simulate jumping rope backwards. As the imaginary rope clears under the feet, the motion is similar to the back float recovery to a stand.

- **Back Glide with Kickboard Support:** Hold kickboard on abdomen while assuming back float position for extra support. Then add a glide.

➤ **Corner Support:** Standing against the corner of the pool, rest head on the pool's edge while extending both hands to either side, and grasp the edge of the pool with both hands, and assume a back float position. To recover, draw knees to chest, bring head and shoulders forward, and place feet on pool bottom.

Additional Drills

____

____

WET Drill: *Changing from Prone to Supine*

➤ **Pendulum Switch:** Begin in a back float position with arms at sides. Using the abdominal muscles, bend hips and slowly lower them into the water. Then reach forward with arms, placing face in the water. Keep knees straight or tucked, then extend legs back, finishing in a prone float. Reverse by rounding back and bending hips to return to a back float position. Try to keep body position as streamlined as possible. Squeeze buttocks as float position changes.

Supine to Prone Float

An alternative is to bend knees to a *tuck* position when changing from one floating position to the other.

SWIM TIP: *Some people have great difficulty learning to float. The temptation is to become very discouraged. With an instructor's guidance, add the flutter kick leg motion to the float to help streamline the body into a glide position.*

HOW AM I DOING?

Dates	Name of Skill	I Did It!	Needs Work	Comments
	Prone float			
	Recovery from prone float			
	Back float			
	Recovery from back float			
	Prone push-off to wall			
	Prone push-off from wall			
	Back glide with kickboard support			

PRACTICE TIP: *For safety and comfort, practice the back (supine) float and recovery with a partner who is behind you and whose arms are under your shoulder blades for support.*

Sculling and Treading

Sculling

Sculling provides continuous support and propulsion for almost all swim skills and helps to provide a better feel for the water. Sculling is creating a continuous "figure 8" motion with arms, moving them simultaneously away from the center of the body to the starting point as the palms press against the water in either direction.

Stand in chest-deep water with arms extended in front, just below the water's surface. Begin with thumbs up, palms facing each other. Turn thumbs down and press your hands out and away from each other until they are shoulder-width apart; then turn thumbs up and press hands toward each other until palms almost touch.

WET Drill: *Sculling*

- **Scull and Hug:** Stand in chest-deep water, arms extended in front, with thumbs pointing downward. Sweep arms out, pressing water backward. Then turn thumbs up and press water forward, until arms hug the body. Then bring arms in front again and repeat.

> ***SCULLING WITH HAND PADDLES***
> *Hand paddles are like fins for hands. Like fins, they require additional energy for propulsion, and they should be used carefully to avoid creating muscle strain (or making swimming a contact sport!).*

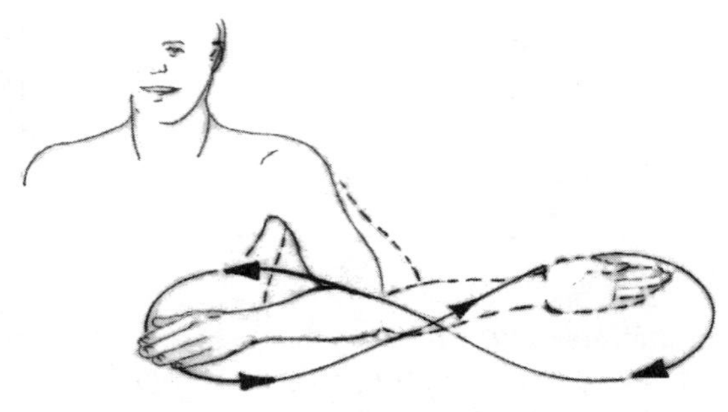

Sculling

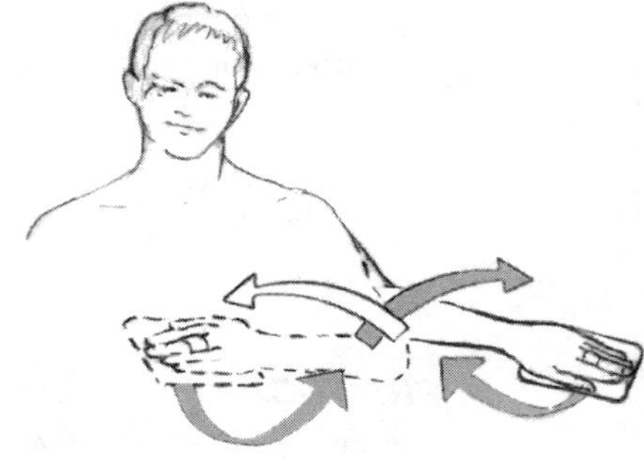

Sculling with Hand Paddles

Treading

Treading is a safety skill that enables a swimmer to stay afloat in deep water in a vertical position, head above water, using as little energy as possible. It is also a water exercise. To tread—let arms and hands use a sculling motion; legs kick in a bicycle-type pedal action. (Use kick leg motions, such as scissors, frog, or whip, which are described in Unit II.)

WET Drill: *Treading*

➤ **Combined Treading Skills:** First practice treading in chest-deep water. Scull, bend forward at the waist, bend knees, and begin pedaling legs as if bicycling. Try not to let feet touch the bottom. Gradually move to deeper water when comfortable. Hold on to pool edge or ladder with one hand for support while sculling with the other arm when first learning to tread.

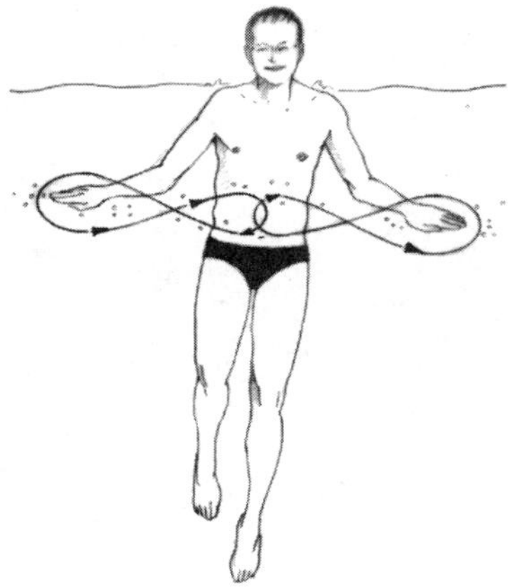

Treading

Unit II

Stroke Techniques

Stroke techniques are the "meat and potatoes" of swimming. This unit presents the major swim strokes and their components, including streamlined body position, arm motion (catch, pull, and recovery), leg motion, breathing, and coordination. One of the major differences among the various swimming strokes is the movement pattern of the arms and legs. The movement pattern is either alternating or simultaneous. The alternating strokes are the crawlstroke and the backstroke. The simultaneous strokes are the elementary backstroke, breaststroke, and the butterfly. A variation of both movement patterns is the sidestroke.

Each stroke has unique characteristics. Prior knowledge and personal preference may guide the swimmer to a favorite stroke. As this unit progresses, you will have the opportunity to learn new skills and to perfect stroke techniques with stroke-specific WET drills, additional stroke drills, and swimming tips.

Each stroke chapter concludes with three evaluation checklists for the swimmer to record progress and to note instructor's tips for successful swimming.

Chapter 4

Crawlstroke

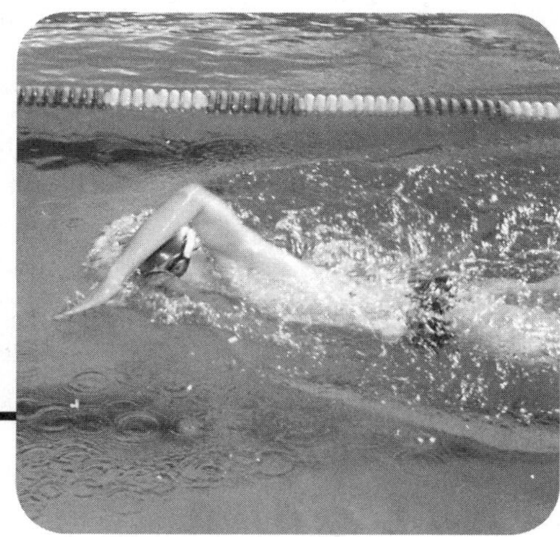

The crawlstroke was brought to public attention in 1844 by two Native Americans who, during a swimming competition, used the alternating arm motion and beat the water with their feet. Flying Gull won England's National Society of Swimming medal by swimming a 130-foot pool in 30 seconds. This alternating stroke was the natural stroke not only of Native Americans but also of the aborigines of South America, West Africa, and the South Pacific islands. The stroke evolved as the crawl, sometimes known as freestyle, and is the fastest and now the most popular of all the strokes used by swimmers in North America.

Body Position

The **crawlstroke** begins in a streamlined prone float body position. Arms are extended straight overhead with ears covered by upper arms. The face is submerged forward to mid-forehead level.

Arm Motion

There are three main components of any arm motion: the catch, the pull, and the recovery. The main power for the crawlstroke comes from the arm motion.

The **catch** occurs when the hand enters the water. The hand should glide into the water—not splash. The key to efficient swimming is being sure that the elbow always remains higher than the hand, providing the best leverage against the water's resistance. Keeping the hand relaxed and the palms slightly outward, straighten the arm at the elbow as the hand enters the water so that the hand is about 8 inches below the water's surface.

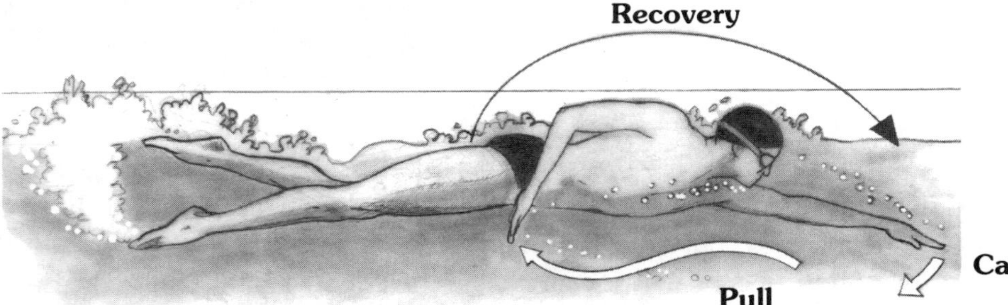

Crawlstroke Arm Motion Components

The **pull** propels the body forward by pushing the water backward. The standard straight arm pull begins from the catch position. With fingers pointed downward, the arm draws water straight downward and backward toward the thigh.

The **recovery** returns the arm above the water back to the catch position. Bend the elbow and lift the hand out of the water, keeping the elbow higher than the hand, with fingers pointed forward and downward.

IS THIS YOU?
Many beginner swimmers make a common mistake by not pulling completely back during the arm motion for the crawlstroke.

SWIM TIP: *Another common error that novice swimmers may encounter is the following. At the point that the arm is extended for the catch the elbow is dropped into the water and the wrist is bent upwards. But this motion prevents the swimmer from forcefully pushing backward on the water to go forward. It also causes extra water resistance, with the elbow dragging through the water, further impeding progress. To remedy this, extend the arm forward, always keeping the elbow higher than the hand, and move the forearm and the hand as one unit. Once the hand is in the water, use the palm to forcefully push the water back in order to move forward.*

Leg Motion

The **flutter kick** is the leg motion for the crawlstroke. It provides balance and some propulsion. The legs alternate—one is up and the other is down—using the power of the hip and the thigh muscles. Ideally, the legs should separate, and move past each other with a maximum separation of 12 to 18 inches. The knees are slightly bent, the ankles loose, and the toes pointed inward. The legs are just below the surface of the water. When doing the kick, it looks as if the water is boiling.

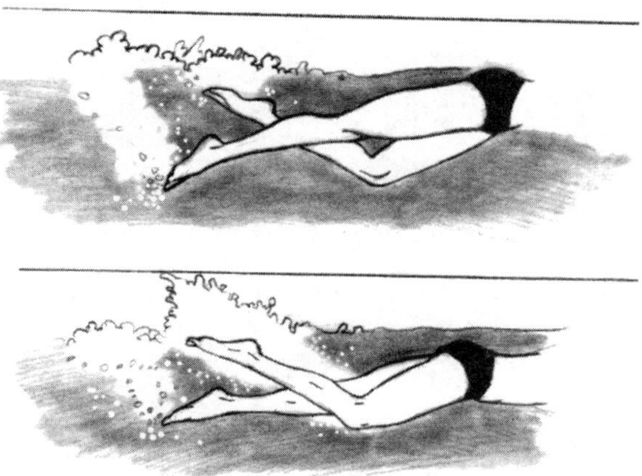

Flutter Kick

SWIM TIPS: *Wearing goggles allows swimmers to keep their eyes open and see where they are going.*

Do not hold breath underwater. Exhale continuously, forming bubbles in the water.

Rhythmic Breathing

The secret to comfort while swimming the crawl is receiving a steady supply of air. Rhythmic breathing is the technique that enables the swimmer to obtain a continuous supply of air. Rhythmic breathing coordinates with the crawl (hand-over-hand) arm stroke. Inhale air in a frequent, regular pattern. As the head turns to one side to inhale, the arm of the opposite side of the body is extended in front of the head, and the other arm is at the hip. Take a breath and turn face front into the water and exhale (forming bubbles). While exhaling, the opposite arm pulls down under the body. Make sure to pivot the head just enough to get a "bite" of air. Exhale continuously, never holding the breath.

Crawlstroke and Rhythmic Breathing

Stroke Coordination

Swimming correctly is coordinating the components of the stroke together. Begin by combining the arms and the legs. Then add rhythmic breathing. As the head turns to the breathing side, the arm on that side has just finished its pull and is ready to recover. At the same time the opposite arm is extended forward for the catch, ready to pull.

WET Drills for Crawlstroke

WET drills teach swimmers to learn to practice correctly and to overcome faulty swim habits. The following WET drills highlight ways to learn and perfect the basic crawlstroke.

WET Drills: *Arm Motion*

➤ **Alternating Arm Circles:** Stand in waist-deep water, then walk forward, moving the arms alternately in forward circles, simulating the crawlstroke arm motion.

➤ **Splashback:** Standing in chest-deep water, with body bent forward from the waist, place arms in water. Walk forward using crawlstroke arm motion with thumb brushing past thigh and splashing water back to finish pull. This gives an exaggerated feeling of the correct crawl arm stroke pulling motion. Once the drill is comfortable, incorporate it into the crawl arm motion *without* splashing.

WET Drills: *Flutter Kick*

➤ **Leg Switch:** Stand with one leg forward, the other back. Jump and switch leg positions, brushing big toes together at the height of the jump.

➤ **Wall Kick:** Hold on to the wall in the prone bracket position and practice the flutter kick. Keep legs underwater. Make the water "boil." (See explanation of bracket position on p. 50.)

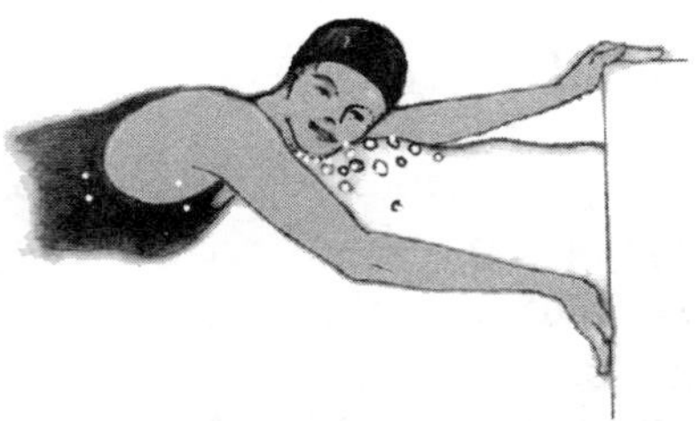

Bracket Position

> ***SWIM TIP:*** *The bracket position is used by swimmers to practice the flutter kick while holding on to the pool wall. Grasp the edge of the pool with one hand, and place the other hand flat against the pool wall with fingers pointed downward. The bracket position is often used for other kicking drills as well as breathing drills.*

WET Drill: *Rhythmic Breathing*

➤ **Head Pivot:** Determine breathing side. Stand in waist-deep water, with head in center position. Bend from the waist and place face in water. Inhale as head moves 90 degrees over right or left shoulder. Turn head back to center position, face in water, exhaling continuously. Repeat on same breathing side, maintaining continuous pivoting motion.

> ***SWIM TIP:*** *To determine the rhythmic breathing side, experiment by pivoting the head in either direction in the water. Begin rhythmic breathing for the crawlstroke on the side that feels the most comfortable.*

WET Drills: *Coordination*

➤ **Arm and Leg Combo:** Use both legs to push off pool bottom and/or wall to assume a prone position. Then do the flutter kick and add one complete crawl arm stroke cycle, that is, one right-arm pull and one left-arm pull.

➤ **Walk and Stroke:** In chest-deep water, practice the crawl arm motion combined with rhythmic breathing. Practice first while stationary, then while walking forward. When the arm stroke and rhythmic breathing are working together, add the flutter kick and you are swimming.

➤ **Fingertip Entry:** Walk in chest-deep water practicing crawlstroke arm motion. Lift elbow upward and out of the water, with forearm and hand following. The arm should move upward, outward, and forward during the first half of the recovery. Then move hand forward and inward, with fingertips pointing downward to begin the entry. Hand and forearm should enter the water's surface at a 30- to 40-degree angle. As the arm recovers, bend and lift the elbow just high enough so that the fingertips skim the water's surface. The arm recovers forward to the catch or starting position. During the recovery the arm should be relaxed as much as possible.

➤ **Wide Hand Entry:** Hold kickboard sideways with hands on each end. Stroke with one arm at a time, extending arm forward at shoulder width and grasping outer edge of kickboard. This drill helps to correct a narrow pull.

*FINA (Federation Internationale Natacion Amateur) is the international governing body for aquatic competitions. In competitive swimming, the event in which swimmers generally do the crawlstroke is called the **freestyle.** There are no restrictions as to how the freestyle is done, so the crawlstroke is almost always used in competition because it is the fastest stroke.*

Swimming Faster and Better: Refined Crawlstroke

Techniques are not static in any sport. The challenge to athletes at all levels is to attain greater speed and strength and to best harness the body's energy and momentum. In swimming, the development of the S-shaped arm pull for the crawlstroke is an important example of this process.

S-Shaped Arm Pull

In the crawl arm stroke, the arm pushes water straight down and back from the catch position like a paddle wheel. The new swimmer often starts off the arm pull with a fast motion and then slows down. A more efficient arm motion to propel the body forward is called the **S-shaped arm pull.** The S-shaped pull displaces still water rather than water that is already in motion. This pull enables the swimmer to move an increased volume of water, increases resistance against the water with each stroke, and propels the swimmer forward with greater efficiency per stroke.

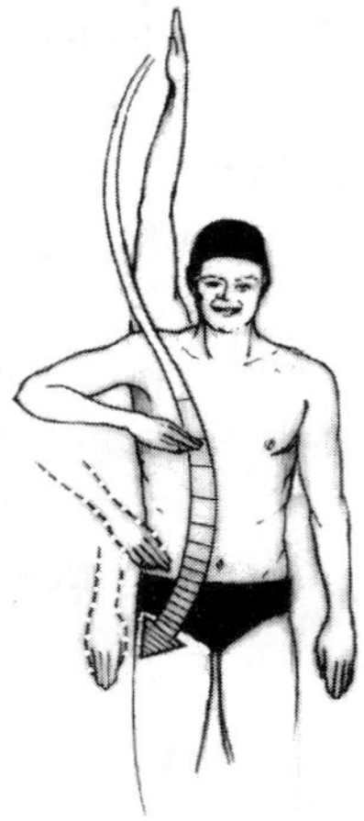

To perform the two-part S-shaped arm pull, trace a reverse letter S or question mark with the right hand by first pulling water outward and downward. As the hand passes the head, pull the hand inward toward the waist. Next, press the hand back, moving it diagonally toward the thigh. Straighten and extend the arm, accelerating the movement, as if throwing a ball in the direction of one's feet. Repeat with the left arm, tracing a letter S or reverse question mark.

Body Roll

The **body roll** and the S-shaped arm pull together refine the traditional crawlstroke into a more efficient and powerful stroke. The body roll uses strong back and shoulder muscles, so that each pull becomes more forceful and carries the swimmer a greater distance with the same energy expenditure.

Pulling with the left arm, rotate the left shoulder down into the water approximately 45 degrees. The added leverage from the back and shoulder muscles during this rotation creates momentum for the shoulder to roll and follow the hand into the water at the catch. When the right hand enters the water for the catch, the body roll reverses to the right side. This also makes it easier to turn the head for a breath as well as for the opposite arm to recover.

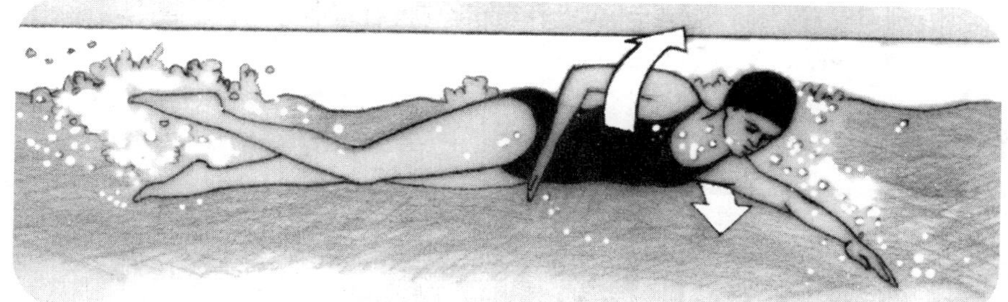

Refined Crawlstroke Body Roll

Crossover Kick with Hip Roll

As each shoulder follows the arm into the water with the S-shaped pull, the hips naturally follow the roll of the shoulder, allowing the body to roll in the direction of the forward arm. The feet then cross at the lower part of the leg. To take advantage of this rotational momentum, the flutter kick is modified so that it becomes a balancing force for the refined crawl. As the right shoulder rolls downward and the arm pulls, the right hip will also dip down, and the left foot will cross behind the right foot. For left-arm pull, the opposite occurs. This slower leg motion is called the **crossover kick,** and, with an accompanying hip roll, acts more to stabilize and balance the body than to propel the body.

SWIM TIP: *To streamline the body in the water, kick just below the surface of the water. The shoulders can then ride higher. This position creates more efficiency and speed.*

Alternate Breathing

Another feature of the crawlstroke and refined crawlstroke, especially for advanced swimmers, is **alternate or bilateral breathing.** Alternate breathing is inhaling every third arm stroke instead of every other stroke. Alternate breathing helps balance the stroke, strengthens neck muscles equally on both sides, and at the same time increases a swimmer's aerobic capacity.

Table 4.1 highlights the crawlstroke components, their refinements and sequence.

TABLE 4.1 ***Crawlstroke Components and Refinements***

Stroke Components	Crawlstroke	Crawlstroke Refinements
Breathing	Rhythmic breathing	Rhythmic or alternate breathing
Pulling	Straight arm pull	S-shaped arm pull
Body Rotation	Minimal body rotation	Body rotation up to 45° on each side
Kicking	Six-beat flutter kick	Two- to four-beat flutter with crossover kick

A crawl arm stroke cycle consists of one right arm pull and one left arm pull. The flutter kick is technically a six-beat kick consisting of three kicks (downbeat, upbeat, downbeat) per arm stroke cycle. In the crossover kick, the action is slower and can be either a two-beat (per arm stroke cycle) or a four-beat kick with hip roll.

WET Drills for Refined Crawlstroke

WET Drills: *S-Pull Arm Motion*

- **Single-Arm S-Pull:** Standing in waist-deep water, place left hand on the pool edge. Trace a reverse S pattern or question mark through the water with right arm. Change arms and repeat.

- **Catch-Up S-Pull:** Begin with arms extended, holding on to a kickboard turned widthwise for support. Walk in shallow water, tracing the S-pull pattern, one arm at a time. Wait or catch up before starting the stroke with the other arm. The catch-up S-pull drill can also be done without a kickboard.

Crawlstroke Sequence and Coordination

WET Drills: *Body Roll*

- **Trunk Turn:** In chest-deep water, stand with hands on hips. Turn body and shoulders from side to side.

- **Stroke Punch:** In chest-deep water, alternately punch each arm forward underwater, allowing shoulders and hips to follow the full extension of the arm.

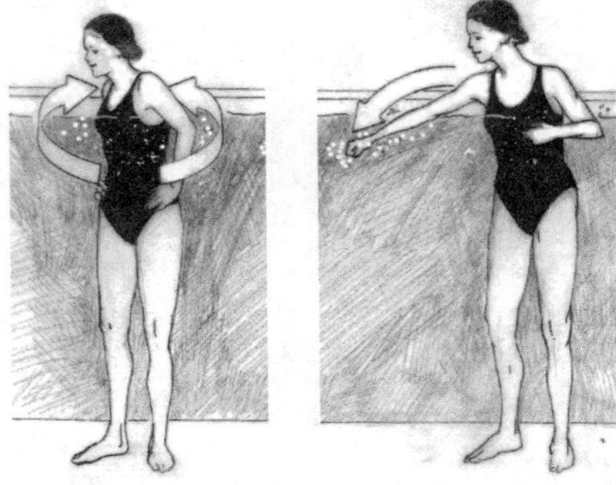

Trunk Turn and Stroke Punch

WET Drills: *Crossover Kick*

- **Sit and Roll:** Sit on the edge of the pool and alternately roll hips from left to right. As body rolls to the left, cross the right leg over the left. Alternate and roll to the right side.

- **Fin Kick with Hip Roll:** Hold on to pool edge, and practice crossover kick while wearing fins. Repeat the drill this time using a kickboard. Remember to turn hips alternately from side to side.

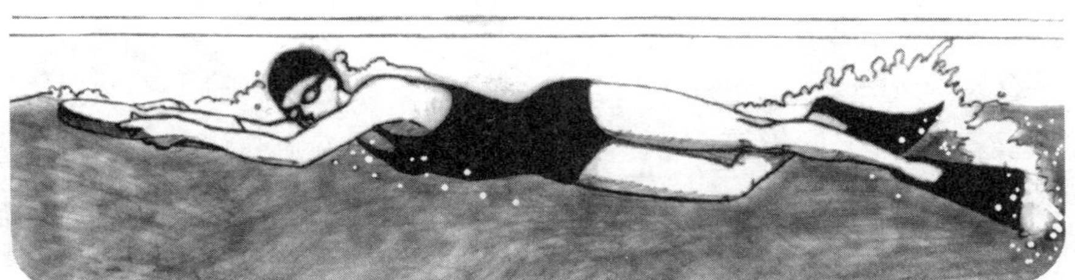

Crossover Fin Kick with Hip Roll with Kickboard

WET Drills: *Alternate Breathing*

➤ **Three Strokes and Breathe:** Turn head to inhale and breathe every third arm stroke. Alternately turn head to inhale on both right and left sides. First practice this drill in a standing position; then walk forward. Continue drill using a pull buoy, then swim, and finally breathe every third stroke on alternate sides.

Mastering the Crawlstroke Swim Drills

There is a difference between managing and mastering the water. Use the following swimming drills to fine tune the crawlstroke.

Distance per Stroke (DPS)

Distance per Stroke (DPS) is a drill to check stroke efficiency by measuring the distance the swimmer propels forward with each stroke. Count the number of strokes to complete one pool length (counting each hand entry as one stroke). Then try to lower the number of strokes for additional pool lengths. It is possible to increase the distance forward by moving more water backward and with greater force. DPS can be applied to all strokes. The higher a swimmer's DPS, the lower the stroke count.

- **Standing Stroke Count:** Standing in place, count the number of arm strokes in one minute. Rest one minute. Then repeat and lower the standing stroke count by pulling with more power.
- **Glide Crawlstroke:** This drill develops a "feel" for using the momentum of the stroke to coast through the water. Starting from a streamlined body position, take one stroke. After one pull, allow arm to remain extended at thigh ready to recover and hold the other arm which is now forward in the catch position. Glide as long as possible with a body roll to the side of the forward arm. Then, as the forward arm pulls, recover the opposite arm to the catch position, and glide, with a body roll to that side. Continue to swim the lap with a glide at each catch, and count the number of

strokes taken. The aim is to lower the stroke count each lap by increasing the distance per stroke.

- **Salute and Stroke:** Walk forward using crawl arm motions in which the elbows recover very high, similar to a salute position at forehead. Begin with these short arm strokes and gradually extend successive arm strokes. Then allow legs to lift from bottom and swim.

Arm, Leg, Breathing Swim Drills

The following arm, leg, and breathing swim drills can be incorporated during practice workouts to help improve the crawlstroke and refined crawlstroke.

- **High Elbow-Fingertip Skim:** To maintain proper arm position on recovery of arms. As arm finishes pull, elbow bends and lifts high enough for thumb to skim side of body up to arm pits when standing. Then, keeping elbow higher than hand, fingers skim forward on surface of the water until entering water for catch position, when swimming.
- **Splashback Glide:** To emphasize the final press of arm and hand at the end of stroke and to feel the S-pull. Finish stroke with hand pressing close to thigh, splashing water backward, just prior to lifting arm out of the water. As the splash occurs, forward arm should pause in the catch position and glide over head.
- **One-Arm Pull:** To even out stroke pulls so they are equally powerful and efficient. This pulling drill trains the arm to avoid crossing the midline of body. Pull with one arm at a time. Pause or catch up to nonpulling arm with four flutter kicks between strokes.
- **Fist Closed Pull:** To reinforce the proper positions of hand and elbow placement during the S-pull. Swim with hands clenched into fists and experience the difference in propulsion provided by the arms.
- **Streamlined Flutter Kick:** To practice correct head and body position with arms. Kick with arms stretched overhead (no kickboard). Keep water line at hairline, lifting head quickly for a breath.

- **Spiral Flutter Kick-Body Roll:** To emphasize the body roll. This drill helps to create a crossover kick and a more powerful arm pull as well. Begin with one shoulder out of the water and the other shoulder pointing to bottom. After eight to twelve kicks, roll shoulders and body to the other side, maintaining a prone position. This body roll creates a hip roll and crossover leg motion. Use fins or a kickboard, and vary arm positions as part of drill.

CHECKLIST FOR CRAWLSTROKE

If You Are Doing This . . .	Try This . . .	Personal Comments
1. Lifting head out of the water for breath on one or both sides.	**1.** Practice rhythmic breathing, turning head to one side only. In the water, keep ear on the surface of the water as turn for a breath.	_______________
2. Letting hands enter and arms pull across midline of body.	**2.** Hold kickboard widthwise and practice stroking, arms shoulder-width apart.	_______________
3. Kicking too high and hard above the surface, splashing water.	**3.** Make the water "boil." Use wall, kickboard, and/or fins for practice. Do not overkick.	_______________
4. Pulling inefficiently and with many strokes per lap.	**4.** Focus on catch position, keeping elbow higher than hand, and push hands past hips before recovery. Practice DPS drill, focusing on moving hand, wrist, and forearm as one unit.	_______________

CRAWLSTROKE SKILL CHECKLIST

Date	Swim Skills	Comments
	Crawlstroke	
____________	Streamlined prone float	____________
____________	Crawl arm motion (catch, pull,	____________
	& recovery)	____________
____________	Flutter kick	____________
____________	Rhythmic breathing	____________
____________	Stroke coordination	____________
	Refined Crawlstroke	
____________	S-shaped arm pull	____________
____________	Body roll	____________
____________	Crossover kick with hip roll	____________
____________	Alternate breathing	____________
____________	Combined stroke coordination	____________
	WET Drills	
____________	Alternating arm circles	____________
____________	Splashback	____________
____________	Leg switch	____________
____________	Wall kick	____________
____________	Head pivot	____________
____________	Arm and leg combo	____________
____________	Wall walk and stroke	____________
____________	Fingertip entry	____________
____________	Wide hand entry	____________
____________	Single-arm S-pull	____________
____________	Catch-up S-pull	____________
____________	Trunk turn	____________
____________	Stroke punch	____________
____________	Sit and roll	____________
____________	Fin kick with hip roll	____________
____________	Three strokes and breathe	____________
	Mastering Drills	
____________	Distance per stroke	____________
____________	Standing stroke count	____________
____________	Glide crawlstroke	____________
____________	Salute and stroke	____________
____________	High elbow-fingertip skim	____________
____________	Splashback glide	____________
____________	One-arm pull	____________
____________	Closed fist pull	____________
____________	Streamlined free flutter kick	____________
____________	Spiral flutter kick-body roll	____________

CRAWLSTROKE SKILL EVALUATION CHART

Name ______________________________ Class ________________

Dates	Stroke Component	Common Errors	How to Correct Them

General Comments: ____

____

____

____

Chapter 5

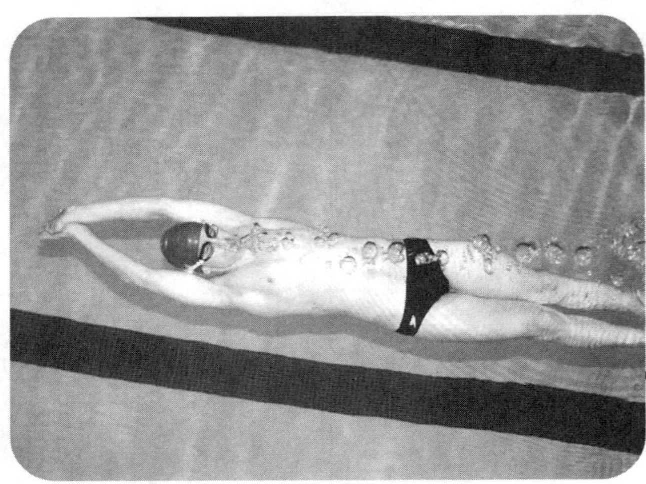

Backstrokes

There are several backstroke variations. The first—the elementary backstroke—is a relaxing and relatively simple stroke. The arms and legs move simultaneously.

Elementary Backstroke

Body Position

The **elementary backstroke** begins in a back float (supine) position. Review back float and recovery in Chapter 3 on page 37.

Arm Motion

From a back float position, move arms simultaneously underwater, through the *catch, pull,* and *recovery*. Begin the catch with the arms extended overhead underwater in a V position. Then pull both arms straight down to thighs into a streamlined body position. Recover after the glide by drawing hands up toward arm pits to begin another catch in the V position.

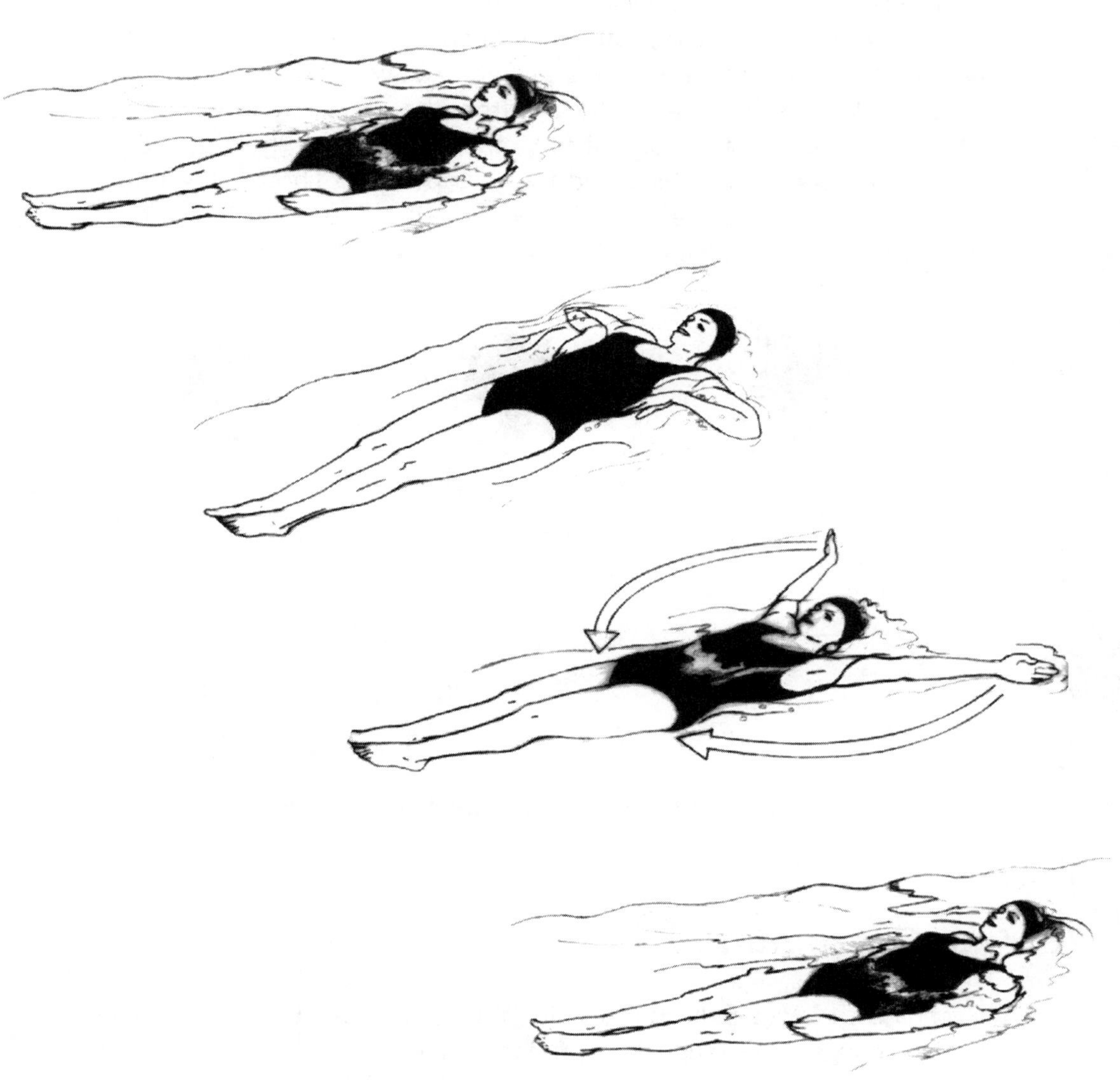

Elementary Backstroke Arm Motion

Leg Motion

The leg motion for the elementary backstroke is simultaneous and symmetrical. The legs should remain underwater throughout the kick. The leg motion is either a frog kick or a whip kick.

Historically, the **frog kick** has been used with the elementary backstroke arm motion—the knees bend outward beyond hip width with feet flexed. Then the legs extend from the knees into a wide V position. The legs are then brought together quickly and straightened so that the ankles are touching and toes are pointed. Though the **whip kick** has superseded the frog kick because it is more efficient, many people find the frog kick to be a more comfortable leg motion.

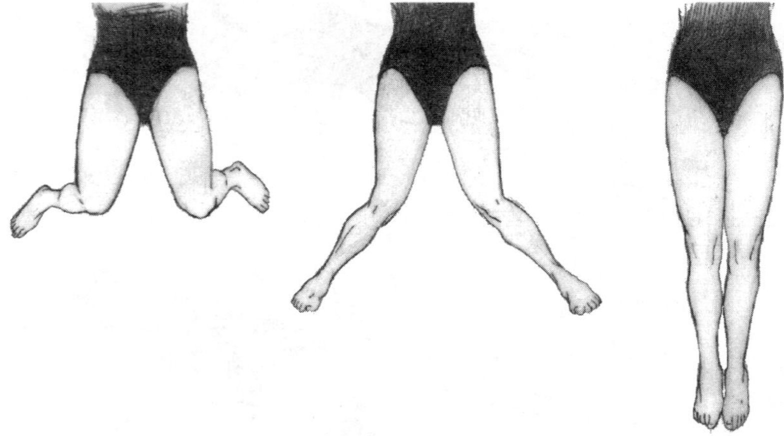

Elementary Backstroke Whip Kick

Stroke Coordination

Combine the arm pull and kick for the elementary backstroke. The arms and legs provide equal propulsion during this stroke. Push off into a back float with arms at sides; always begin the stroke this way. Legs should be straight and together.

Begin moving arms and legs simultaneously. As the arms bend, the knees bend. The arms extend as the feet flex. As the arms pull down to the sides, the legs squeeze together at the same time, propelling the body head first. The sequence is bend, extend, together, and glide. Glide or coast through the water propelled by the momentum of the stroke.

SWIM TIP: *Throughout the elementary backstroke arm motion, the arms remain below the water's surface.*

WET Drills for Elementary Backstroke

WET Drill: *Arm Motion*

- **Scratch and Stretch:** Practice the elementary backstroke arm motion in a standing position. Starting with arms at sides, bend elbows outward, drawing thumbs up toward armpits, as if scratching sides of the body upward. Then stretch arms above shoulders in a V position. Pull straight down to sides and repeat.

WET Drill: *Leg Motion*

- **Frog Kick on Wall:** Place back against the wall, grasp pool edge with hands, and assume a back float position. Do frog kick, keeping knees underwater by dropping heels toward the pool bottom.

TIP: *Modify the frog kick by keeping the knees narrower than a hip width apart. This kick is also used for the breaststroke and is called the whip kick.*

WET Drill: *Coordination*

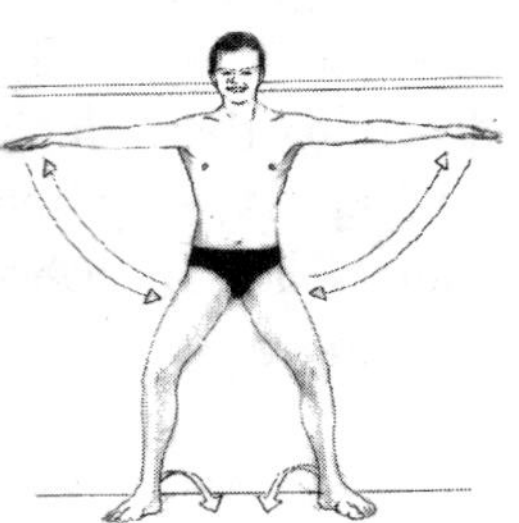

➤ **Aqua Jumping Jack:** Jump and separate legs into a V position. Simultaneously use elementary backstroke arm motion, stretching arms out. Jump again, bringing arms down to sides and legs together.

Mastering the Elementary Backstroke Swim Drills

The following elementary backstroke drills can be incorporated during the workout to help improve the stroke.

- **Bend and Push:** To experience a greater feel for the propulsion of the arm motion. Walk backward in waist-deep water as arms push water downward. Arm motion begins with elbows close to waist and forearms extended outward from the sides of the body.
- **Arm Motion with Flutter Kick:** To practice proper body position and arm motion. Assume the back float position and start to flutter kick. Next add the elementary backstroke arm motion. Arms remain underwater throughout stroke.
- **Seated Kick:** To practice the kick technique slowly and properly. Sit close to pool edge with legs together and extended over water. Bend the knees, dropping heels toward the pool wall. Flex feet and rotate them outward, separating them to approximately hip width, while knees remain together. For the propulsion phase of the kick, move lower legs in an outward circular motion, snapping them back together as they straighten at the knees. End with legs together in a fully extended position, with toes pointed.

- **Corner Kick:** To practice proper kicking technique. Place back in the corner. Hold on to pool edge with each hand and let legs and hips float. Legs bend (with knees close together), extend, snap, and glide. For a more comfortable position, try to keep shoulders underwater.
- **Just the Kick:** To feel the propulsion of the kick. Hold a kickboard, one hand grasping top edge and one hand holding bottom edge. Press across chest. Assume a supine float and begin kicking.

CHECKLIST FOR ELEMENTARY BACKSTROKE

If You Are Doing This . . .	Try This . . .	Comments
1. Not gliding after each stroke.	1. Wait for a count to three before starting next stroke cycle. Place greater emphasis on pull phase of arms and snap of legs as they press together.	
2. Splashing when pulling and/or recovering above water.	2. Keep hands close to body on recovery and extend arms underwater, especially during pull.	
3. Breaking surface of water with feet.	3. Flex feet as knees bend, and drop heels to bottom. Practice kicking with back to the wall so you can watch your feet.	
4. Sinking or sagging in the middle of the body.	4. Keep chest upward by arching slightly. Be certain arms pull underwater.	

Backstroke

The conventional **backstroke** is sometimes called the backcrawl or the windmill backstroke. It is basically the crawlstroke done on the back. The swimmer breathes freely with face out of the water. This backstroke is an alternating stroke.

Body Position

Begin in a supine or back float streamlined body position. Keep chin close to chest and look at feet. The water line is at ear level.

Arm Motion

As in any arm motion, the backstroke arm motion consists of the *catch,* the *pull,* and the *recovery.* Lift one arm straight overhead while continuing to keep the other at the side. With the pinky finger (little finger) leading, place the overhead extended arm downward into the water for the catch.

For the pull, sweep this arm straight down under the water toward the thigh. Brush past thigh with the thumb to complete the pull.

Recover by lifting arm out of the water, leading with the pinky to continue straight back to the catch position.

While one arm is in midair during recovery, the other arm is pulling. Continue the alternating arm stroke motion with arms moving continuously and in opposition to each other.

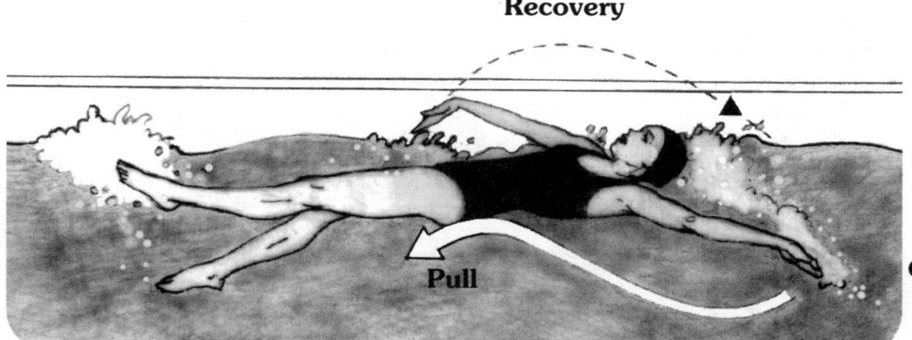

Backstroke with Arm Motion Components

Leg Motion

The backstroke flutter kick is similar to the crawl flutter kick. Legs are close together and move in an alternating up and down motion, separated by about 12 inches. Knees should stay loose and flexible. Knees and top of feet should just barely break the water's surface. As with the crawl, the arm motion provides more forward movement than the leg motion.

Stroke Coordination

Begin in a back float position with arms at sides, extending both arms, palms facing outward. Begin the recovery with one arm by bringing it out of the water, pinky finger up, lifting it straight overhead at shoulder width. Press the arm back another six inches into the water for the catch; then sweep arm down through the water for the pull. As thumb brushes thigh, rotate arm so that the pinky faces up again. Then begin the stroke with the other arm. Continue alternating arm stroke with arms moving continuously and in opposition to each other. Add the flutter kick, six beats (three kicks) to a stroke cycle. Breathe fully and continuously with face out of the water.

WET Drills for Backstroke

WET Drill: *Arm Motion*

➤ **Alternate Backward Arm Circles:** Standing in waist-deep water, alternately circle the arms backward, pulling them under the water, and recover above the water. Touch the ears as arms circle backward.

WET Drill: *Leg Motion*

➤ **Back Kick on Wall:** Hold onto the pool edge, with arms extended to either side. Bring legs up to the surface, adding the back flutter kick. Just barely break the surface, making water "boil."

Backstroke Sequence and Coordination

Refined Backstroke

As the S-shaped arm pull makes the crawlstroke more efficient, the backstroke is improved by adding the **bent-arm S-pull.**

Bent-Arm S-Pull

As arms move alternately, the body rolls naturally. The left arm enters and catches under the water, causing the body to dip down to the left at a 45-degree angle. The arm then pulls downward and backward. The pull continues, as the elbow bends and moves toward waist. The accelerated or final part of the pull occurs when the hand passes shoulder level. With elbow close to waist, the same forearm sweeps inward, then rotates and presses "still" water straight down to the feet (as if throwing a ball down to the feet). Simultaneously, the right shoulder, with arm at the side, breaks the water's surface. The arm then *recovers* overhead, with pinky up, and enters the catch position, creating a body roll to the right side.

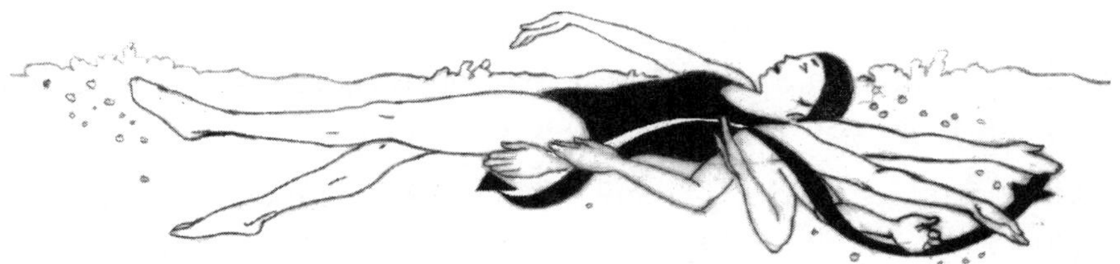

Bent-Arm S-Pull

WET Drills for Refined Backstroke

WET Drills: *Body Roll*

- **Trunk Turn:** With hands on hips, inhale and turn body at the waist to one side. Exhale as you turn to the center position. Inhale and turn to the opposite side.

- **1/4 Turn Jump:** Stand in chest-deep water with elbows bent and palms down on water's surface. Jump and turn 90 degrees to the right by thrusting both hands to the left at full arm's length, thus moving the water in the direction opposite to the turn. Reverse direction.

➤ **Rock and Roll at the Wall:** Float on back parallel to the pool wall, with inside arm holding on to the edge of the pool for support. Arms should be extended. Bring the outside arm overhead to the catch position. Using the refined bent-arm S-pull, the arm pulls and the body rolls in the direction of the pulling arm. The body rotates and the hips, heels, and shoulders touch the wall. The shoulder of the supporting arm rotates outward out of the water. As the pull is completed, the body rotates to the opposite direction, so that the chest, hips, and thighs graze the wall. The head stays centered throughout the drill. Repeat on the opposite side.

Mastering Backstroke Swim Drills

Use the following drills to improve the backstroke.

- **Propulsion Press:** To get a greater feel for the most propulsive phase of backstroke arm motion. Begin with back flutter kick, hands at sides. Bend elbows, keeping hands underwater at hip level. Then move hands away from body in a position similar to that of dribbling a basketball. From this position, you can create a powerful press with hands and forearms.
- **Backstroke Glide:** To slow down the arm stroke, to be attentive to the body roll, and accentuate the press at the end of the arm pull. Move arms alternately, but at each catch (hand entry), hold the glide with arm extended. Shoulders roll simultaneously and in opposite directions as each hand pushes water just prior to lifting arm for recovery.
- **Roll and Kick:** To practice the backstroke shoulder roll. Keep arms at side and flutter kick on back. Alternately roll body, allowing one shoulder to break the surface of the water. Keep head centered.

* **Backstroke Flutter Free Kick:** To practice proper body position and good flutter kick form. Flutter kick on back with both arms extended overhead. Keep body as stretched and streamlined as possible with arms held straight and close together.

* **Backstroke Distance per Stroke:** To increase the efficiency of each stroke. Pull backstroke with a pull buoy. Count the strokes needed to complete one pool length. On successive laps, try to lower the number of strokes.

CHECKLIST FOR BACKSTROKE

If You Are Doing This . . .	Try This . . .	Comments
1. Bending at the hips, and riding low in the water.	**1.** Streamline body position by keeping head back in line, while arching back slightly, pushing hips up, squeezing buttocks.	
2. Swimming with stiff ankles, with feet flexed and toes turned outward and upward.	**2.** Turn feet inward with big toes brushing past each other. Use fins to improve ankle flexibility	
3. Bending arms on recovery.	**3.** Keep elbows straight throughout recovery. Pinky finger enters water first for the catch.	

BACKSTROKE SKILL CHECKLIST

Date	Swim Skills	Comments
	Elementary Backstroke	
________	Back float and recovery	________
________	Arm motion	________
________	Frog kick	________
________	Stroke coordination	________
	Backstroke	
________	Back float	________
________	Arm motion	________
________	Backstroke flutter kick	________
________	Stroke coordination	________
	Refined Backstroke	
________	Bent-arm S-pull	________
	WET Drills	
________	Scratch and stretch	________
________	Frog kick on wall	________
________	Aqua jumping jack	________
________	Alternate backward arm circles	________
________	Back kick on wall	________
________	Trunk turn	________
________	1/4 turn jump	________
________	Rock and roll at the wall	________
	Mastering Skills	
________	Bend and push	________
________	Arm motion with flutter kick	________
________	Seated kick	________
________	Corner kick	________
________	Just the kick	________
________	Propulsion press	________
________	Backstroke glide	________
________	Roll and kick	________
________	Flutter free kick	________
________	Distance per stroke	________

BACKSTROKES SKILL EVALUATION CHART

Name ______________________________ Class ______________

Dates	Stroke Component	Common Errors	How to Correct Them

General Comments: ____

____

____

____

Chapter 6

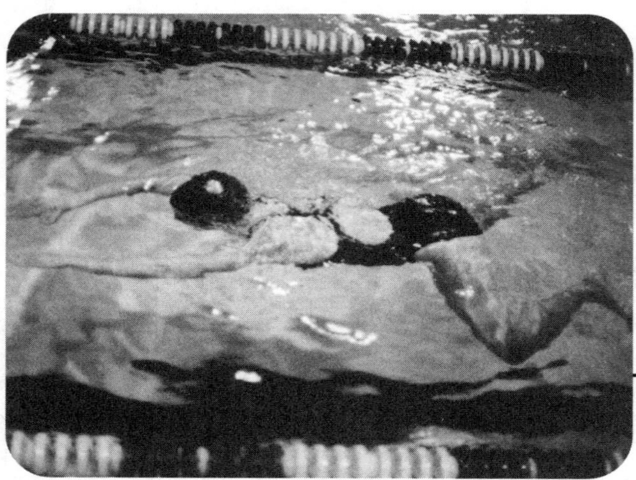

Breaststroke

The **breaststroke** is one of the oldest swimming strokes. It is slower than other strokes, but it is also relaxing. In Europe, the breaststroke is usually learned first. The breaststroke is a symmetrical stroke where the movement of one side of the body is mirrored by the other side in both timing and position. In addition, in this stroke, the arms and legs are equally as important for propulsion or forward movement.

Body Position

Begin in a prone streamlined body position.

Arm Motion

The breaststroke is a flowing stroke in which the arms move simultaneously underwater in a motion called the **heart-shaped arm motion.** For the *catch,* extend arms forward, thumbs pointing down. Press arms outward and downward, palms leading, for the *pull.* Bend elbows, keeping them up, and pull them back to shoulder level. Then bring forearms together under chest to complete the shape of an upside down heart.

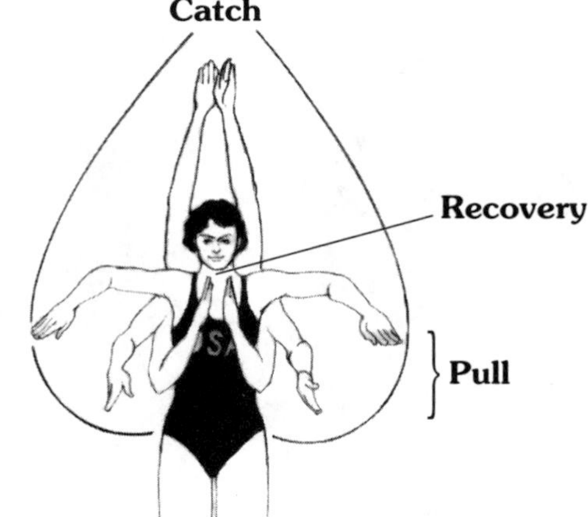

Heart-Shaped Arm Motion

From this prayerlike position of the hands and arms, *recover* to the starting position underwater by extending arms forward.

Leg Motion

The breaststroke leg motion utilizes the whip kick executed from a prone position. The legs begin in an extended streamlined position. Bend knees simultaneously toward pool bottom and simultaneously bring heels up to buttocks. Separate knees approximately hip width apart, then rotate flexed feet outward with lower legs forming a V. The propulsion of the kick is achieved by straightening knees and bringing lower legs together in an accelerated snapping motion, with feet and ankles touching and toes pointed.

FROG KICK FOR BREASTSTROKE

Some breaststroke swimmers prefer the frog kick rather than the whip kick, especially when concerned about possible knee strain. In the frog kick, the knees bend, and the legs separate wider than hip width, while the feet remain close together. The legs then extend into a wide V and are brought together with a snapping motion.

Frog Kick

Stroke Coordination

Start in a streamlined glide position, arms and legs fully extended. As the arm pull begins, bend knees to begin the kick. The shoulders and head will rise up naturally and ride high, enabling the swimmer to take a breath. As legs finish the kick, recover arms to an undulating glide with body streamlined and with face in the water exhaling.

SWIM TIP: *During the arm pull of the stroke cycle, the shoulders and the head rise naturally. This is the time to inhale deeply. During the glide when face returns to the water, exhale completely.*

WET Drills for Breaststroke

WET Drills: *Arm Motion*

- **Walk and Pull:** Stand, then walk in chest-deep water, while practicing the breaststroke arm motion. Begin with arms in front of body just below water's surface. Keep elbows straight and thumbs touching. Pull hands outward, then inward toward chest in heart-shaped motion. Recover them underwater by extending arms into glide position.

➤ **Forward Scull:** Stand in chest-deep water, with arms extended in front of body and thumbs pointed downward. Sweep arms out to shoulder level, pressing water backward. Then turn thumbs up and press water forward, until palms almost touch. Next turn thumbs downward and repeat, creating a figure-8 sculling motion in front of you. Imagine hands simultaneously drawing an infinity sign (∞) underwater.

WET Drills: *Leg Motion*

➤ **Whip Kick:** Practice whip kick on wall with arms in bracket position. Bring heels as close as possible to buttocks, dropping knees without breaking water. Then flex feet, separate and extend legs in a V position, keeping knees hip width apart. Flex and rotate feet outward with lower legs forming a V. Straighten knees and bring lower legs together in a snapping motion so that ankles touch and toes are pointed. This snap causes forward propulsion.

➤ **Plié and Jump:** Stand in chest-deep water with knees bent as in a plié position. Jump up, using leg muscles to explode off the bottom, straighten legs, and point toes. Return to starting position and repeat.

➤ **Karate Kick:** Stand in waist-deep water, with back to the pool wall and arms fully extended. Hold on to the pool edge for support, keeping knees close together. Bend the right knee and bring the right foot up close to the right buttock. Rotate the knee outward and touch the wall with the heel. Then rotate the leg in a circle and resume the starting position. Repeat with the left leg.

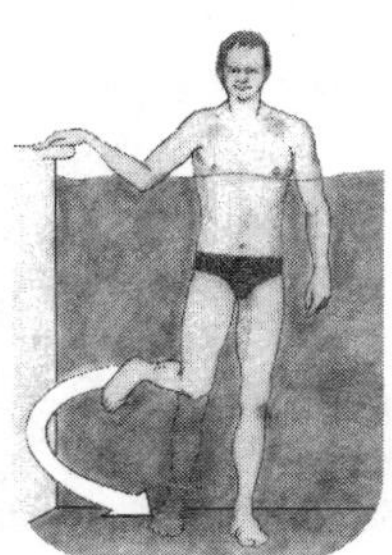

WET Drills: *Coordination*

➤ **Heart-Shaped Pull with Knee Bend:** Combine the heart-shaped pull with a knee bend in a standing position. At start of the pull, bend knees. As hands come together for the recovery, straighten legs.

➤ **Stroke Coordination:** Standing in chest-deep water, begin with arms extended in front, shoulders under the water. Move arms simultaneously and symmetrically underwater and trace the shape of an upside-down heart. With thumbs pointing down, press hands outward and downward. Bend elbows and press palms back toward feet. When hands are at shoulder level, bring forearms together under chest to complete the heart shape. From this prayerlike position of the hands and arms, recover to starting position underwater by extending arms forward.

SWIM TIP: *After the heart-shaped arm pull, recover arms together quickly in a streamlined glide.*

Refined Breaststroke

Experienced swimmers who use the breaststroke as a serious fitness exercise or in competition use the refined stroke which has a quicker arm motion.

Arm Motion

Compared to the breaststroke, the arm motion of the refined breaststroke can be described as a sculling action. At the catch, the arms pull by sculling outward, followed by an inward scull. Propulsion is obtained equally from both the outward and the inward scull. Recovery occurs

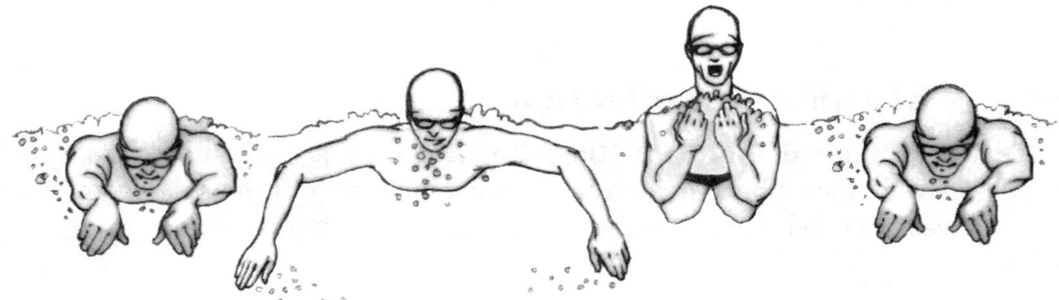

Refined Breaststroke Arm Motion

with hands breaking the surface of the water and reaching forward to the catch position after a short glide. Head and shoulders follow, riding high in the water.

Leg Motion

Bring heels up toward buttocks, dropping knees without breaking the water surface. Then flex and rotate feet outward with lower legs forming a V. Effect propulsion by straightening knees and bring lower legs together (soles touching) in a snapping motion so that ankles and pointed feet touch.

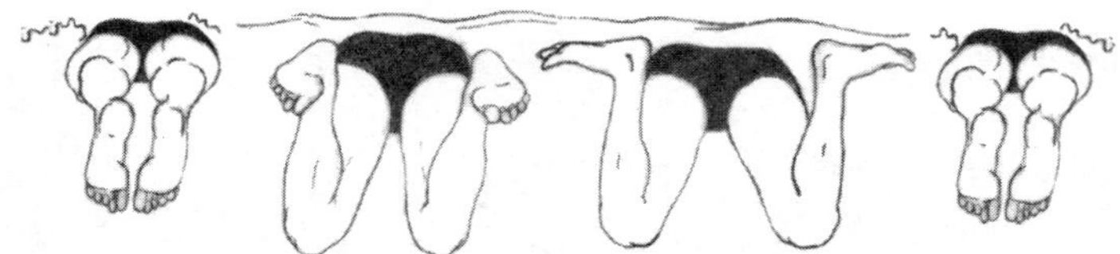

Refined Breaststroke Whip Kick Leg Motion

Mastering Breaststroke Swim Drills

Use these drills to improve the basic components of the breaststroke.

- **Pull-Kick-Kick:** To develop an undulating body motion with proper timing of pull, kick, and breathing. Alternate one arm pull with two whip kicks. As first kick is completed, drive arms and head underwater so body is completely immersed for second kick.
- **Whip Kick:** To practice kicking with proper body position to increase power. Extend arms straight in front and glide, with or without kickboard, and do the whip kick. When using a kickboard, either keep head above water and breathe normally or coordinate the inhalation and exhalation with kick. When not using a kickboard, face remains in the water. To take a breath, scull hands outward to get a quick lift of head and shoulders.

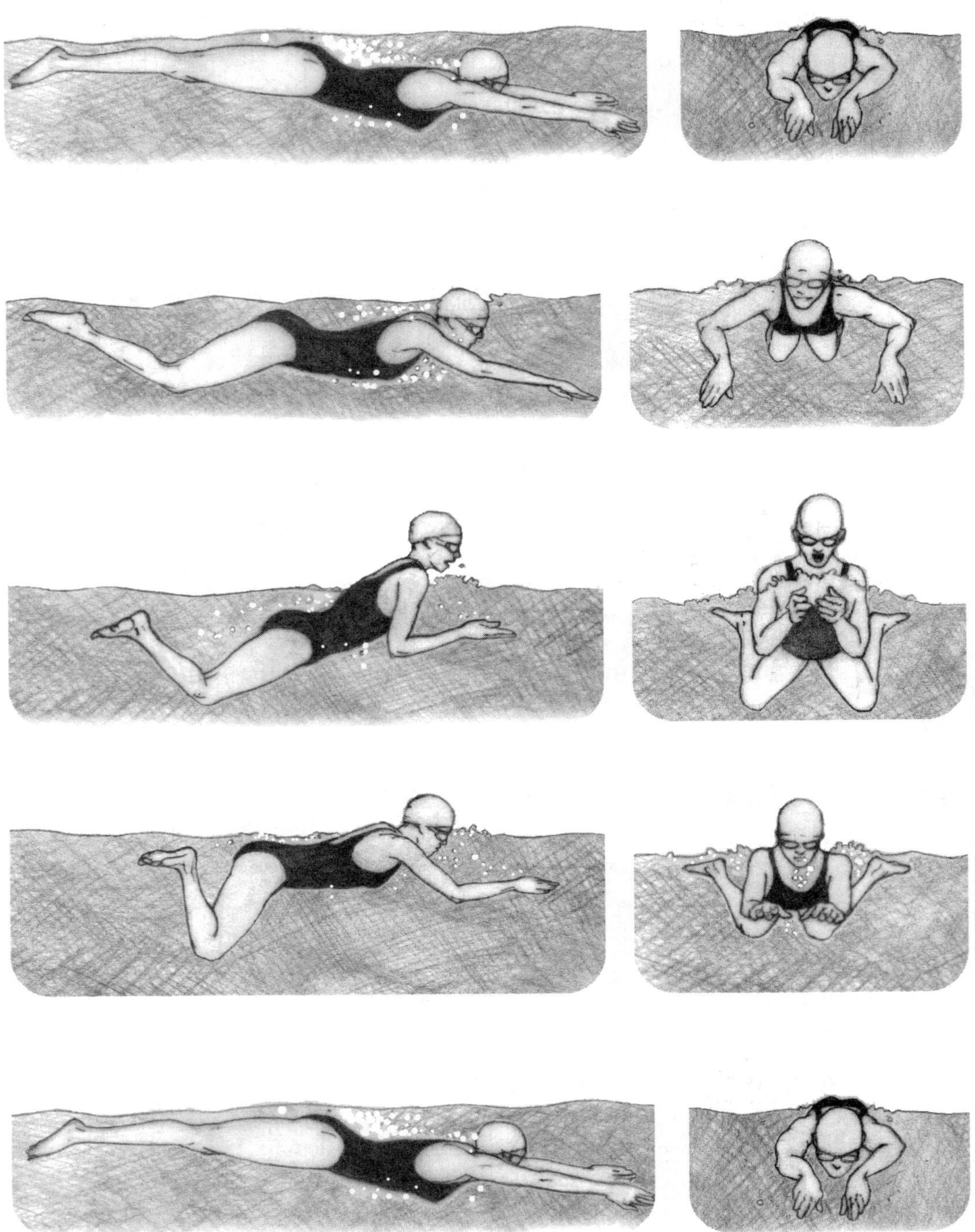

Breaststroke Sequence and Coordination

- **Wade with Pull:** To practice arm pull. Walk in chest-deep water, using the breaststroke arm motion to assist in walking across the pool. Keep both hands in sight at all times. Hands should never go behind the body. For variation try drill with hand paddles.
- **Vertical Kick:** To strengthen the kick. Practice the whip kick while in a vertical position in deep water. To make drill harder, decrease arm motion for minimal or no sculling support. Use a flotation device for support when first practicing the drill.
- **Distance per Stroke:** To maximize the efficiency of stroke. Count the strokes needed to complete one length. On successive lengths, decrease the number of stroke cycles.

CHECKLIST FOR BREASTSTROKE

If You Are Doing This . . .	Try This . . .	Comments
1. Pulling hands below shoulders and beginning recovery at waist.	1. Keep hands in sight throughout pull and recovery.	
2. Lifting head for breath after pull.	2. At the catch, press downward as well as slightly outward. Head will lift as shoulders rise up naturally.	
3. Kicking without propulsion.	3. Flex feet and position them outside knees during propulsion phase of kick. Practice whip kick.	
4. Not attaining a glide after the kick.	4. Recover hands quickly by squeezing elbows and forearms together and then extend arms overhead with a slight downward thrust.	

BREASTSTROKE SKILL CHECKLIST

Date	Swim Skills	Comments
	Breaststroke	
________	Prone body position	________
________	Heart-shaped arm motion	________
________	Whip kick	________
________	Frog kick	________
________	Stroke coordination	
	Refined Breaststroke	
________	Sculling arm motion	________
________	Whip kick leg motion	________
	WET Drills	
________	Walk and pull	________
________	Forward scull	________
________	Whip kick	________
________	Plié and jump	________
________	Karate kick	________
________	Heart-shaped pull with knee bend	________
________	Stroke coordination	________
	Mastering Breaststroke Drills	
________	Pull-kick-kick	________
________	Whip kick	________
________	Wade with pull	________
________	Vertical kick	________
________	Distance per stroke	________

BREASTSTROKE SKILL EVALUATION CHART

Name ______________________________ Class ______________

Dates	Stroke Component	Common Errors	How to Correct Them

General Comments: ____

____

____

____

Chapter 7

Butterfly

The **butterfly** is the most energetic and the most challenging of all the strokes. It is also graceful, exhilarating, and sensuous. Considered the most difficult, the butterfly is, in fact, the S-pull arm motion done with each arm. The symmetrical arm and leg motion pattern is similar to the breaststroke, except that the arms recover above the water's surface.

The butterfly evolved in competition from the breaststroke as an over-the-water recovery. Remember Pablo Morales' 1992 Olympic 100-meter butterfly win? Try it. It is a challenge that is worth the effort.

Body Position

The butterfly stroke begins in a prone streamlined position.

Arm Motion

The arms move simultaneously in a **double S-pull** or **keyhole arm motion** and recovery is above the water. Hands *catch* or enter the water, shoulder width apart. Extend hands forward, outward, and

Butterfly Keyhole Arm Motion

downward for the *pull*. Then bring hands together under the abdomen near the waist, elbows bent about 90 degrees and press backward toward the feet. When arms are almost fully extended, hands near hips, *recovery* begins. Arms clear the water, elbows leading as they swing forward to return to catch or starting position.

SWIM TIP: *Keep elbows higher than hands throughout the keyhole arm pull, especially during the recovery.*

Leg Motion

The leg kick for the butterfly is known as the **dolphin kick.** It is similar to the flutter kick, but the legs move in unison. A wave-like body motion is created by bringing the hips up, buttocks breaking the surface as legs kick downward. On upward leg motion, the feet should just break the surface.

Stroke Coordination

To coordinate the keyhole arm motion and the dolphin kick, start with the single-beat kick. Pull and inhale; then kick and exhale while arms are recovering. Although the butterfly is normally done with a two-beat kick per arm stroke, the coordination of arm and leg motion is best learned by starting with a single-beat kick per arm stroke.

Begin in a face-float position, arms extended underwater and shoulder-width apart for the catch. Bend legs as arms press outward, then inward, then back past hips. Extend legs for propulsion as arms lift above the water for the recovery. As shoulders rise during the pull, head lifts just enough to get a bite of air. Then lower head immediately.

When the single-beat kick feels comfortable, the next step is a two-beat kick per arm cycle. Coordinate the butterfly stroke in the following sequence: catch and kick, pull and kick, inhale and recover.

WET Drills for Butterfly

WET Drills: *Arm Motion*

➤ **Double-Arm Circle:** In waist- or chest-deep water, stand, then walk, practicing the double-arm S-pull with keyhole pattern. Brush thumbs past thighs before recovering arms out of water. This is similar to the arm motion used for the jump rope.

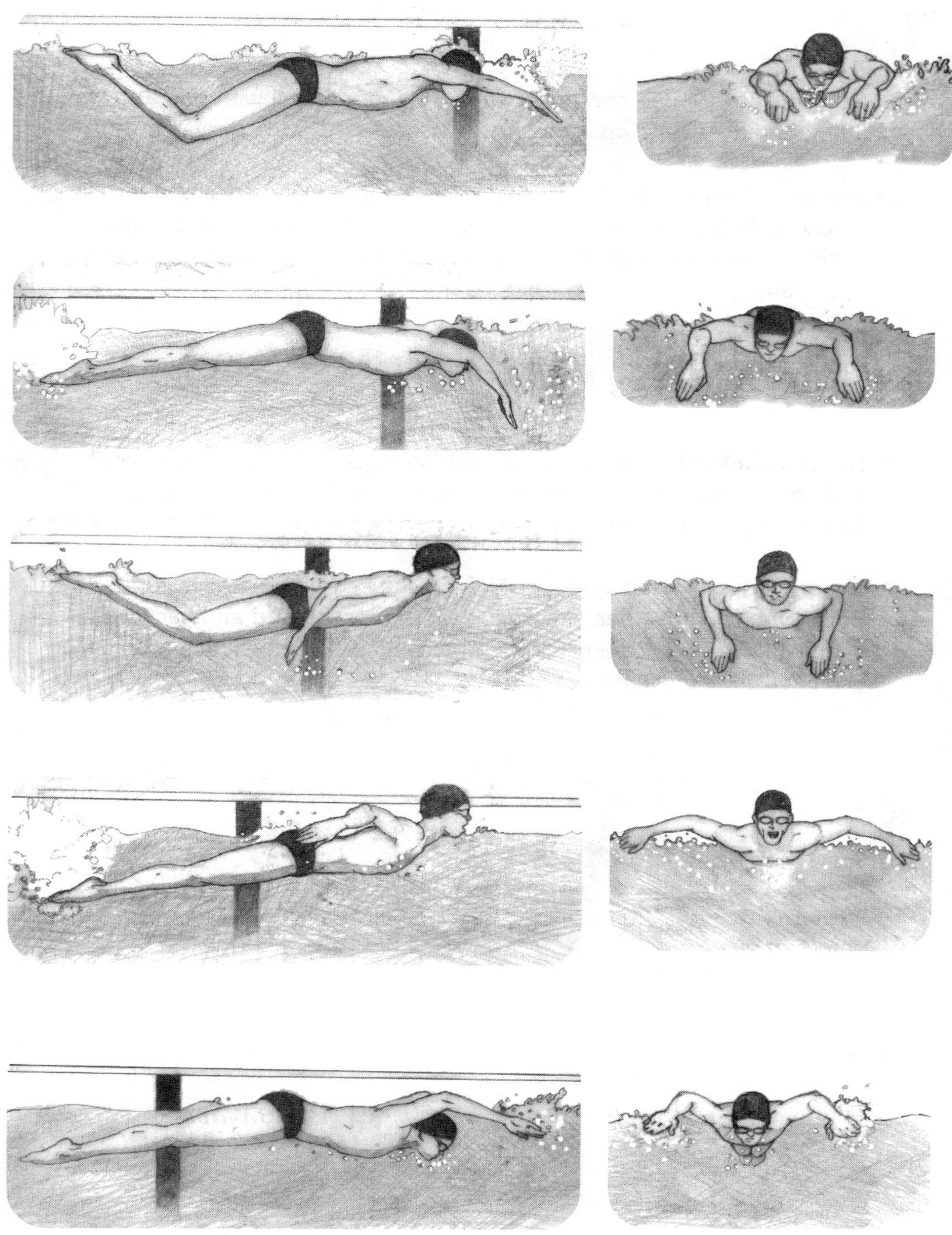

Butterfly Sequence and Coordination

- **Single-Arm Fly:** In chest-deep water, stand and pull with one arm at a time as knees bend and straighten twice. Repeat with other arm.

- **Lunge:** Stand with back against pool wall. Place feet on wall with arms extended backwards, holding on to deck, with back arched slightly. Push off from wall with legs, and lunge forward with arms recovering over water.

WET Drills: *Leg Motion*

- **Seated Kick:** Sit on pool's edge, with knees bent. Drop heels to touch wall, then simultaneously straighten knees and lift legs to water's surface, toes pointed downward.

- **Body Wave:** In deep water, hold edge of pool with one arm for support. With legs together, press hips alternately forward and backward, keeping knees relaxed and allowing hips and legs to move in a dolphin-like undulating movement.

Seated Kick

Body Wave

WET Drills: *Coordination*

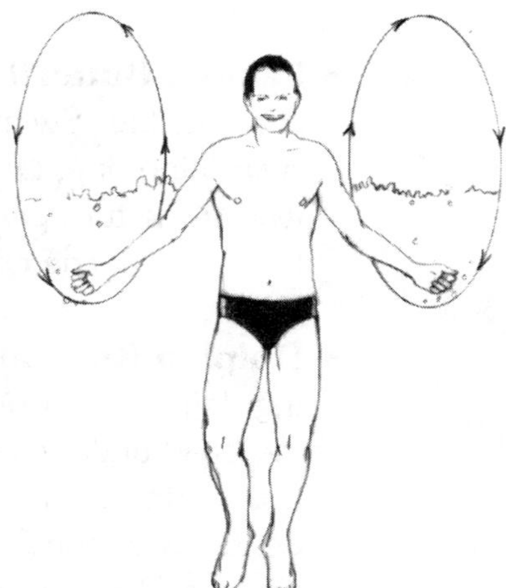

➤ **Jump Rope:** Simulate jumping rope, without actually jumping or clearing a rope. Start in a standing position, arms forward on water's surface. As arms circle downward into water, bend knees. As arms brush by legs and recover, straighten legs. This is similar to the coordination for the single-beat kick and the butterfly arm pull.

> ***SWIM TIP:*** *While the butterfly uses the S-pull that is used for the crawlstroke, without the body roll, arm recovery is more difficult. Stretches and WETS will help to increase flexibility and strength.*

Mastering Butterfly Swim Drills

- **Walk and Pull:** To provide coordination of arm pull with breathing. Walk in waist-deep water and bend at waist to place face in the water. Practice butterfly arm motion. As arms press back, lift head for a breath, and as arms recover above the water, the head is in the water.

- **One-Arm Butterfly:** To practice the coordination of arms and dolphin kick in a less exhausting manner. Swim with one arm at a time and keep the other arm stretched overhead. Breathe on the side of the stroking arm. The dolphin kick and the undulation of the body remain the same in the simultaneous arm stroke. Change arms every few strokes or at the end of every lap.

- **Limited Butterfly:** To swim the butterfly according to each person's ability. Swim laps using the crawl and after each turn, try swimming one, two, or three strokes of butterfly. The glide off the wall at the turn gives momentum to the swimmer for effective butterfly form. The crawl gives the swimmer time to rest.

- **Dolphin Kick on Side:** To improve body undulation by practicing dolphin kick on the side. Extend bottom arm overhead, keeping head underwater. Lift and turn head quickly for air. Think how a dolphin swims. Flex and extend hips, allowing knees to bend gently, with equal forward and backward movement. Change sides while pulling with bottom arm, and breathe.

- **Body Wave with Fins:** To feel the undulating body motion that comes from the dolphin kick. In deep water, wearing fins, perform the dolphin kick by flexing and extending hips, allowing knees to bend naturally (moving hips backward and forward equally). This hip action creates a wave-like motion of legs and fins. Fins that move equally forward and backward keep the swimmer in one place and provide necessary support for keeping the head above water.

SWIM RX: *It is unwise for swimmers who have had back injuries or pain to swim the butterfly.*

CHECKLIST FOR BUTTERFLY

If You Are Doing This . . .	Try This . . .	Comments
1. Keeping head up too long during inhalation.	1. Nod head forward in water after inhalation to allow arms to recover easily. Exhale fully underwater.	______
2. Dragging arms during overwater recovery.	2. Keep elbows higher than hand throughout recovery; improve flexibility by stretching; improve upper body strength.	______
3. Bending knees excessively, with feet breaking surface of the water.	3. Practice body wave WET drill.	______
4. Gliding too long or experiencing a "dead" spot in stroke after catch.	4. Begin catch sooner. Add second kick later. Keep body undulating continuously. If tired, stop and rest.	______

BUTTERFLY SKILL CHECKLIST

Date	Swim Skills	Comments
	Butterfly	
______	Body position	______
______	Arm motion	______
______	Leg motion–dolphin kick	______
______	Single-beat kick	
______	Double-beat kick	
______	Stroke Coordination	______
	WET Drills	
______	Double-arm circle	______
______	Single-arm fly	______
______	Lunge	______
______	Seated kick	______
______	Body wave	______
______	Jump rope	______
	Mastering Butterfly Drills	
______	One-arm butterfly	______
______	Limited butterfly	______
______	Dolphin kick on side	______
______	Body wave with fins	______
______	Walk and pull	______

BUTTERFLY SKILL EVALUATION CHART

Name ______________________________ Class ______________

Dates	Stroke Component	Common Errors	How to Correct Them

General Comments: ____

____

____

____

Chapter 8

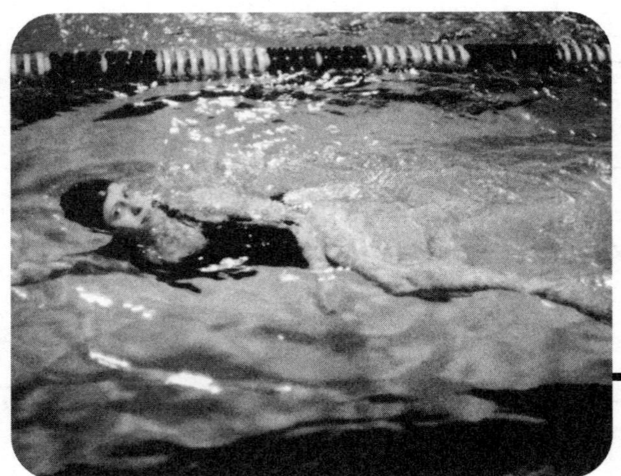

Sidestroke

The **sidestroke** is a relaxing stroke. The body is extended sideways with the head just above the surface of the water while the arms and legs remain underwater. It can be swum on either side. The sidestroke is frequently used for lifesaving rescues.

Body Position

The sidestroke begins in a streamlined body position on either the right or left side, with the bottom arm extended overhead but under the water.

Arm Motion

Begin in a streamlined glide position, lying on either side. The bottom arm is extended overhead in line with the ear. The top arm rests on the thigh. The bottom arm *catches* in the extended position and *pulls* with elbow bending underneath the face as the hand moves toward the chest. At the same time the top arm *recovers* upward and both arms

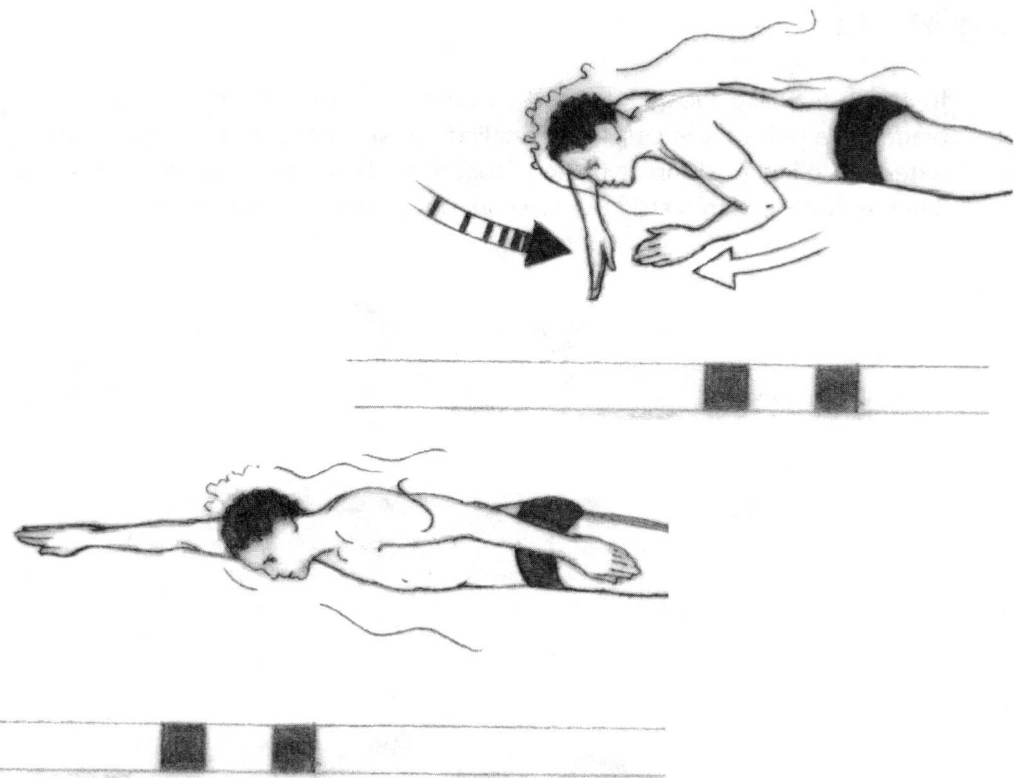

Sidestroke Arm Motion

move simultaneously toward each other, with both hands meeting at chest level. The top arm then pushes down toward the feet as the bottom arm recovers, extending overhead. A glide phase follows and the stroke cycle begins again. This motion is similar to picking an apple from a tree. After picking the apple, place it in the other hand, throw it down, and then reach for another apple.

To swim sidestroke on the other side, tuck knees to chest and extend legs to the side in the opposite direction.

OVERARM SIDESTROKE TIP: *For variety, recover the bottom arm over the surface of the water to the catch position.*

Leg Motion

In the sidestroke kick, the legs separate and come together like the blades of a pair of scissors. This is called the **scissors kick.** Begin in an extended glide position, with legs together. Tuck knees toward chest. Then extend legs in a stride or scissors position with top foot flexed and

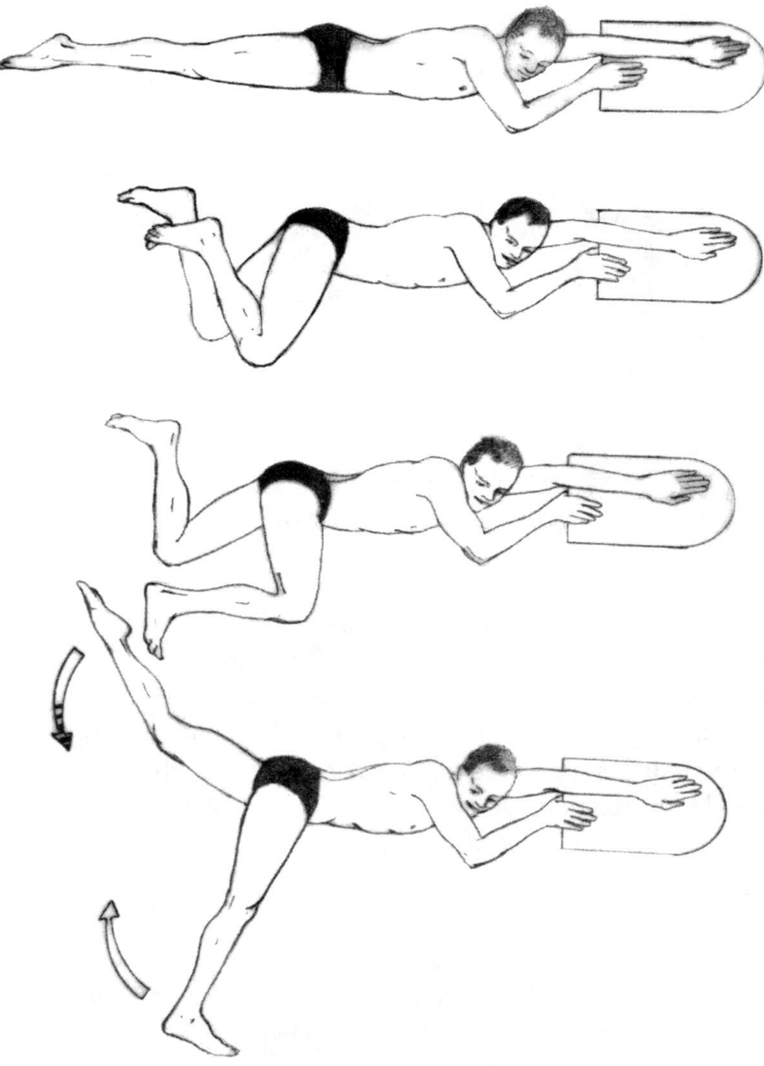

Scissors Kick Leg Motion

forward, and bottom leg back with toes pointed. Snap legs together sharply for propulsion and finish in the glide position with legs together.

In an **inverted kick** the top leg moves back and the bottom leg forward.

SWIM TIP: *Try both the scissors kick and the inverted kick and choose one that is comfortable.*

Stroke Coordination

This stroke has two distinct steps. In the first step, the arms, legs, and body all contract together in the middle of the body as swimmer inhales. In the second step, the body extends and straightens into a streamlined glide. The bottom arm initiates the first step by pulling down as the legs bend and the arms meet at chest level. In the second step, the bottom arm extends to recover, the top arm extends overhead and presses toward the feet, and the legs straighten and squeeze together, as the swimmer exhales.

WET Drills for Sidestroke

WET Drill: *Body Position*

➤ **Float Position:** This float position is preparation for swimming the sidestroke. Hold a kickboard lengthwise under each arm. Extend the bottom arm in a side-glide position with the ear resting on the arm. The top arm rests along the other side of the body on the hip, the legs are together and extended. The body is on its side and balanced in a float position .

WET Drills: *Arm Motion*

➤ **Apple Picking:** This drill simulates the sidestroke arm motion. Begin by standing in chest-deep water. Extend one arm overhead, reach up, and pick an apple from a tree. Place it in the other hand at chest level

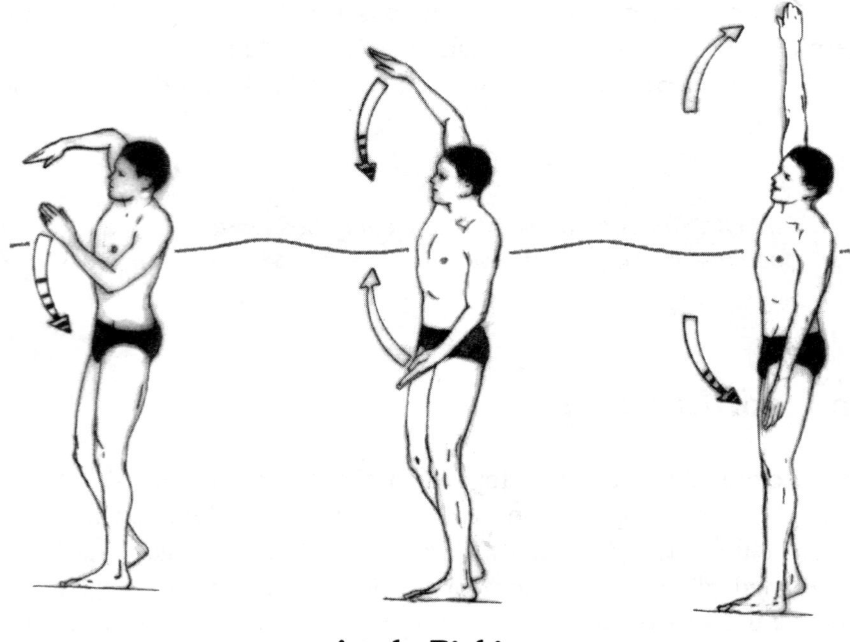

Apple Picking

and throw the apple downward (as if into a basket). Reach for another apple. Then bring both hands underwater, arms extended sideways and practice apple picking underwater.

- **Accordion Squeeze:** Simulate playing the accordion by expanding arms to full width and then contracting arms, hands meeting at chest level.

- **Rope Tug:** Walk sideways, facing a real rope (either a lifeline or safety line) or an imaginary one. Pull body in one direction along the rope, leading with the bottom arm. Then reverse direction and change arms.

WET Drills: *Leg Motion*

➤ **Scissors Kick in Bracket Position:** Lie on side with both hands on the wall in bracket position. Begin in extended glide position, legs together. Bend knees toward chest. Then separate and extend legs, one moving backward with toes pointed, the other leg underwater and parallel to the surface to make a "giant step" position. Then squeeze or whip legs together.

➤ **Scissors Lunge:** Stand in chest-deep water with feet together. Take a long lunge sideways with lunging leg bent at the knee, and the standing leg straight. Draw standing leg up to meet the lunging leg as it straightens. Continue lunging forward; then change directions.

WET Drills: *Coordination*

➤ **Gallop:** Leap forward with one leg, straighten legs on height of jump, squeezing them together. Repeat with other leg.

➤ **Walk:** Combine scissors lunge with accordion squeeze. Stand with legs together and arms extended to the sides at shoulder level, palms facing forward. Take a large step sideways with lunging leg bent at knee, while bringing arms together to meet underwater at chest, keeping elbows bent. Then stretch arms out to the side and bring legs together and straighten. Repeat, stepping in the same direction. Then reverse direction.

Mastering the Sidestroke Swim Drills

- **Vertical Scissors Kick:** To strengthen the kick. Practice the scissors kick while in a vertical position in deep water, using arm sculling for support. If needed, use flotation device while in the learning stage. Then reduce support for a more challenging drill.
- **Distance per Stroke:** To maximize the efficiency of the stroke. Count the strokes needed to complete a length while swimming. On successive lengths try to decrease the number of stroke cycles.

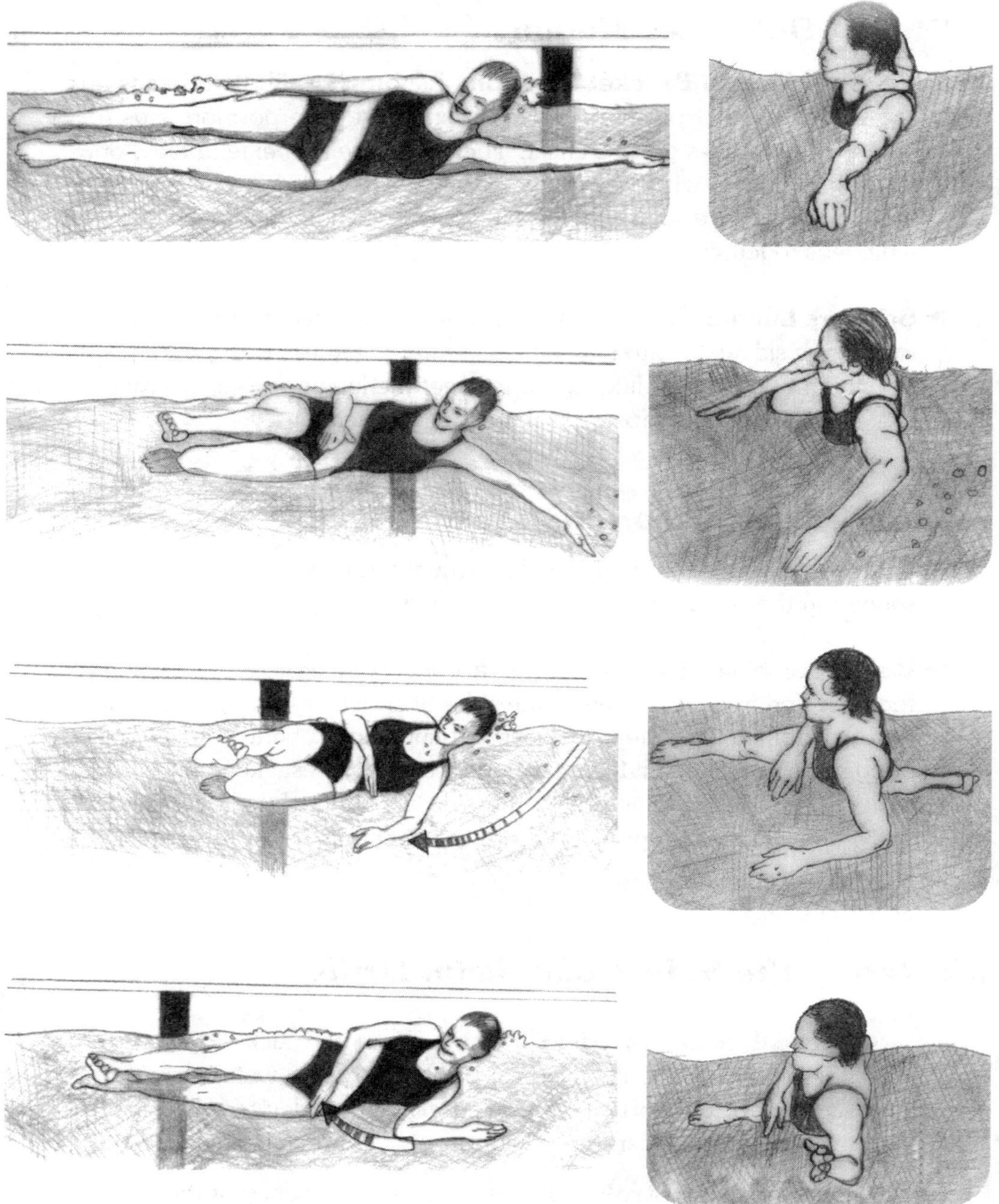

Sidestroke Sequence and Coordination

- **Arm and Leg Motion Coordination:** To coordinate bottom arm motion with kick. Hold a pull-buoy at chest with top arm. Bottom arm is extended overhead in catch position. Begin arm pull as knees are brought to chest in tuck position. This is the end of the first step. Complete the kick by snapping legs together as bottom arm recovers underwater back to its catch position. This is the end of the second step.

CHECKLIST FOR SIDESTROKE

If You Are Doing This . . .	Try This . . .	Comments
1. Continuously moving arms and legs without gliding.	1. Allow pause for glide phase (counting to 3) after each kick to streamline body. Keep lower ear in the water.	
2. Splashing water with arms and legs.	2. Flex foot of forward leg to press water backward on scissors kick. Keep hands underwater.	
3. Swimming sidestroke off balance.	3. Use kickboard under bottom arm for support to stabilize body on side (rather than on front or back).	
4. Holding head completely out of water.	4. Place lower ear on surface of water.	

SIDESTROKE SKILL CHECKLIST

Date	Swim Skills	Comments
	Sidestroke	
________	Body position	________
________	Arm motion	________
________	Leg motion	________
________	Scissors kick	________
________	Inverted kick	________
________	Stroke coordination	________
	WET Drills	
________	Float position	________
________	Apple picking	________
________	Accordion squeeze	________
________	Rope tug	________
________	Scissors kick in bracket	________
________	Scissors lunge	________
________	Gallop	________
________	Walk	________
	Mastering Sidestroke	
________	Vertical scissors kick	________
________	Distance per stroke	________
________	Arm and leg motion coordination	________

SIDESTROKE SKILL EVALUATION CHART

Name ______________________________ Class ________________

Dates	Stroke Component	Common Errors	How to Correct Them

General Comments: ____

____

____

____

Stroke Summary

The following chart highlights the strokes and components described in Unit II. It provides the relative arm and leg power contribution to the overall propulsion of the swim strokes.

Pattern	Stroke	Arm Motion	Leg Motion	Approximate % of Stroke's Power from Arms	Approximate % of Stroke's Power from Legs
Alternating	Crawlstroke	Straight	Flutter kick	60	40
	Refined Crawlstroke	S-pull	Flutter kick; crossover kick	80	20
	Backstroke	Straight or bent-arm pull	Flutter kick	70	30
	Bent-arm backstroke	Bent-arm S-pull	Flutter kick	75	25
Simultaneous	Elementary backstroke	V pull	Frog kick	50	50
	Breaststroke	Heart-shaped	Whip kick	50	50
	Butterfly	Keyhole	Dolphin kick	65	35
Variable	Sidestroke	Regular (or overarm)	Scissors or inverted kick	50	50

Chapter 9

Turns and Starts

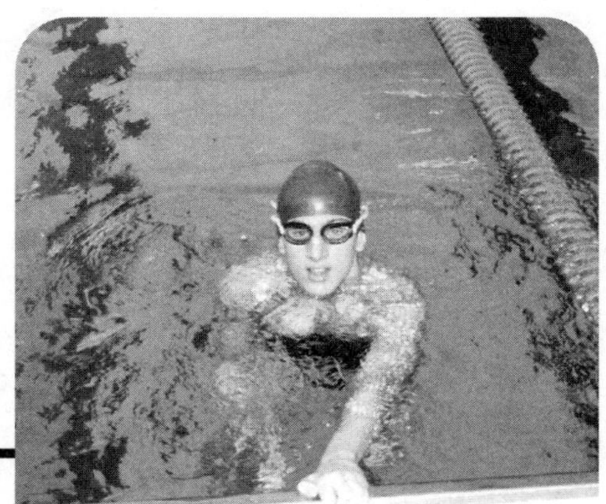

Learning to swim laps without interruption is the key component of swimming for fitness. Continuous swimming becomes possible with a well-executed **turn** and **push-off.** They create the forward momentum needed for the next lap. The forward momentum is further extended by keeping the body in a streamlined position at the beginning of the new lap.

Crawlstroke Turns

Open Turn

Near the end of a lap when approaching the wall, grasp the pool edge with the hand that has just recovered and is extended forward. Pull the body toward the wall, bringing knees into a **tuck** position in front of body. Lower the shoulder of the free arm into the water and turn body in the opposite direction, 180 degrees, swinging legs and hips under the body and bringing feet flat against the pool wall. Take a breath, keeping head just above the water. Release hand from the wall, swinging it over the shoulder near the forehead. Extend arm just beneath the water's surface to join the other arm. Both arms are now stretched

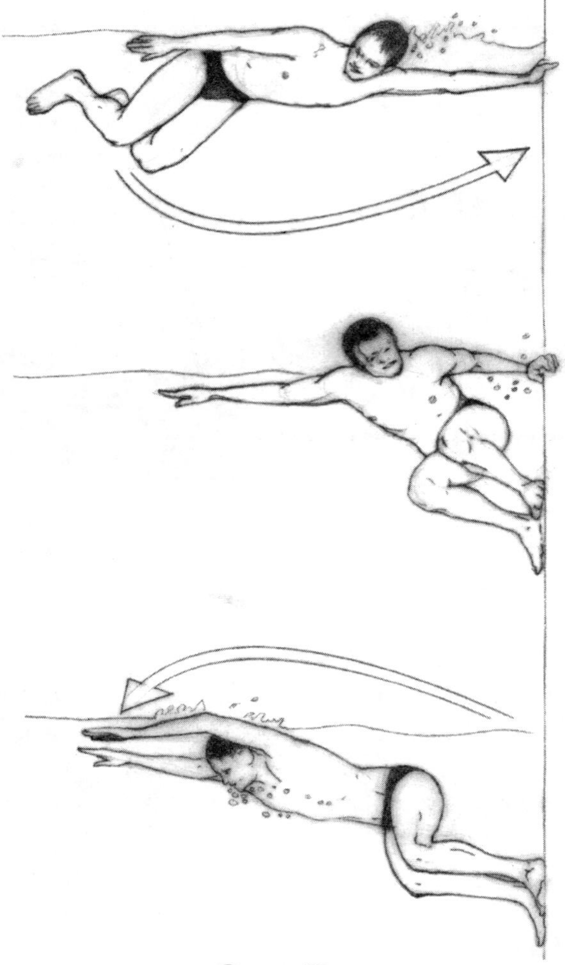

Open Turn

overhead. At the same time, turn toes downward to rotate body to a face float position. Then push off the wall with legs and glide in a streamlined body position. Begin flutter kick and add arm stroke when coming out above surface of water.

SWIM TIP: *For efficient swimming, use the momentum of the glide. During the glide, keep the body in full streamlined position. Remember, gliding is like coasting downhill on a bicycle.*

WET Drills: *Open Turn*

- **Sit-Up:** Place back against the corner of the pool, arms grasping the edge. Bend both knees, bringing them up to chest. Twist body and bring legs toward the right. Extend legs, bend knees up, and return to center. Twist to the left, extend legs, bend knees up again, and return to center. Repeat.

- **Tuck and Turn:** Stand several feet from the pool wall. Push off from the bottom, glide and kick to the wall, arms stretched overhead. Grasp the pool edge with one hand, then tuck your knees to your chest. Turn 180 degrees, adding the push-off from the wall. Practice the open turn with alternating the lead arm.

- **Quick Lightning Turn:** Stand with one hand touching pool edge, arm extended, while other arm is extended in the direction of push-off. Tuck knees up and place feet on wall. With body in side position, submerge head underwater as arm on the pool edge bends and quickly brushes past forehead in a salute position. Hands then meet overhead and legs straighten for push-off. Repeat with opposite arm leading. Then begin with both hands touching wall simultaneously as in breaststroke and butterfly stroke. Extend one arm in direction of push-off and continue quick lightning turn.

Quick Lightning Arm Turn

Closed Turn

As the crawlstroke improves, increase the number of laps and replace the open turn with the more efficient closed turn. Approach the wall as in the open turn, making sure to inhale deeply. First, grasp the wall with the extended arm, tuck knees, and place feet on wall to turn keeping head underwater during turn. Rotate feet against the wall and push off into a streamlined glide position.

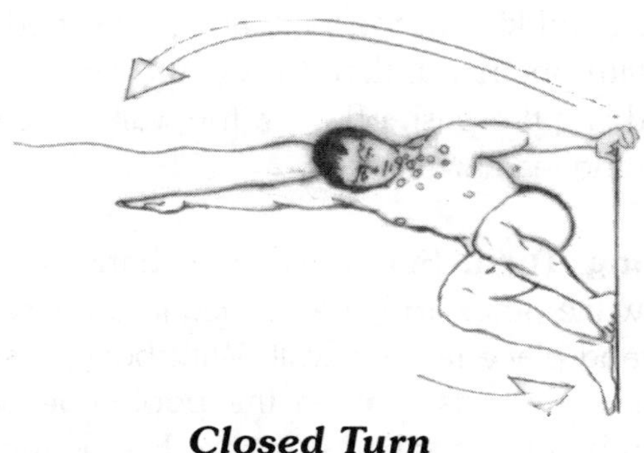

Closed Turn

WET Drill: *Closed Turn*

➤ **Closed Encounters:** Stand several strokes from the wall. Swim into the wall and practice the closed turn, keeping face underwater throughout the turn.

Flip Turn

The flip turn is used by swimmers who want to add speed and splash to their lap swimming. This somersault turn optimizes momentum at the wall and adds power to the push-off. Swim toward the wall and tuck chin to chest. The extended arm pulls downward as legs dolphin kick to initiate the tuck or flip. The arms push water overhead, which helps to lift or flip the hips over. The body twists on to its side as feet touch wall. The push-off follows as body is in streamlined position with arms extended overhead.

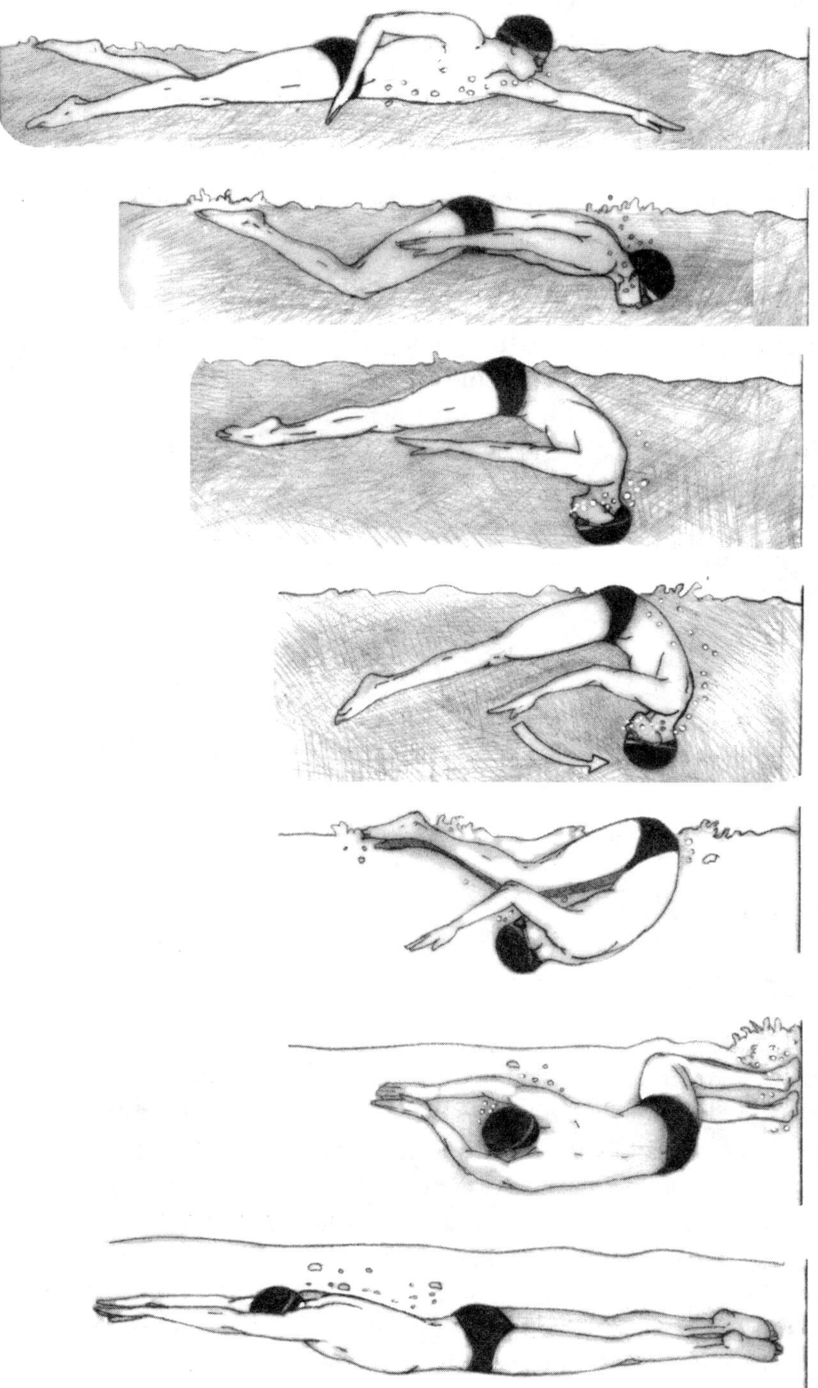

Flip Turn Sequence

WET Drills: *Flip Turn*

- **Face Splash:** Stand in chest-deep water with hands at sides. Bend at knees as hands simultaneously splash water upward toward face. Then extend hand overhead and straighten knees. Return hands to side and repeat.

- **Front Tuck Somersault:** In deep water, start in a face float position with hands at sides. Drop chin to chest, tuck knees to chest, and push water backward with a scooping arm circle motion that begins at the hips and goes toward the head, as if splashing water in face. This movement flips body over in a somersault.

- **Swim and Tuck:** Begin five yards from the wall. As swimmer approaches the wall, do a front tuck somersault.

> ***SWIM TIP:*** *Take a good breath of air before starting the flip turn and continuously exhale through the nose throughout the front tuck somersault.*

Backstroke Turns

Open Turn

A good turn preserves the momentum of forward motion. To begin the backstroke turn, grab the gutter or deck edge with one hand or press hand to the wall at water level with palm flat and thumb up. Begin to bend and drop elbow of arm on the wall to bring head and body close to the wall and turn in the direction of that arm on the wall. Tuck knees in close to chest, and keep free arm extended in the original direction, turning 180 degrees on back. The swimmer ends up facing the wall with feet touching it. Inhale while bringing arm at the wall overhead to meet the extended one.

For the push-off, stretch arms and upper body as knees are straightened. Keep head tucked between arms, slightly underwater. Glide to the surface of the water, exhaling continuously.

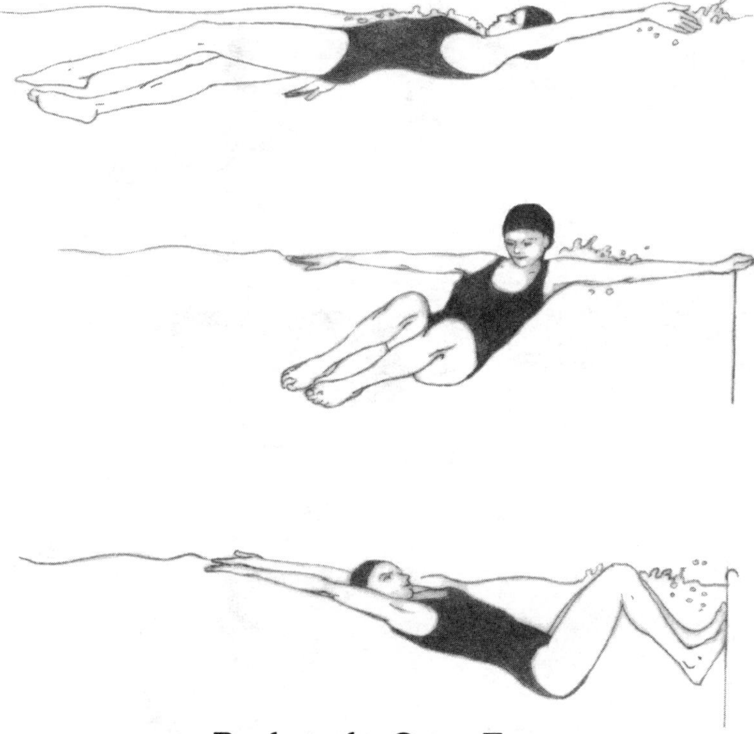

Backstroke Open Turn

Flip Turn

The flip for the backstroke is similar to the crawlstroke flip turn. Approach the pool wall with one arm extended overhead. Roll over into a prone position in the direction of the extended arm. Pull both arms under body. With both arms at sides and palms facing pool bottom, begin to flip. Scoop hands overhead, flipping legs out of the water so that feet touch the wall. Push off from the tuck position, staying on back and extending into a streamlined body position.

Breaststroke and Butterfly Turn

For each stroke, approach the wall and continue looking in forward direction to be able to judge the distance from the wall. Maintain speed and rhythm and arrive at the wall with both arms extended in front of

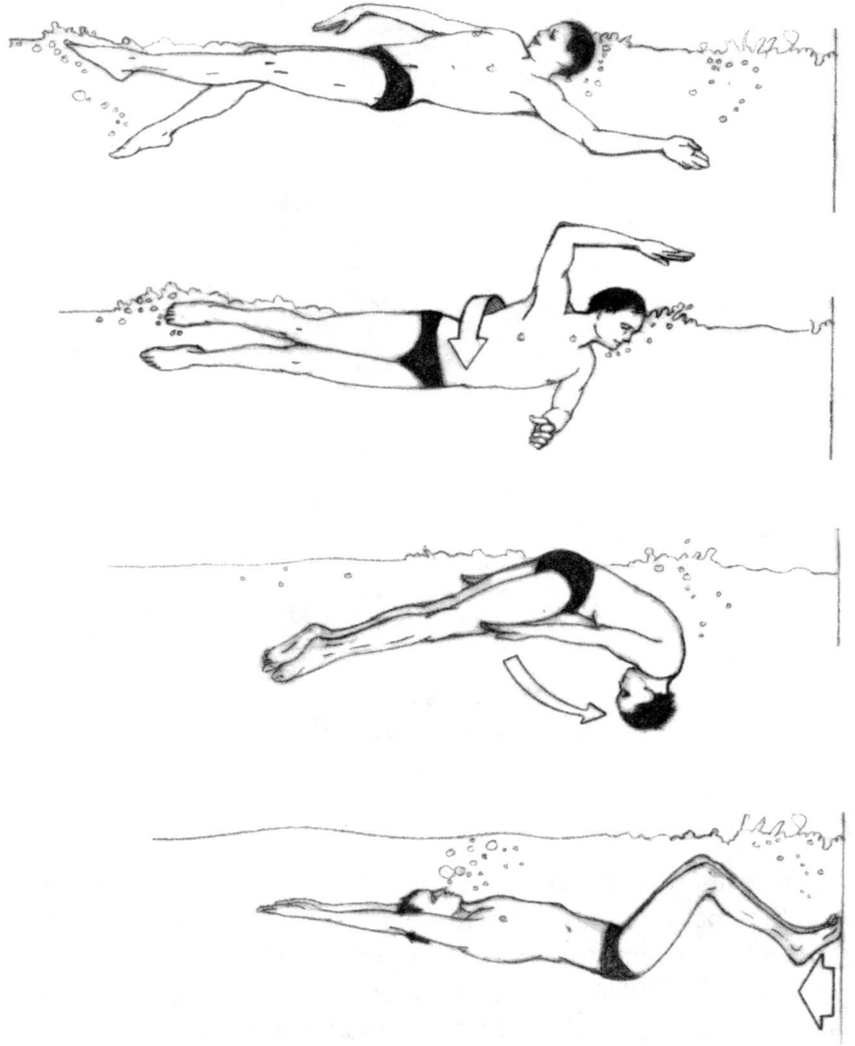

Backstroke Flip Turn Sequence

body and under the water. For both turns, hands touch the wall parallel to the water's surface and each other; be sure to touch the wall with both hands simultaneously. Immediately inhale and turn toward one side by dropping the shoulder into the water at a 90-degree angle and draw the same elbow to the side. Then, at the turn, extend the

Breaststroke Turn

other arm over the head away from the wall and turn 180 degrees. Be certain inhalation is complete before head drops into the water. Release the other hand from the wall during the pivot. Then bend legs and bring them under body, placing feet firmly on the wall, one higher than the other. Extend both arms out front; the body is still slightly tilted or rolled to the side of the dropping shoulder.

The push-off is accomplished by straightening the legs and extending the body into a streamlined, fully prone position. For the breaststroke, push off at a slight angle downward and take one strong pull. Pull hands under chest and abdomen and extend them all the way under thighs. During recovery of arms, take one kick; as breaststroker begins to surface, take second arm pull to continue the breaststroke. (In competition, only one arm pull and one kick are allowed before head must return to the water's surface.)

Breaststroke Push-Off and Pull Out

For the butterfly push-off, do not push off at a downward angle as in the breaststroke. During the glide, extend body into a streamlined, fully prone position, and keep arms extended in front. Do one or more dolphin kicks immediately to help return to the surface.

Sidestroke Turn

For the sidestroke, use a variation of the crawl open turn. Touch the wall with the leading arm. Then shift weight, bringing feet under body around to touch the wall, driving the shoulder of the free arm into the water at a 90-degree angle. Push off and begin the stroke, swimming on the side opposite the one used during the previous lap.

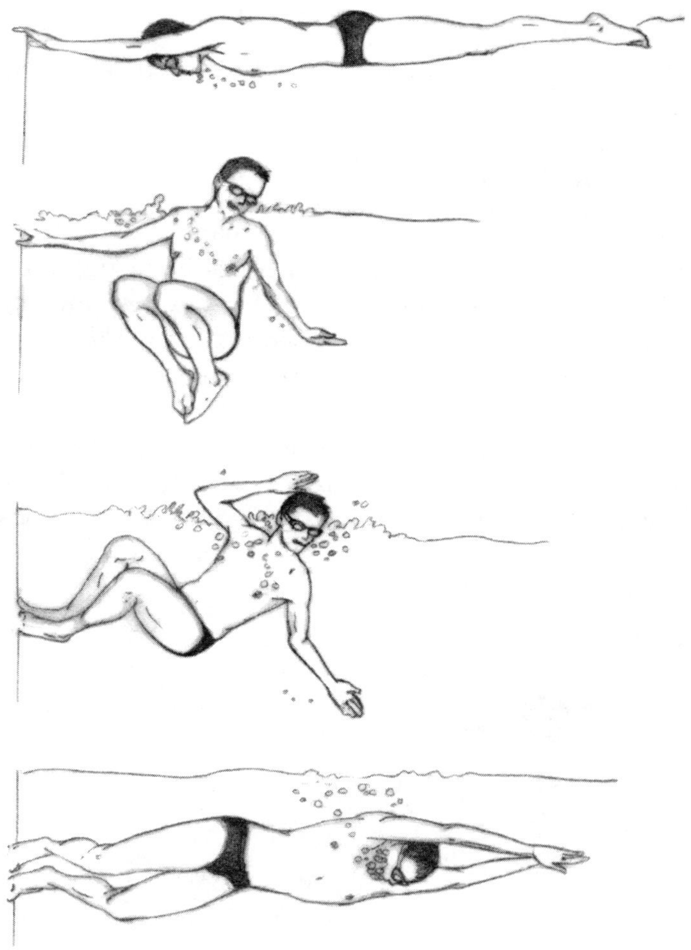

Butterfly Turn

TRANSITIONAL TURNS

Transitional turns are used to change direction from one stroke to another; for instance, from the backstroke to the crawl.

Starts

There are prescribed swimming starts for each stroke.

Crawlstroke Start

Stand in the water with knees bent and back foot braced against the wall. Extend arms straight out in front of the body in the glide position and take a bite of air. Immediately drop underwater, bracing other foot against the wall, and straighten both legs as forcefully as possible. During the glide, keep body stretched and streamlined and toes pointed. Just before momentum starts to fade, flutter kick and rise to the surface. Begin first pull with the arm opposite from the breathing side. Then, the arm on the breathing side recovers, take first inhalation. This in-the-water start technique can be applied to push-offs, just after the turn.

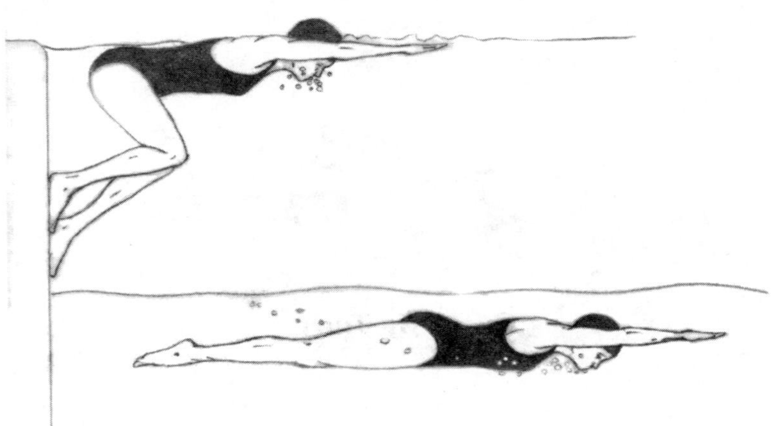

Crawlstroke Start

Sidestroke Start

The sidestroke start is similar to the crawl start, except that the push-off is shallower so that the body barely submerges. (The one-arm push-off variation is best for this stroke.)

Backstroke Start

Grasp the gutter of the pool, or the backstroke bar on the starting block if there is one. Place feet against the wall just below the water surface (one foot slightly higher than the other, if easier), and bend knees, bringing body into a tuck position. Bend elbows and pull up body so that the surface of the water approaches hip level. To push off, swing arms around and overhead in a continuous sweeping motion, head tilted slightly backward. Arch back and stretch body during leg push-off. Shoulders and hips stay above the water during the start, but feet remain underwater at all times. Exhale forcefully through the nose while gliding below the surface in a streamlined position. Begin to flutter kick as momentum of the glide fades, and take first arm pull when head emerges from the water; leave the other arm in the catch position until it is time to pull.

Backstroke Start and Push-Off

START TIPS

All starts have these basic principles:

- Push off aggressively and with force.
- Practice jumping jacks to improve starts. The power of the push-off comes from the legs. (This is also known as plyometric training.)
- Keep the body streamlined and stretched, with legs straight, toes pointed, and muscles tightened. Head is in line with body. Keep ears covered by arms during the glide.

Virtual Reality

Now that you've learned to swim, and swim better, step into your own virtual reality of a more active aquatic lifestyle with competent swimming skills. This virtual reality includes boating, water skiing, skin and SCUBA diving, and other water sports. But this is not virtual reality. Now for you, it's the real thing.

TURNS AND STARTS SKILL CHECKLIST

Date	Swim Skills	Comments
	Turns and Starts	
______	Crawlstroke open turn	______
______	Crawlstroke closed turn	______
______	Flip turn	______
______	Backstroke open turn	______
______	Backstroke flip turn	______
______	Breaststroke/butterfly turn	______
______	Sidestroke turn	______
______	Crawl start	______
______	Sidestroke start	______
______	Backstroke start	______
	WET Drills	
______	Sit-up	______
______	Tuck and turn	______
______	Quick lightning turns	______
______	Closed encounters	______
______	Face splash	______
______	Front tuck somersault	______
______	Swim and tuck	______

TURNS AND STARTS SKILL EVALUATION CHART

Name ______________________________ Class ________________

Dates	Stroke Component	Common Errors	How to Correct Them

General Comments: ____

____

____

____

Unit III

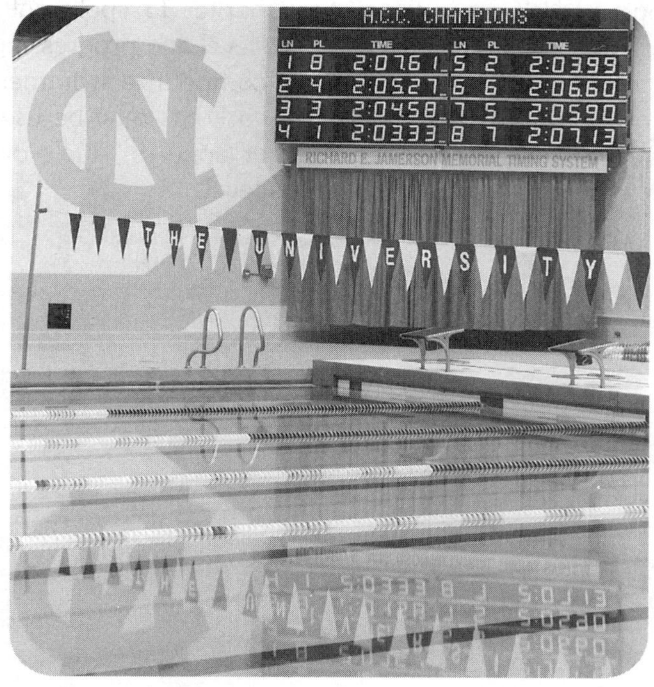

Courtesy of Colorado Timing Systems

Lap Fitness Training

Unit III brings together the swim skills, WET drills, and stroke techniques that were presented in the first two units of this book and applies them to lap workouts. This unit serves as a fitness program that can stand alone or can be adapted to any swimmer's proficiency and fitness level.

An aquatic workout has its own language. Chapter 10 highlights definitions of terms to help the swimmer customize and maximize his or her workouts and efforts in the water. Chapter 11 spells out 50 main-set lap workouts, starting with the novice level and progressing through five levels to the level of an experienced competitive swimmer—that is, going from 50 to 2,500 yards. These workouts may be used in conjunction with a workout/class agenda, or done on one's own to improve both swimming and overall fitness level.

Chapter 10

Lap Lingo for Conditioning

© Laimute E. Durskis

Workout Description

Aquatic conditioning and swimming involve learning a new language. This is true of all sports and, like all sports, swimming has its particular nomenclature and verbal shortcuts. While definitions of strokes, drills, and skill components have been discussed in the beginning chapters of the book, the terms listed below, alphabetically, are specifically relevant to aquatic conditioning and workouts.

Distance Notation

In aquatic conditioning, the workout is defined by distance notation. Note meters and yards are interchangeable even though the measurement is slightly different (36 inches vs. 39.37 inches).

1 × 50 = swim 50 yards/meters, 1 time

2 × 50 = swim 50 yards/meters, 2 times (with a rest in between)

1 × 100 = swim 100 yards/meters, 1 time

Terms

Pulling: The arm motion (coordinated with breathing) of the stroke without the kick. Pulling helps to build upper body strength; it is frequently used for warm-ups. During pulling drills, training devices such as pull-buoys help support the lower portion of the body. Other equipment, such as hand paddles, focus arm motion and help to increase resistance. Combinations of pulling and kicking with swimming laps can add variety to the main set.

Catch: When the hand enters the water and the palm first recognizes resistance against the water. The catch begins the arm pulling motion.

Kicking: Kicking drills isolate the leg motion of a given swim stroke by keeping the arms stationary (frequently with the assistance of a kickboard or other flotation device), and using the legs to propel the body forward. In kicking drills, training devices, such as swim fins and kickboards, help a kicking practice, as well as increase leg muscle strength and power.

Pull-Kick-Swim Set: Dividing the given stroke first into the individual components (i.e., pulling, then kicking), and then implementing them both together (i.e., swimming). By isolating and then combining the components, the swimmer refines and improves the total stroke.

Controlled Breathing: Training technique in which the body does more while breathing less frequently. Fewer breaths taken during swimming increase the body's ability to function efficiently with less oxygen. By training the body to do more while breathing less frequently, cardiovascular fitness improves as well as an ability to get a "second wind."

Alternate Breathing: A type of controlled breathing used in the crawlstroke. It is also known as bilateral breathing and is introduced by inhaling on every third pull. Alternate or bilateral breathing allows the swimmer to turn his face out of the water on both the left and right side in alternate succession. It is used to balance the stroke and increases the training effect by limiting the number of breaths per distance.

Individual Medley (IM): A competitive swimming event that involves swimming the butterfly, backstroke, breaststroke, and freestyle or crawlstroke. The strokes are swum in this exact order in a standard IM. In training they are usually swum in the same order, although, occasionally, they are swum in reverse (reverse IM)—the crawlstroke, breaststroke, backstroke, and butterfly.

Broken Swims: Timed swims that are broken up into small distances and interrupted by short rests of a specified length (e.g., 10 seconds). After completing the entire swim, subtract the total resting time from the final time to determine swim time. An individual medley (IM) of 400 yards (1 × 400), for instance, can be broken into 100 yards for each stroke with rest intervals in between each stroke.

Lap: One length of a pool, from one end to the other end. The actual length is determined by the size of the pool, i.e., 25 yards, 25 meters, 50 meters.

Long Course: 50-meter Olympic-size pool.

Short Course: 25-yard pool length. A 25-meter pool is usually referred to as short course meters.

Build-Ups: A training technique in which the swimmer begins each lap slowly and gradually builds up speed by the end of the lap. The build-up allows the swimmer to establish technique at a slow swim pace and maintain it as speed is increased.

Circle Swimming: In lap swimming, circle swimming is the pattern arranged to accommodate several swimmers within a lane at the same time. Most pools in the United States circle in the counterclockwise direction—the swimmer swims on the right side of the lane for the first lap and the left side of the lane for the second lap.

Crescendo Set: A set of several swim laps of regular increasing distances (for example: 1 × 25, 1 × 50, 1 × 75).

Ascending Interval Set: A set of several swims in which the intervals become longer as the set progresses. For example, during a set of ten 100-yard swims (10 × 100), the first three 100-yard swims could begin on a 2:00 interval, the next four on a 2:15 interval, and the last three would on a 2:30 interval. Generally, speed increases as the intervals increase.

Conversely, a descending interval set is when the intervals become shorter as the set progresses. This set is a more advanced training technique.

Pyramid Set: A set of several swims of regularly increasing, then regularly decreasing, distances (1 × 25, 1 × 50, 1 × 75, 1 × 50, 1 × 25). This is also known as an ascending/descending set.

Main Set: The main portion of the workout, where the aerobic training effect occurs. The main set is between the warm-up and the cool-down or stretching. It is the "meat and potatoes" of the workout.

Warm-Up: The 5- to 10-minute period at the beginning of the workout that prepares a swimmer's muscles and cardiovascular system for work. This period is a gradual loosening and stretching of muscles and elevation of the heart rate. The warm-up allows the swimmer to adjust mentally and physically from a land environment to a water workout. A water fitness warm-up usually consists of easy swimming, water exercises, and stroke drills.

Cool-Down: The period of time (approximately 5-10 minutes) at the end of the water fitness workout that allows the swimmer's cardiovascular system to return to its resting state. Cool-downs can consist of easy swimming, water exercises, and easy stretching.

Swim-Down: Easy swimming often done after a part of the main set of the workout. The swim-down, like the cool-down, allows the cardiovascular system to return to a lower heart rate.

Split: The time it takes a swimmer to complete a portion of a workout. For example, the time it takes to swim the first 50 yards of a 100-yard swim is called the first 50 split.

Stroke Counting: The number of strokes used to complete a certain distance (usually one lap or 25 yards/meters). It is good practice to try to lower the stroke count during subsequent swims (while maintaining speed). Do a stroke count periodically to check if efficiency and power are improving. This is also referred to as DPS or distance per stroke.

Pace: The amount of time consistently applied for a swimmer to cover a given distance. Pace is expressed in terms of the amount of time it takes a swimmer to cover each 50 yards/meters.

Paced Swims: A typical training technique is to compare times of both halves of a swim. By swimming the same time for each half, the swimmer develops a feel for pacing. This is known as even splitting. If the second half is faster than the first, it is called negative splitting.

Target Heart Rate: One method of determining whether a swimming is exercising aerobically within the THR (Target Heart Rate) range is to check pulse immediately after a main set or timed swim. This will eventually be a way of measuring fitness progress, because the lower the resting rate, the more efficient the cardiovascular system.

Fartlek Training: A favorite training technique of runners that breaks a swim into alternating slow and fast laps. The Fartlek technique varies the number of laps swum at each speed; for instance, when swimming pyramid style: 1 fast, 1 slow; 2 fast, 2 slow; 3 fast, 3 slow; 2 fast, 2 slow; 1 fast, 1 slow.

Interval Training: A series of swims of the same distance that are repeated, each within a specified length of time. The amount of rest between each swim is determined by how fast each swim is accomplished. For instance, if the *interval set* is four 50-yard swims in 1 minute, 15 seconds each (4 × 50 on 1:15), and it takes 1 minute to swim the first 50, there are 15 seconds of rest before beginning the next 50-yard swim. If it takes 45 seconds to swim 50 yards, there are 30 seconds to rest, and so on.

This training method can increase heart rate to approximately 70 percent of maximum heart rate during the swim. At this training rate the rest period is fairly short so that the heart rate does not return completely to the resting rate. Intervals are widely used as part or all of the main set of a workout.

Reading the Clock: How to time a swim. An analog pace clock is available at most pools. When timing a swim, the first interval or swim will be on the 60-second mark. If the interval is 1 minute, 15 seconds, the second swim will begin on the 15-second mark, the third on the 30-second mark ("the bottom"), and so on. Many state-of-the-art aquatic facilities feature digital timing systems as well.

Repetitions: Sets of swims of the same distance done at close to maximum effort (up to 90 percent of maximum heart rate), but with a long rest period between swims (usually equal to the swimming time). This allows the heart rate to come back down to nearly normal. This type of swimming develops speed and anaerobic capacity (the ability to work at intense levels by using stored oxygen for moderate periods of time). Since it is fatiguing, this method is used sparingly and usually to prepare competitive swimmers for peak performances, and only after a thorough warm-up.

Sprints: Short, fast swims done at maximum speed (up to 100 percent effort) to simulate the conditions of a competitive race. The amount of rest is usually very long to allow the heart rate to approach the resting rate. Sprinting creates more muscle power and strength than it does endurance. Like repetition swimming, sprints improve anaerobic capacity.

Timed Swim: Recording of the time required for a swimmer to cover a given distance and used as a benchmark for comparison against future swims. It is usually done near the completion of a workout after resting. Timed swims accustom the swimmer to refer to the clock, and work towards improved and more efficient swimming.

Taper: Competitive swim training seasons corresponding to the time of competitions by decreasing distance and increasing the quality of each swim workout. During the taper period of the season, rest is encouraged in order to produce the best performance at the time of competition.

Open Water/Distance Swimming: Swimming in a natural body of water, such as an ocean or a lake, as opposed to a swimming pool. The shortest distance in open water competition is usually one mile; other events go up to 28 miles.

Chapter **11**

Fifty Ways to Leave the Gutter

© Laimute E. Durskis

This chapter contains 50 progressive lap swim workouts, divided into five levels. Levels I, II, and III highlight one or two swim strokes. Levels IV and V are useful for experienced fitness or competitive swimmers. Level V includes workout sets of Individual Medleys, where butterfly, backstroke, breaststroke, and crawlstroke are swum in succession. Each level adds 500 yards in 10 workout increments.

Level	Workout Number	Stroke	Main Set (in yards
I	1–10	Crawlstroke	50–500
II	11–20	Backstrokes	550–1000
III	21–30	Breaststroke/Sidestroke	1050–1500
IV	31–40	Crawlstroke Refinement	1550–2000
V	41–50	Butterfly and Individual Medley (IM)	2050–2500

Each level contains sample WETs to use as warm-ups and cool-downs. It is recommended to mix and match these exercises to vary the workout.

PEP TALK: WHAT IS A WORKOUT?
A workout is part physical exertion and part self-discipline. The hard part is getting started; once started, it is easy.

Level I: Crawlstroke Warm-Ups/Cool-Downs (Sample WETs)

Level I brings the new swimmer from 2 laps (50 yds/meters) to just over one quarter of a mile (500 yards/meters) using the crawlstroke.

- Water Walk/Jog—Forward, backward, sideward
- Bobbing with Breathing—Standing, walking
- Prone and Supine Kick—On wall
- Prone Float, Glide, and Flutter Kick
- Crawl Arm Stroke—Walking
- Rhythmic Breathing
- Combine Rhythmic Breathing and Crawl Arm Stroke

Notes for Warm-Ups/Cool-Downs: Level I

____

____

____

Level I: Crawlstroke Main Set Workouts

Workout Number	Workout Distance	Workout		Total Laps
➤ 1	50 yds	1 × 25 yds	1 Lap Crawl	2 laps
		Rest		
		1 × 25 yds	1 Lap Crawl	

Comments: ______________________________

____

Workout Number	Workout Distance	Workout	Total Laps
➤ 2	100 yds	4 × 25 yds 4 Laps Crawl Rest in between laps	4 laps

Comments: ____________________

Workout Number	Workout Distance	Workout	Total Laps
➤ 3	150 yds	2 × 25 yds 2 Laps Crawl Rest in between laps 1 × 50 yds 2 Laps Crawl Rest 2 × 25 yds 2 Laps Crawl Rest in between laps	6 laps

Comments: ____________________

Workout Number	Workout Distance	Workout	Total Laps
➤ 4	200 yds	2 × 25 yds Crawl Rest 1 × 50 yds Crawl Rest 1 × 75 yds Crawl Rest 1 × 25 yds Crawl	8 laps

Comments: ____________________

Workout Number	Workout Distance	Workout	Total Laps
➤ 5	250 yds	2 × 25 yds Crawl 3 × 50 yds 2 × 25 yds	10 laps

Comments: ____________________

PEP TALK: *REST as needed. As conditioning improves, distance will increase and resting time will decrease.*

Workout Number	Workout Distance	Workout		Total Laps
➤ 6	300 yds	1 × 75 yds 1 × 25 yds 2 × 50 yds 1 × 75 yds 1 × 25 yds	Crawl	12 laps

Comments: ______________________________

____

Workout Number	Workout Distance	Workout		Total Laps
➤ 7	350 yds	1 × 25 yds 1 × 50 yds 1 × 75 yds 1 × 50 yds 1 × 75 yds 1 × 50 yds 1 × 25 yds	Crawl	14 laps

Comments: ______________________________

____

Workout Number	Workout Distance	Workout		Total Laps
➤ 8	400 yds	1 × 25 yds 1 × 50 yds 1 × 75 yds 1 × 100 yds 1 × 75 yds 1 × 50 yds 1 × 25 yds	Crawl	16 laps

Comments: ______________________________

____

Workout Number	Workout Distance	Workout		Total Laps
➤ 9	450 yds	1 × 100 yds	Crawl	18 laps
		1 × 75 yds		
		1 × 100 yds		
		1 × 50 yds		
		1 × 100 yds		
		1 × 25 yds		

Comments: ____

____

Workout Number	Workout Distance	Workout	Total Laps
➤ 10	500 yds	Continuous 500 yd crawl Rest as needed	20 laps

Comments: ____

____

Optional Timed Swim (25 yds suggested) Time: ______________

Level II: Backstrokes Warm-Ups/Cool-Downs

Level II highlights the elementary backstroke and the regular backstroke. It brings the lap swimmer's distance from just over 1/4 mile to one kilometer (1000 yards).

Choose from Level I warm-ups and add other sample WETs.

- Prone Flutter Kick (with kickboard)
- Supine Float, Glide, Kick
- Elementary Backstroke Arm Motion
- Whip Kick
- Backstroke Arm Motion

Notes for Warm-Ups/Cool-Downs: Level II

____

____

____

> ***PEP TALK:*** *A workout is a wise use of a swimmer's time and an investment in excellence. It is similar to preparing for life's challenges.*

Level II: Backstrokes Main Set Workouts

Workout Number	Workout Distance	Workout		Total Laps
➤ 11	550 yds	1 × 25 yds	Crawlstroke	22 laps
		1 × 50 yds	Repeat set 2×	
		1 × 75 yds	Repeat set 2×	
		1 × 100 yds	Repeat set 2×	
		2 × 25 yds	Repeat set 2×	

Comments: ____

____

Workout Number	Workout Distance	Workout		Total Laps
➤ 12	600 yds	1 × 150 yds	Crawl	24 laps
		2 × 25 yds	Back	
		1 × 100 yds	Crawl	
		2 × 25 yds	Back	
		1 × 75 yds	Crawl	
		2 × 25 yds	Back	
		1 × 50 yds	Crawl	
		2 × 25 yds	Back	
		1 × 25 yds	Crawl	

Comments: ____

____

Workout Number	Workout Distance	Workout		Total Laps
➤ 13	650 yds	4 × 50 yds 2 × 25 yds 3 × 100 yds 2 × 50 yds	Crawl Back Crawl Back	26 laps

Comments: ______________________

Workout Number	Workout Distance	Workout		Total Laps
➤ 14	700 yds	1 × 200 yds 1 × 100 yds 1 × 50 yds	Crawl Crawl Back	28 laps

Comments: Repeat the workout (set) for total distance.

Workout Number	Workout Distance	Workout		Total Laps
➤ 15	750 yds	1 × 25 yds 1 × 50 yds 1 × 75 yds 1 × 100 yds 1 × 125 yds	Stroke choice Stroke choice Stroke choice Stroke choice Stroke choice	30 laps

Comments: Rest and repeat set in reverse order.

Workout Number	Workout Distance	Workout		Total Laps
➤ 16	800 yds	2 × 200 yds 1 × 50 yds 2 × 100 yds 1 × 50 yds 2 × 50 yds	Crawl Back Crawl Back Crawl	32 laps

Comments: ______________________

Workout Number	Workout Distance	Workout		Total Laps
➤ 17	850 yds	2 × 250 yds	Crawl	34 laps
		4 × 25 yds	Back	
		1 × 250 yds	Crawl	

Comments: ______________________________

____

Workout Number	Workout Distance	Workout		Total Laps
➤ 18	900 yds	1 × 300 yds	Crawl	36 laps
		1 × 50 yds	Back	
		1 × 200 yds	Crawl	
		1 × 50 yds	Back	
		1 × 300	Crawl	

Comments: ______________________________

____

Workout Number	Workout Distance	Workout		Total Laps
➤ 19	950 yds	3 × 100 yds	Crawl	38 laps
		4 × 75 yds	Back	
		7 × 50 yds	Back and Crawl	

Comments: ______________________________

____

____

Workout Number	Workout Distance	Workout		Total Laps
➤ 20	1000 yds	1 × 400 yds	Crawl	40 laps
		8 × 25 yds	Alternate Back and Crawl	
		1 × 200 yds	Crawl	
		8 × 25 yds	Alternate Back and Crawl	

Comments: ______________________________

____

Optional Timed Swim (50 yds suggested) Time: ____________

Level III: Breaststroke and Sidestroke Warm-Ups/Cool-Downs

Level III highlights the breaststroke and sidestroke and brings the lap swimmer's distance from over one-half mile to almost one mile.

Include warm-ups/cool-downs from Level I: crawlstroke and Level II: backstrokes. Add the following WETs.

- Arm Sculling Motion
- Treading
- Breaststroke—Heart-Shaped Arm Motion
- Breaststroke Whip Kick
- Sidestroke Arm Motion
- Sidestroke Scissors Kick

Notes for Warm-Ups/Cool-Downs: Level III

____

____

____

____

____

____

PEP TALK: *A workout is a personal triumph over laziness and procrastination. It can be the badge of a winner—the mark of an organized, goal-oriented swimmer who has taken charge of his or her fitness.*

Level III: Breaststroke and Sidestroke Main Set Workouts

Workout Number	Workout Distance	Workout		Total Laps
➤ 21	1050 yds	1 × 200 yds	Crawl	42 laps
		4 × 25 yds	Alternate Breast and Crawl	
		1 × 100 yds	Crawl	
		4 × 25 yds	Breast	
		1 × 100 yds	Crawl	
		4 × 25 yds	Alternate Sidestroke and Crawl	
		1 × 100 yds	Crawl	
		4 × 25 yds	Sidestroke	
		1 × 100 yds	Crawl	
		1 × 50 yds	Backstroke	

Comments: ______________________________

____

Workout Number	Workout Distance	Workout		Total Laps
➤ 22	1100 yds	1 × 300 yds	Crawl (Pull-Kick-Swim)*	44 laps
		1 × 250 yds	Crawl	
		1 × 200 yds	Crawl Pull	
		1 × 150 yds	Crawl Pull-Kick-Swim	
		1 × 100 yds	Back	
		1 × 50 yds	Breast	
		2 × 25 yds	Sidestroke	

Comments: *Alternate 2 laps pull, 2 laps kick, 2 laps swim and repeat by 50s.

____

____

Workout Number	Workout Distance	Workout		Total Laps
➤ 23	1150 yds	3 × 300 yds	Crawl	46 laps
		3 × 100 yds	Breast	
		3 × 50 yds	Breaststroke	
		4 × 25 yds	Sidestroke	

Comments: ______________________________

____

Workout Number	Workout Distance	Workout		Total Laps
➤ 24	1200 yds	1 × 400 yds	Crawl	48 laps
		4 × 100 yds	Crawl Pull	
		8 × 50 yds	Alternate Strokes	

Comments: Alternate backstroke, breaststroke, sidestroke.

____

____

Workout Number	Workout Distance	Workout		Total Laps
➤ 25	1250 yds	4 × 75 yds	Kick, Swim	50 laps
		1 × 25 yds	Kick	
		1 × 50 yds	Swim	
		4 × 75 yds	Kick, Swim, Breaststroke	
		4 × 75 yds	Backstroke	
		4 × 75 yds	Sidestroke	
		1 × 50 yds	Crawl	

Comments: ______________________________

____

Workout Number	Workout Distance	Workout		Total Laps
➤ 26	1300 yds	4 × 50 yds	Crawl	52 laps
		1 × 500 yds	Crawl	
		1 × 300 yds	Choice*	
		1 × 200 yds	Choice*	
		1 × 100 yds	Choice*	

Comments: *Choose the stroke(s) you wish.

____

____

Workout Number	Workout Distance	Workout		Total Laps
➤ 27	1350 yds	5 × 200 yds	Stroke choice	54 laps
		1 × 50 yds	Kick	
		1 × 50 yds	Pull	
		1 × 50 yds	Kick	
		1 × 50 yds	Swim	
		7 × 50 yds	Stroke choice	

Comments: ______________________________

____

____

Workout Number	Workout Distance	Workout		Total Laps
➤ 28	1400 yds	4 × 50 yds	Crawl	56 laps
		4 × 200 yds	Crawl	
		1 × 100 yds	Breast	
		1 × 100 yds	Back	
		1 × 100 yds	Side	
		1 × 100 yds	Crawl	

Comments: ______________________________

____

____

Workout Number	Workout Distance	Workout		Total Laps
➤ 29	1450 yds	4 × 50 yds	Crawl	58 laps
		1 × 500 yds	Crawl	
		1 × 600 yds	Crawl Every third lap, stroke choice	
		6 × 25 yds	Alternate strokes—choice	

Comments: ______________________________

____

____

Workout Number	Workout Distance	Workout		Total Laps
➤ 30	1500 yds	1 × 1000 yds continuous swim	Crawl	60 laps
		10 × 50 yds	Alternate strokes	

Comments: ______________________________

____

Optional Timed Swim (100 yds suggested) Time: ____________

Level IV: Crawlstroke Refinement Warm-Ups/Cool-Downs

During Level IV, the swimmer refines the crawlstroke, employing stroke-specific drills and training techniques. These drills help increase speed and efficiency. The swimmer's lap distance exceeds the mile—it goes from 1500 yards to 2000 yards.

At this level, it is advisable to conduct swims more precisely by using interval training. This level includes the 4 × 50 yards crawlstroke at the beginning of each workout. By using less rest between 50s, and increasing speed on each 50, the swimmer builds up and progresses faster.

The warm-ups/cool-downs increase the target heart rate for the main set. Include warm-ups/cool downs from Level I: crawlstroke, Level II: backstrokes, and Level III: breaststroke, sidestroke.

Add the following WETs and add fins for kicking:

- S-pull arm stroke drills
- Fingertip drill
- Fist drill
- Bilateral breathing

Notes for Warm-Ups/Cool Downs: Level IV

PEP TALK: *A workout makes a swimmer better today than the swimmer was yesterday. It strengthens the body, relaxes the mind, and toughens the spirit. When a swimmer works out regularly, problems seem to diminish and confidence grows.*

Level IV: Refined Crawlstroke/S-Pull Main Set Workouts

Workout Number	Workout Distance	Workout		Total Laps
➤ 31	1550 yds	4 × 50 yds	Freestyle	62 laps
		4 × 25 yds	One-arm drill*	
		4 × 100 yds	Freestyle	
		4 × 100 yds	Choice	
		1 × 300 yds	Breathe on one side	
		7 × 50 yds	(1 × 25 one-arm; 1 × 25 crawl)	

Comments: *Use right arm for one lap; left arm for next.

Workout Number	Workout Distance	Workout		Total Laps
➤ 32	1600 yds	4 × 50 yds	Crawlstroke build up	64 laps
		4 × 25 yds	Catch-up	
		1 × 300 yds	Stroke choice	
		3 × 100 yds	Rest 30 seconds between each—maintain pace	
		4 × 50 yds	25× one-arm/ 25 free	
		1 × 300 yds	Swim	
		4 × 50 yds	Catch-Up	

Comments: ________________________________

____

____

➤ 33	1650 yds	Descending laps from 11 to 1 with 30 sec rest in between 11, 10, 9, 8, 7, 6, 5, 4, 3, 2, 1	66 laps

Comments: Vary strokes, equipment, speed, etc.

____

____

➤ 34	1700 yds	4 × 50 yds	Crawlstroke	68 laps
		4 × 25 yds	Fingertip recovery	
		4 × 100 yds	Swimmer's choice	
		4 × 75 yds	25 drill, 25 swim, 25 drill	
		1 × 200 yds	Swim	
		4 × 125 yds	50 crawl, 25 drill, 50 crawl	

Comments: Vary and use drills to improve technique.

____

____

Workout Number	Workout Distance	Workout		Total Laps
➤ 35	1750 yds	4 × 50 yds	Drills	70 laps
		1 × 500 yds	(Optional for time)	
		10 × 50 yds	Rest 30 secs between each	
		1 × 500 yds	(Optional for time)	
		1 × 50 yds	Timed swim	

Comments: 1st 500—Time: ; 2nd 500—Time ;

1 × 50—Time:

Workout Number	Workout Distance	Workout		Total Laps
➤ 36	1800 yds	4 × 50 yds	Crawl	72 laps
		4 × 25 yds	Crawl-glide drill	
		1 × 500 yds	Crawl	
		1 × 400 yds	Crawl	
		1 × 300 yds	Crawl	
		1 × 200 yds	Crawl	
		1 × 100 yds	Crawl	

Comments: Rest 1 minute between swims.

Workout Number	Workout Distance	Workout		Total Laps
➤ 37	1850 yds	2 × 50 yds	Crawl	74 laps
		4 × 25 yds	Fist drill swim	
		1 ×1000 yds	Crawl	
		6 × 50 yds	25 Fist drill/ 25 Crawl	
		1 × 200 yds	Stroke choice*	
		1 × 100 yds	Stroke choice	
		1 × 50 yds	Stroke choice	

Comments: *Choose stroke other than Crawl.

Workout Number	Workout Distance	Workout		Total Laps
➤ 38	1900 yds	2 × 50 yds	Crawlstroke	76 laps
		Rest 5 secs for each 25-yd swim		
		1 × 25 yds (5 sec rest)		
		1 × 50 yds (10 sec rest)		
		1 × 75 yds (15 sec rest)		
		1 × 100 yds (20 sec rest)		
		1 × 125 yds (25 sec rest), etc.		
		1 × 150 yds		
		1 × 175 yds		
		1 × 200 yds		
		Rest; repeat set in reverse order		

Comments: ______________________________

____

____

Workout Number	Workout Distance	Workout		Total Laps
➤ 39	1950 yds	4 × 50 yds	Crawlstroke	78 laps
		4 × 25 yds	Fist, drill	
		4 × 100 yds	Kick-Pull-L Swim	
		5 × 200 yds	Free, rest 1-2 min between each	
		5 × 50 yds	Stroke choice	

Comments: ______________________________

____

____

Workout Number	Workout Distance	Workout		Total Laps
➤ 40	2000 yds	4 × 50 yds	Crawlstroke	80 laps
		1 ×1650 yds*	(Optional Timed Swim)	
		1 × 150 yds	Stroke Choice	

Comments: *1,650 yards — Time: ______________________

____

____

Optional Timed Swim (100 yds suggested) Time: ____________

Level V: Butterfly and Individual Medley Warm-Ups/Cool-Downs

Level V introduces the challenging butterfly and then puts all the strokes together into the individual medley. This final level brings the swimmer from 2000 yards/meters to 2500 yards, which is almost one and a half miles). Include warm ups/cool downs from Level I—crawlstroke, Level II—backstrokes, Level III—breaststroke and sidestroke, and Level IV—freestyle.

Add the following skills and WETs.

- Butterfly Keyhole Arm Pull
- Dolphin Kick—Jump Rope
- Turns
- Easy Swims

Notes on Warm-Ups/Cool Downs: Level V

____

____

____

____

> ***PEP TALK:*** *A workout is a form of renewal. When finishing a challenging workout, you not only feel better physically, YOU FEEL BETTER ABOUT YOURSELF!*

Level V: Butterfly and Individual Medley Main Set Workouts

Workout Number	Workout Distance	Workout		Total Laps
➤ 41	2050 yds	1 × 200 yds	Crawlstroke	82 laps
		1 × 200 yds	Backstroke	
		1 × 200 yds	Crawlstroke	
		1 × 200 yds	Breaststroke	
		2 × 25 yds	Dolphin Kick	
		2 × 25 yds	Crawlstroke	
		2 × 25 yds	Dolphin Kick (kickboard optional)	
		4 × 25 yds	Crawlstroke	
		4 × 25 yds	Dolphin Kick	
		1 × 150 yds	Crawlstroke	
		1 × 150 yds	Pull	
		1 × 150 yds	Flutter Kick	
		3 × 100 yds	Pull-Kick-Swim (Backstroke or Breaststroke)	
		1 × 150 yds	Medley (50 backstroke, 50 breaststroke, 50 Free)	

Comments: Optional: Use fins for dolphin kick.

Workout Number	Workout Distance	Workout		Total Laps
➤ 42	2100 yds	1 × 100 yds	Choice	84 laps
		1 × 25 yds	Dolphin Kick	
		1 × 200 yds	Swim	
		1 × 25 yds	Back	
		1 × 300 yds	Swim choice	
		1 × 25 yds	Kick	
		1 × 200 yds	Swim	
		1 × 25 yds	Kick	
		1 × 100 yds	Swim	
		6 × 25 yds	Pull set (no pull buoy); alternate Butterfly and Crawl	
		1 × 200 yds	Kick; alternate Dolphin Kick Choice by 25s	
		8 × 25 yds	Pull; alternate Butterfly and Crawlstroke (no pull buoy)	
		8 × 25 yds	Medley of strokes by 25s: Backstroke, Breaststroke, Crawl	

Comments: Emphasize Butterfly Keyhole Arm Pull.

➤ 43	2150 yds	1 × 400 yds	Crawl	86 laps
		1 × 300 yds	Pull	
		1 × 200 yds	Swim	
		1 × 100 yds	Kick	
		4 × 50 yds	Crawlstroke (breathe on non-breathing side)	
		4 × 50 yds	Crawlstroke (alternate breathing—every 3 arm pulls)	

Workout Number	Workout Distance	Workout		Total Laps
		4 × 50 yds	Crawlstroke (breathe on non-breathing side)	
		10 × 25 yds	One-arm Butterfly*	
		4 × 75 yds	Medley—25 Backstroke, Breast, Crawlstroke	

Comments: *Extend left arm overhead. Breathe to the opposite side (right side) as in Crawlstroke. Change arm and breathing sides, each 25.

Workout Number	Workout Distance	Workout		Total Laps
➤ 44	2200 yds			88 laps
		6 × 75 yds	Each 75 1 × 25 one-arm Butterfly, 1 × 50 Crawlstroke	
		6 × 75 yds	Each 75 1 × 25 Butterfly, 1 × 50 choice	
		10 × 50 yds	Alternate 1 × 25 Kick, 1 × 25 Swim—Crawlstroke	
		1 × 300 yds	Swim choice (every 4th lap Butterfly)	
		8 × 25 yds	Crawlstroke (alternate breathing)	
		12 × 25 yds	Medley of strokes (choice)	

Comments: Emphasize coordinated Butterfly stroke.

Workout Number	Workout Distance	Workout		Total Laps
➤ 45	2250 yds	20 × 25 yds	Alternate Butterfly, Backstroke, Breastroke, Crawlstroke	90 laps
		1 × 400 yds	Kick (every other lap Dolphin Kick)	
		1 × 75 yds	25 Butterfly, 50 Crawlstroke	
		1 × 75 yds	25 Backstroke, 50 Crawlstroke	
		1 × 75 yds	25 Breaststroke, 50 Crawlstroke	
		1 × 75 yds	All Crawlstroke	
		4 × 75 yds	Repeat above set	
		1 × 350 yds	Crawlstroke (every 4th lap alternate breathing)	
		16 × 25 yds	Alternate 1 × 25 Kick, Swim; follow IM order (Butterfly,Backstroke, Breaststroke, Crawlstroke)	

Comments: Individual Medley of all competitive strokes.

➤ 46	2300 yds	24 × 50 yds	Alternate IM order: 1 × 25 stroke, 1 × 25 Crawlstroke	92 laps
		1 × 500 yds	Crawlstroke—every 3rd lap alternate breathing	

Workout Number	Workout Distance	Workout		Total Laps
		1 × 50 yds	Butterfly	
		1 × 100 yds	Crawlstroke	
		1 × 50 yds	Backstroke	
		1 × 100 yds	Crawlstroke	
		1 × 50 yds	Breaststroke	
		1 × 100 yds	Crawlstroke	
		1 × 150 yds	Kick choice	

Comments: Individual Medley of all competitive strokes.

Workout Number	Workout Distance	Workout		Total Laps
➤ 47	2350 yds	12 × 25 yds	Alternate 25 Dolphin Kick on right side, left side	94 laps
		6 × 150 yds	Stroke choice 150 Pull-Kick-Swim set (50 each)	
		4 × 100 yds	100 IM—25 each Butterfly, Backstroke, Breaststroke, Crawlstroke	
		1 × 150 yds	Choice	
		12 × 50 yds	Alternate easy/hard 50 Crawlstroke	

Comments: Easy/hard—Fartlek training.

Workout Number	Workout Distance	Workout		Total Laps
➤ 48	2400 yds	3 × 100 yds	Individual Medley—100 Swim, 100 Kick, 100 Choice	96 laps
		1 × 600 yds	Crawlstroke Swim 1-arm butterfly drill every 4th lap	
		2 × 200 yds	Individual Medley- 1st & 3rd swim 2nd IM Kick	
		1 × 400 yds	Crawlstroke Dolphin kick on side every 4th lap	
		20 × 25 yds	Crawlstroke with controlled breathing/ 25 with alternate, 25 with 5 breaths, 25 with 4, 25 with 3, 25 with 2, 25 with 1 Repeat controlled breathing pattern 4 times.	

Comments: 100 and 100 Individual Medley; controlled breathing or fewer breaths per lap.

Workout Number	Workout Distance	Workout		Total Laps
➤ 49	2450 yds		Drill: Rola cupa	98 laps
		6 × 100 yds	Crawlstroke 25 right arm, 25 left arm, 25 catch-up, 25 swim	
		1 × 100 yds	Dolphin Kick	
		5 × 100 yds	Individual Medley	
		1 × 100 yds	Back Flutter Kick	
		2 × 200 yds	Choice	

Workout Number	Workout Distance	Workout		Total Laps
		1 × 100 yds	Whip Kick	
		3 × 100 yds	Crawlstroke—alternate breathing	
		1 × 100 yds	Flutter Kick	
		1 × 200 yds	Choice—Backstroke or breathing	
		1 × 50 yds	Timed Swim	

Comments: Rola Cupa drill = right arm/left arm/catch-up/swim

1 × 50; timed swim: ____________

Workout Number	Workout Distance	Workout		Total Laps
➤ 50	2500 yds	1 × 100 yds	IM	100 laps
		1 × 200 yds	Stroke Choice—Pull	
		1 × 300 yds	Crawlstroke	
		1 × 400 yds	2nd Stroke Choice	
		1 × 500 yds	Crawlstroke (Optional Timed Swim)	
		1 × 400 yds	Stroke Choice	
		1 × 300 yds	Crawlstroke	
		1 × 200 yds	Stroke Choice	
		1 × 100 yds	IM	
		Rest 30 seconds per 100 yds (i.e.,1st 100, Rest 0:30; 200 yds, rest 1:00; 300 yds, 1:30, etc.)		

Comments: Swim up and down the ladder.

Optional Timed Swim Time: ____________

To estimate the number of laps or lengths, refer to Table 11.1.

Here is a guide to estimate the number of laps by types of pool.

TABLE 11.1 ***Lap Guideline Chart***

Length in Feet	Length in Yards	Approximate Number of Laps per 100 Yards
37.5	12.5	8
60	20	5
75	25	4
100	33	3
165	55	2

Standard pool = 75 ft
Olympic pool = 50 meters

To calculate mileage

- In a 20-yard pool:
  - 1/4 mile is 22 laps (440 yards)
  - 1/2 mile is 44 laps (880 yards)
  - 1 mile is 88 laps (1,760 yards)
- In a 25-yard pool:
  - 1/4 mile is 18 laps (450 yards)
  - 1/2 mile is 36 laps (900 yards)
  - 1 mile is 70 laps (1,750 yards)
- In a 25-meter pool:
  - 1/4 mile is 16 laps (400 meters)
  - 1.2 mile is 32 laps (800 meters)
  - 1 mile is 64 laps (1,600 meters)
- In a 33-1/3 yard pool:
  - 1/4 mile is 13 laps (433 yards)
  - 1/2 mile is 26 laps (866 yards)
  - 1 mile is 52 laps (1,732 yards)
- In a 50-meter/55-yard pool:
  - 1/4 mile is 8 laps (400 meters)
  - 1/2 mile is 16 laps (800 meters)
  - 1 mile is 32 laps (1,600 meters)

The following main set workouts equal approximately the magic mile. Refer to Table 11.1 for exact measurements. Mix and match according to individual needs and ability. If the pool is less than 20 yards, swim laps for time.

1800 yards (72 laps) = approximately 1 mile

Alternate each swim with crawl/freestyle and stroke choice.

2 × 25	(2 × 1 lap = 2 laps)
2 × 50	(2 × 2 laps = 4 laps)
2 × 75	(2 × 3 laps = 6 laps)
2 × 100	(2 × 4 laps = 8 laps)
2 × 125	(2 × 5 laps = 10 laps)
2 × 150	(2 × 6 laps = 12 laps)
2 × 175	(2 × 7 laps = 14 laps)
2 × 200	(2 × 8 laps = 16 laps)

1800 yards (72 laps) = approximately 1 mile

Divide mile into thirds

1 × 600	(24 laps)	Swim
1 × 600	(24 laps)	Pull
1 × 600	(24 laps)	Kick

1800 yards (72 laps) = approximately 1 mile

Divide mile in half. Try to pace each 1/2 mile evenly.

1 × 900 yards	(36 laps)	Time:
1 × 900 yards	(36 laps)	Time:

1760 yards (70.4 laps) = exactly 1 mile

1 × 1760 yards (70.2 laps)

> ***SWIM TIP:*** *The Create Your Own Workout in Appendix A may help record a personal workout.*

Personal Aquatic 26.2 Mile Marathon Fitness Chart

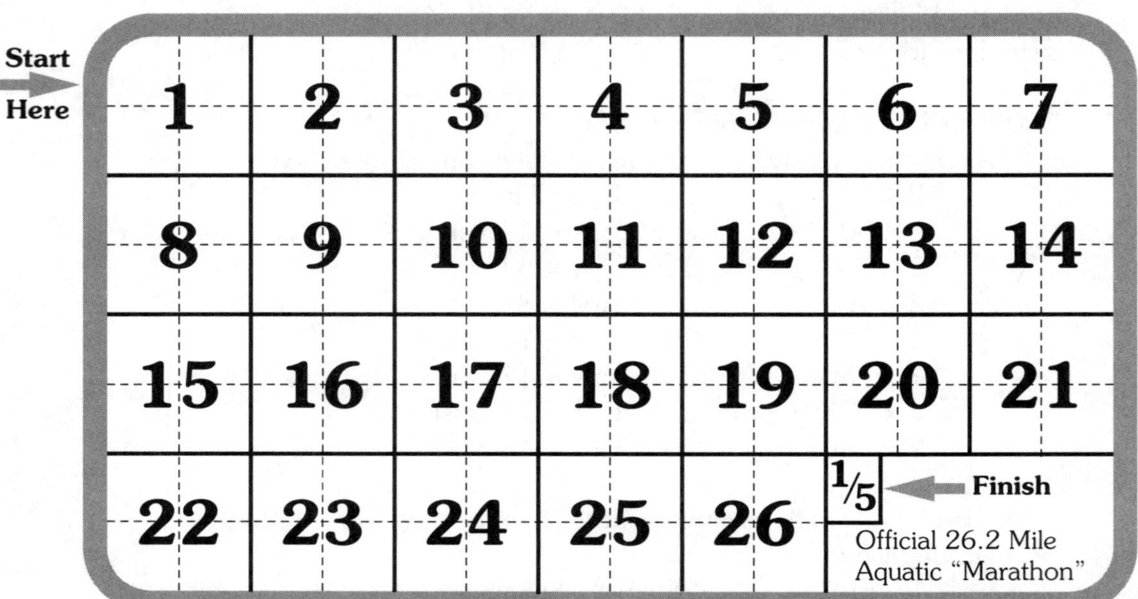

Instructions: Fill in each "small box" as 1/4 mile of swimming or 1/4 hour of aquatic exercise completed.

Unit IV

Water Exercise

During the 1970s, a connection was made between sustained physical activity and good cardiovascular health. It became evident that a lower incidence of heart disease occurred when people exercised on a regular basis. This fact spurred on many people who seldom participated in sports or fitness programs to add physical fitness workouts to their daily or weekly routines. These workouts covered a wide range of aerobic and nonaerobic pursuits, such as jogging, tennis, basketball, and body building.

However, as the exercise boom of the 1970s and 1980s peaked, a large number of high-impact exercise injuries came to the attention of fitness professionals. They determined that a fitness activity was needed that would combine stretching, aerobic conditioning, strength training, and flexibility. Water exercise was the answer.

An offshoot of rehabilitation therapy and nineteenth-century "water cures" combined with dance movement and calisthenics, water exercise has brought millions of people into the pool. This population includes the 50 percent who either did not swim at all or did not swim well enough to get an aerobic workout in the pool. Water exercise became the "no-excuse" exercise for people who had reasons for not swimming, such as "I don't want to get my hair wet," "I'm overweight," and "I'm embarrassed to be seen exercising."

Since the 1980s, water exercise classes have become very popular. At first they were called hydro-calisthenics or hydro-slimnastics. Later, aquarobics or aquacise classes began to appear and now are standard at Ys, community pools, and health clubs throughout the country. Over 5 million people in the United States now participate in some form of water exercise (including lavish spas) to exercise and relax.

In 1979, the author sustained injuries in a serious auto accident. Rehabilitation therapy began with a Hubbard tank in the hospital, where the resistance of water pumped from jets in all directions was used to assist in healing and regaining strength. At the time the author was a top competitive swimmer. After the accident she was not strong enough to resume regular swimming workouts. Out of frustration, she took the hospital water therapy a step further—into the spa and swimming pool—and created exercises to restore strength and flexibility. In the pool she was able to rebuild her fitness conditioning, which led to the beginning of WETs or Water Exercises Techniques®, the basis of this aquatic fitness handbook.

Equipment for water exercise has proliferated, enabling the water exerciser to obtain a fully balanced workout. In addition, sports medicine specialists have increasingly adopted the therapeutic aspects of water to help athletes stay in condition while they are recovering from injuries and now often prescribe skill-specific water workouts to top athletes in all sports to optimize training time and to minimize injuries occurring from overuse.

Unit IV comprises many aspects of water exercise. Chapter 12 introduces WETs as they pertain to full body workout in shallow water; Chapter 13 offers a sample water exercise workout in deep water, and Chapter 14 and Chapter 15 detail aquatic equipment and cross-training for other sports, including the plyometrics movement.

Chapter 12

Water Exercise Techniques (WETs) for Shallow Water

What Are WETs?

Water Exercise Techniques are described as a program of land-based movements adapted for the water and performed in a vertical or standing position (as differentiated from swimming, which is done in a horizontal position). Water exercise workouts can be divided into shallow-water exercises and deep-water exercises. Ideally, the water temperature should be a bit warmer than it is for lap swimming, from low- to mid-80 degrees (F).

Exercise Tips

Repeat each WET exercise a certain number of repetitions or for approximately one minute, and then follow with rest. Then the cycle—exercise and rest—continues. While exercising, keep arms under the water for maximum resistance, unless otherwise noted. Breathe regularly, rhythmically, and deeply. Do not hold breath. Unless otherwise noted, inhale and exhale through both the nose and the mouth.

Use the warm-up and cool-down exercises introduced in Chapter 3, both before and after the WET main set workout.

Water exercise techniques are organized by body area: upper body, middle body, and lower body. In addition, total body exercises can be added to the workout. Below is a list of muscles exercised in different body areas.

TABLE 12.1 ***Muscle Groups by Body Area***

Body Area	Muscle Group
Upper Body	
• Head and neck	Sternocleidomastoid
• Wrist and forearm	Pronators, Supinators
• Upper arm	Biceps
• Back of arm	Triceps
• Shoulders	Deltoids
• Chest	Pectoralis major
• Upper back	Trapezius Latissimus dorsi
Middle Body	
• Sides of trunk	External obliques Latissimus dorsi
• Middle back	Latissimus dorsi Erector spinae
• Rib cage	Intercostals
• Waist	Abdominals
• Lower back	External obliques Gluteus medius and maximus
• Pelvic area	Gluteus maximus, medius, and minimus
Lower Body	
• Thighs	Hamstrings Quadriceps
• Groin, inner thigh	Sartorius Abductors Adductors
• Buttocks	Gluteus maximus
• Hips	Ilo-psoas Gluteus medius
• Calves	Soleus (front) Gastrocnemius (back)
• Ankle and foot	Achilles tendon Peroneus
Total Body	
• All muscle groups	

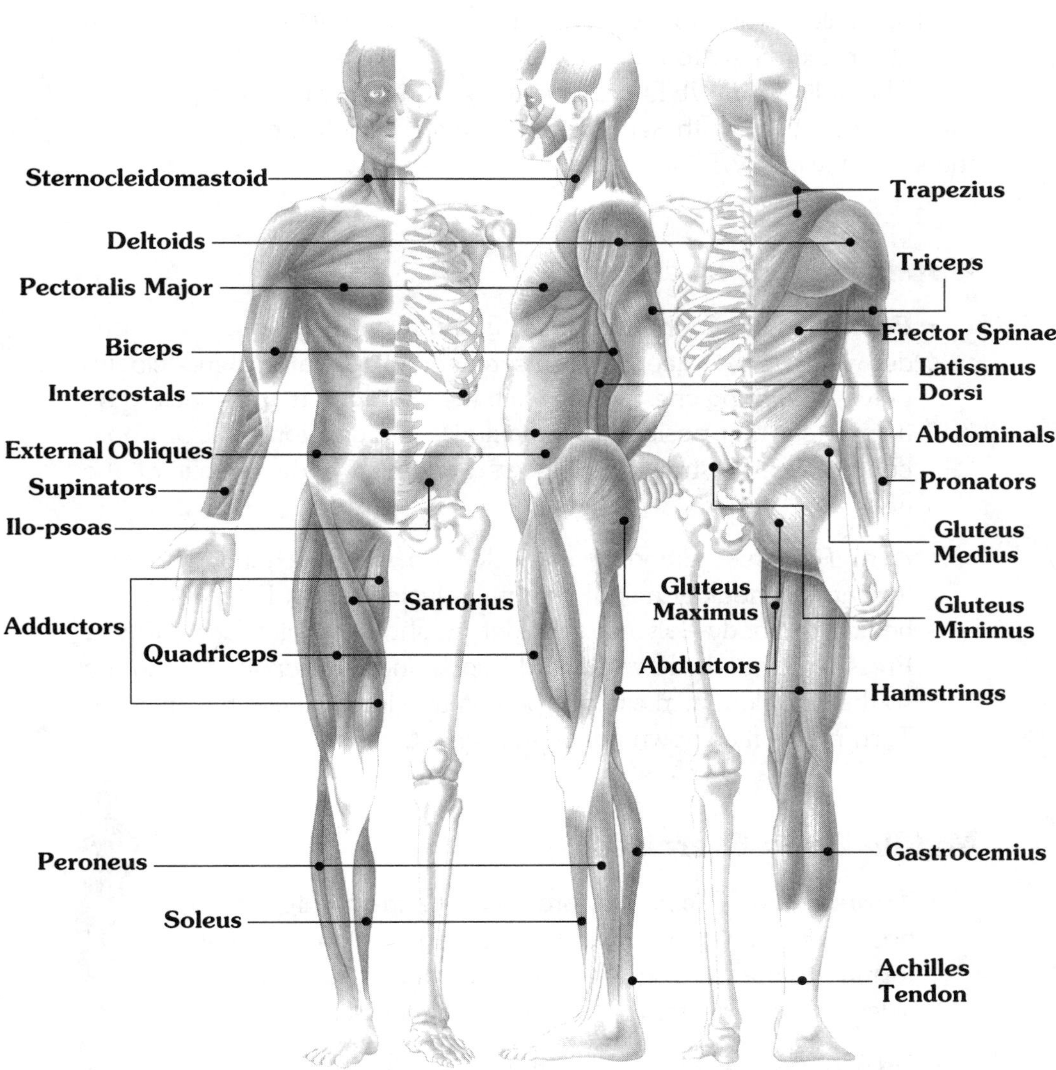

Source: Adapted from Tortora, G. J. *Principles of human anatomy.* New York: Harper and Row, 1989.

Muscle Groups

WETs for Shallow Water

Ideally, shallow-water exercises should be done in waist- to chest-deep water (approximately four feet deep).

The following WETs can be done with or without equipment. Refer to the chart at the end of the chapter to note progress through the shallow-water WETs.

Upper Body Exercises

- **Push-Ups:** Face the wall placing hands on the pool edge, shoulder-width apart, keeping arms extended forward. Bend elbows outward to bring chest to the wall, then straighten arms back to return to starting position. To maximize the development of upper body strength, straighten elbows and push body up out of the water.
- **Arm Presses:** Standing in neck-deep water, extend right arm forward at shoulder height with palm facing down. Extend left arm behind the body—also at shoulder height with palm facing down. Press both hands down toward thighs and then upward in an arc so that the right arm extends behind and left arm extends in front. Turn palms face down again and repeat.

Middle Body Exercises

- **Trunk Turn:** Facing forward, place hands on hips. Turn body to the right and return to starting position. Repeat, turning to the left side. For added resistance, extend arms sideways underwater and use hand paddles.
- **Sit-Ups:** Place back against the pool wall with arms stretched out and hands on pool edge to support body in a back float position. Bend knees and bring them toward chest. Then extend and straighten knees.

Lower Body Exercises

- **Rockette Leg Lift:** Place back against the pool wall with arms extended on the pool edge for support. Alternately, raise legs as close as possible to the water's surface, keeping each leg straight. Use a pull-buoy under heel, or use fins, for extra resistance.
- **Leg Crossover:** Place back against a corner of pool with arms extended on deck for support. Keeping back against the wall, lift legs straight and together at a 90 degree angle to body. Separate legs into a V position, then bring legs together, crossing at ankles.
- **Knee Bend:** Place back against wall for support. Bring one knee up to chest. Return leg to pool floor and repeat with other leg. This is particularly beneficial to help relax lower back.

Total Body Exercises

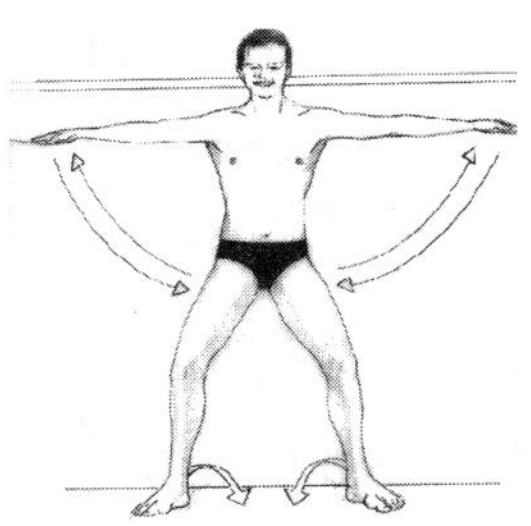

- **Aqua Jumping Jack:** Stand with arms down and palms touching thighs. Simultaneously bring arms to water's surface while separating legs into a V position. Return to the starting position by turning palms downward, bringing arms back to sides, and jumping and bringing the legs together.
- **Arm and Leg Stretch:** Grasp the pool edge with right hand. Raise right leg toward hand as close to the wall as comfortable. Reach with left arm overhead in an arc toward right side. Hold the stretch. Return to starting position, and reverse.
- **Side Hip Touch:** Stand at arm's distance perpendicular to the pool wall, feet together with hand grasping the edge. Touch the wall with the hip that is close to the wall, then swing hips as far as possible away from the wall. For a stretch, bring free arm overhead in an arc. Return to standing position and repeat on other side.

SAMPLE WET WORKOUT CHART

Workout Component	WETs Skills	Number of Repetitions and/or Time	Pulse Check	Comments
Warm-Ups				
Main Set				
Upper Body				
Middle Body				
Lower Body				
Total Body				
Cool-Downs				

Chapter 13

WETs for Deep Water

Ask a group of runners why they are in the pool, and a frequent answer will be that they are runners who are recovering from an injury and want to keep running during the rehabilitation period. Some runners begin deep-water running as a therapeutic process and then run in deep water in the pool as a complement to their resumed land-running program.

Deep-water running attracts a wide range of participants; it meets the needs of the marathoner, the triathlete, and the cross-trainer and provides these athletes with the opportunity to maintain aerobic conditioning and specificity of training while preventing injury from overuse. Also, deep-water running is an alternative fitness regimen for professional or elite level athletes concerned about extending their careers.

Deep-water running is also helpful to the arthritis patient who is able to move more freely in water than on land, as well as to the person who is looking for a pleasant, effective way to keep in shape.

Use an appropriate flotation support for deep-water jogging.

Equipment for Deep Water

The most common kind of equipment for deep water is the flotation device. Flotation devices are primarily used to provide safety and neutral buoyancy, that is, to keep the chin out of the water with ease without having to work at it. Flotation belts and vests enable an exerciser of any ability to simulate jogging in deep water and concentrate on the exercise of running. Exercise in deep water can also be done without equipment.

The best devices are foam rubber flotation belts (e.g., Speedo® Flotation Belt, AquaJogger®, Sprint Aqua Belt® and/or the Wet Vest®, a lightweight, snug-fitting vest made of neoprene, which keep the swimmer upright as well as buoyant. Equally serviceable is a tethered rope attached to a poolside anchor, allowing a swimmer to water jog in a small space, and simulating a sprint or downhill running in water.

Other flotation equipment helpful for deep-water jogging are buoyancy resistance cuffs, such as HydroFit®, which are worn on the wrists, ankles, and/or shoulders. These can be used by aquatic exercisers who are not naturally buoyant.

Deep-Water Exercises

Deep-Water Running

- **Deep-Water Running:** Run or jog exactly the same way as on land. Keep elbows close to body, moving arms in opposition to legs. Maintain good posture.

- **Hurdles:** Simulate the leg position running a hurdle course. Begin in vertical position with legs together and knees bent. Then separate knees and extend one leg straight forward as close to hip level as possible. Simultaneously extend the other leg behind the body, with knees slightly bent.

- **Cross-Country Skiing:** Simulate cross-country skiing with arms and legs moving in opposition to each other and fully extended.

Work on improving range of motion by increasing arm/leg reach both in front and in back of body. Arms and legs should be kept equidistant from each other.

Deep-Water Exercises with Upper Body Flotation Support

- **Deep-Water Sit-Up:** Begin in a vertical position with arms outstretched and grasping a flotation device in each hand (kickboard, floaties, aqua barbell). Bend knees and use abdominal muscles to bring knees toward the water's surface. Then extend legs downward. Repeat.

- **Propeller:** Begin in a streamlined vertical position, with legs together and straight, and ankles crossed; use a flotation device, belt, or vest for buoyancy. Rotate from the waist, sweeping legs right, back, and left, and then return to the streamlined vertical position. Repeat in the opposite direction.

- **Treading:** Treading water is a deep-water exercise as well as a safety skill. Practice treading in its various forms, e.g., bicycle pedal leg motion, egg beater leg motion. For variety use equipment such as hand paddles.

Deep-water exercise workouts can utilize training techniques. For example, using a pace clock or wristwatch, count the number of strides in a given time period. This is called a cadence check. Rest, then repeat jog or run, but at each repeat, try to increase the number of strides.

Another training technique is interval training. Interval training simulates a running workout with sets of fast and slow runs (known also as the Fartlek method). This technique works well with treading.

Following are two sample deep-water interval workouts. Be certain to warm up and cool down before and after each workout.

SAMPLE DEEP-WATER WORKOUTS

Workout 1

Time	Exercise
15 sec	Run with thumbs up
15 sec	Rest
15 sec	Run with thumbs up
15 sec	Rest
30 sec	Run with chin out of water
15 sec	Run with right arm out
15 sec	Run with left arm out
1:00 min	Rest
30 sec	Run forward with right arm out
30 sec	Run backward with left arm out
1:00 min	Rest
1:00 min	Sit-ups in water, alternating left to right
1:45 sec	Jog forward, alternating to left, right, back
2:00 min	Jog
30 sec	Exercise
1:30 sec	Sit-ups
1:15 sec	Jog with hands pushing down, alternate every 15 sec
1:00 min	Jog with hands out last 15 sec
30 sec	Horizontal kick
15 sec	Vertical kick
15 sec	Vertical kick (fast)
15 min	TOTAL TIME

Workout 2

Time	Exercise
30 sec	Tread water
30 sec	Rest
45 sec	Tread water
45 sec	Rest
1:00 min	Walk forward and backward
1:00 min	Rest
1 min/15 sec	Jog in a circle
1 min/15 sec	Rest
1 min/30 sec	Jog toward diving board and raise left hand
1 min/30 sec	Rest
1 min/45 sec	Jog around edge of pool and raise right hand
1 min/45 sec	Rest
2:00 min	Tread water (optional exercises)
1 min/45 sec	Rest
1 min/45 sec	Sit-ups and leg lifts
1 min/30 sec	Rest
1 min/30 sec	Jumping jacks, right hand up, left hand up
1 min/15 sec	Rest
1 min/15 sec	Jog across pool
1:00 min	Rest
1:00 min	Jog across pool with one hand up
45 sec	Rest
45 sec	Jog and turn in place
30 sec	Rest
30 sec	Sprint in place
1:00 min	Easy jog
30 min	TOTAL TIME

FARTLEK WORKOUT SET (Easy/Hard)

30 sec	Easy jog
30 sec	Hard
25 sec	Easy
25 sec	Hard
20 sec	Easy
20 sec	Hard
15 sec	Easy
15 sec	Hard
10 sec	Easy
10 sec	Hard
5 sec	Easy
5 sec	Hard

Suggested variation: Rest and repeat set in reverse order, starting with 5 seconds and progressing to 30 seconds.

WORKOUT SUGGESTION: *Try vertical kicking as part of the main set of a deep-water workout. Vertical kicking is similar to flutter kick or back flutter kick in a vertical position. Begin with vertical kicking for 15 seconds and then rest for 15 seconds, and then continue alternating between kicking and resting. Progress up to 60 seconds vertical kicking and 60 seconds of rest. This pattern can be used as a portion of the main set, i.e., 5 to 10 minutes of a 20- to 30-minute main set. Another variation is to count flutter kick cycles per given time period (one right/one left equals one kick cycyle). Try to better the number of kicks per time period after resting.*

Chapter 14

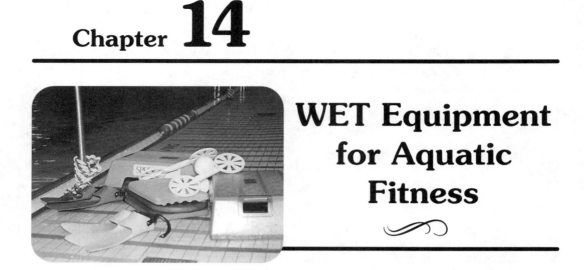

WET Equipment for Aquatic Fitness

Many kinds of conventional swimming equipment can be used for water exercise as well as for swim training. Among the most common and popular are kickboards, pull-buoys, fins, and hand paddles. Using equipment often brings immediate comfort and enjoyment, especially for the non-swimmer and the new swimmer. Appendix B contains a listing of equipment sources.

As discussed in earlier chapters, swimming equipment is used primarily to increase resistance, add variety to workouts, increase intensity (to enhance calorie burn), provide extra buoyancy, and refine specific components of individual swimming strokes. Listed below are examples of frequently used swim training equipment and ways to use them in an aquatic fitness program.

The Kickboard

Kickboards are a basic swim training device, usually available at aquatic facilities. They are made of buoyant materials and are designed to lift and stabilize the arms and upper body during kicking drills. Their size and shape can also be useful for water exercises.

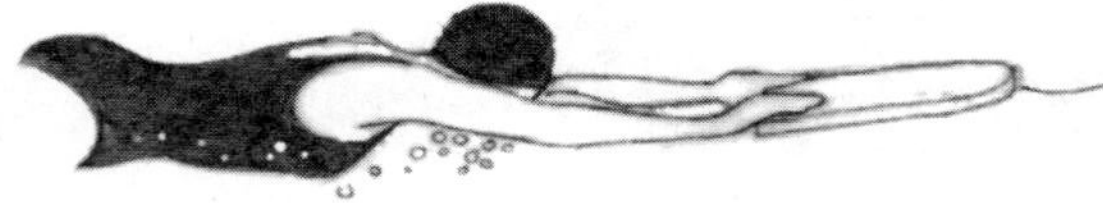

- **Kickboard Presses:** Stand in chest-deep water with hands on a kickboard held widthwise. Remain standing and slowly straighten arms and lower the board under the water. Keeping hands on board, slowly allow the board to surface. As exercise becomes easier, use two boards placed one on top of the other. Then, to increase intensity further, do the kickboard press with just the fingertips.

- **Kickboard Waterfall:** Stand in chest-deep water, holding board widthwise on water's surface with arms extended forward. Submerge board. Then lift board and water until arms are extended overhead to create a waterfall keeping board parallel to water's surface.

- **Ocean in a Pool:** Stand in chest-deep water and hold kickboard widthwise or hold board in a vertical position (perpendicular to the water's surface). Bring board close to body, submerged as much as possible. Extend arms, pushing water and board away from the body. Then bring board quickly toward chest and repeat. Alternate the moving board with equal energy to maximize wave action. In this exercise, the deeper the kickboard is submerged, the greater the resistance and thus the greater the muscle strength to be expended.

- **Triceps Posture Press:** Stand in chest-deep water, with shoulder blades back and chest forward. Hold kickboard behind back in vertical position with curved edge upward. Elbows face outward and the board is close to the body. Extend arms downward and press board as far as possible under the water against the buoyancy of the water. Then bend elbows and let the board rise to starting position, controlling the kickboard as it moves upward.

- **Flexibility Stretch:** Stand in chest-deep water and hold board widthwise overhead, with arms straight and hands grasping the board at each side. Alternately bend arms sideways to the right and left several times. Then rotate the board lengthwise with hands grasping the width of the board in the middle, keeping arms overhead and straight, and repeat movement from side to side several times. Then complete the flexibility stretch by holding the board at its narrowest width, with palms pressed inward and arms still straight overhead. This simulates the streamlined body position, with arms covering the ears.

The Pull-Buoy

Pull-buoys, by definition, are made of buoyant materials. Although primarily used for swim stroke pull drills, they can offer buoyancy against which the water exerciser can work, helping to increase strength.

- **Rockette Kick:** Place back against pool wall with arms extended on pool edge for support. Place pull-buoy under foot by placing heel between horizontal cords of pull-buoy (or across the thinnest part of one-piece pull-buoy). The buoyancy of the pull-buoy will pull leg up to the water's surface, stretching the hamstring muscles. With knees straight, press extended leg downward toward pool bottom, using the strength of upper leg muscles (quadriceps). Then slowly allow the buoyancy of the pull-buoy to bring leg up to the starting position. Control the movement of the leg so that the rate of speed is the same on both the upward and downward sweep. Do several kicks on each side, then repeat with the other leg.
- **Side Swipe:** Stand in waist-to-chest-deep water, holding on to the pool edge or corner with both arms. Place foot on pull-buoy. Starting at water's surface with one leg out to the side, sweep leg down and in front of body in semicircular pattern and then return to starting position. Remember to keep hips as even as possible. Begin with five sweeps on each side. Remove pull-buoy, replace on other leg and repeat on other side, being sure to do an equal number of sweeps on each side.
- **Swim Pull Set:** Practice the arm motion of standard swim strokes by isolating the arms and keeping the legs stationary during pull drills. Place pull-buoy between upper legs, and cross ankles for lower body support.

Fins

For many years, fins have been standard gear for skin and SCUBA divers. They have now entered the swimmer's arena to aid in developing swim skills, aerobic conditioning, and to add variety to workouts. They are also popular among competitive swimmers as a training tool.

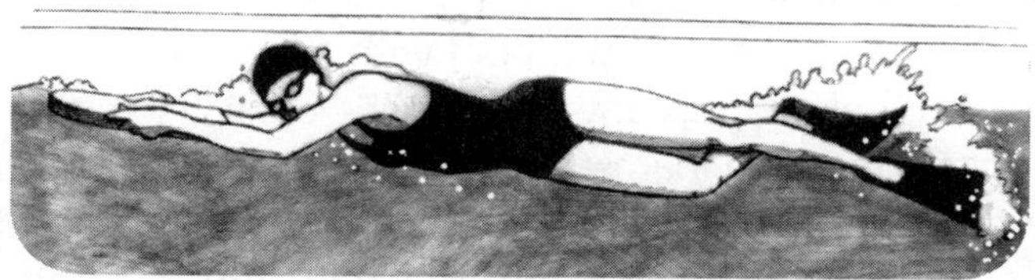

Because the surface area of fins is larger than the foot, more water is displaced by the fin. The extra surface offers greater resistance in all directions. Therefore, kicking exercises with fins build up the large muscles of the leg in a shorter period of training time.

Fins used for many years by deep-sea divers, are no longer heavy and flat. Current state-of-the-art fin technology and design offer swimmers of all levels a range of styles, materials, weights, colors, sizes, fit, comfort, and purpose.

Working out with fins allows the swimmer to experience the exhilaration and sense of riding high in the water; the thrust of the fin extends the force of the leg kick. Wearing fins also keeps the middle section of the body more buoyant and streamlined, which raises the upper body and shoulders higher in the water. By shifting the stress away from the arms and shoulders, fins allow the arm stroke motion to develop power and efficiency, and, therefore, greater swimming speed is more easily accomplished.

Fins are effective for all strokes at almost any level. For the crawlstroke, fins help to strengthen the flutter kick and propel the swimmer faster and farther in streamlined form.

Fins can also be used to develop a more flexible dolphin kick for the butterfly stroke. Using fins during the backstroke raises the hips as well as the whole body to a streamlined position.

Fins are used not just for kicking. For example, if the pool is crowded, use the time to do a medley of stationary kicks with fins while holding on to the edge of the pool.

Exercises and Stretches

- **Quadriceps Stretch:** Standing in chest-deep water, keep knees together. Bend one knee and bring foot as close as possible toward the buttocks and hold on to back of that fin for a quadriceps stretch, then release. Repeat on the other side.

- **Quadriceps Stretch Challenge:** Stand in shallow water, holding on to the edge of the pool with one hand. With the other hand, hold the tip of the fin on the outside leg, and lift that leg so that the hamstring muscles will be stretched. Move the leg outward to the side and then forward, which gives an additional stretch to the inside leg muscles (the abductors and adductors).

Fin Tips

- Progress with fins slowly, especially when using them for the first time.
- Use fins for a portion of rather than for an entire workout.
- Wear socks or diving booties for comfort and fit, if necessary.
- Walk backwards on the pool deck or in the water to avoid tripping or falling while wearing fins.
- Use fins as a morale booster. During a difficult main set, fins help to help slower swimmers keep up with faster ones. Fins will also reinforce the sensation of riding high in the water because of the stronger kick from hips and thighs. Fins are not cheating but strengthening.
- Keep fins just under the surface of the water for best kicking efficiency. While kicking with fins, the legs tend to break through the surface of the water very easily because of the great amount of buoyancy.

For the triathlon participant who is already a trained athlete but who is new to swimming, fins can help to accelerate the process of acquiring correct body position in the water, coordinate arm and leg motions, and train leg muscles other than those used for running and cycling.

Monofin

Introduced by the Italians and the Russians, the monofin is a recent development in fin design. It is a single large fin with two foot pockets side by side. It is ideal for the dolphin kick and for propelling the swimmer with efficiency and speed. However, anyone with back problems should use caution if swimming with the monofin.

Swimmers wearing the monofin often also use a mask and a racing snorkel. Monofin swimming is, as is regular or bifin swimming, a competitive sport and is gaining in popularity.

Fin swimming is fast. Current world record for 50 meters with a Monofin in 14.6 seconds.

Hand Paddles and Mitts

Hand paddles and mitts are commonly used for swim training and water exercise. Most hand paddles and mitts exercises are for strengthening the upper body. Hand paddles and mitts come in a variety of colors, styles, shapes, and thicknesses. Perhaps their most common use is to practice the arm motion, especially in the crawlstroke.

TIP: *Exercise with caution when using hand paddles. The water's resistance against the shoulders can be strong.*

Swimming Stroke Exercises

- **Resistance Check:** Wear a mitt or paddle on one hand and, with wrist flat, place hand in the water, just below the surface. Extend the arm, then bend it backward and forward from the elbow. There will be little resistance. Lower the hand underwater, and feel the resistance of the water by first flexing hand upward and then pronating hand downward.

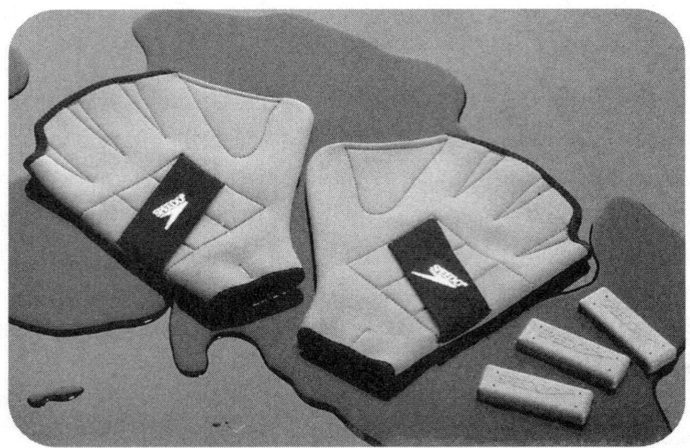

Courtesy of Speedo®/Authentic Fitness

Mitts

- **Crawlstroke Arm Motion:** One of the greatest resistances the swimmer and water exerciser might feel is in a simulated arm stroke for the crawl. Stand in place and with hand in mitt or paddle, pull arm straight through and back behind body (something many swimmers forget to do). Then go on to walking the stroke, pulling arm through. Refer to splashback drill on page 49. Then complete the exercise by swimming crawlstroke (walk, pull, swim).

- **Backstroke Arm Motion:** With hand in mitt or paddle, standing in chest- or waist-deep water, simulate backstroke arm motion, walking backward, then pulling arm through, then swimming. There is a greater pull with the paddle or mitt and greater shoulder rotation.

- **Breaststroke and Butterfly Arm Motions:** The breaststroke and butterfly call for smaller hand paddles or mitts. Standing in chest- or waist-deep water, with hands in mitts or paddles, practice the heart-shaped pull, for the breaststroke, followed by the arm circle motion for the butterfly. Do a small arm circle in place, then a medium arm circle, and then a larger arm circle underwater, feeling the resistance of the water against the paddle or mitt.

  A nice variation for the butterfly arm motion is to simulate jumping rope using paddles or mitts. After simulating the arm motion, move on to jumping and combine arms and legs.

- **Trunk Turn:** Extend arms outward to the side underwater, 180 degrees apart, using appropriately sized hand paddles. Maintaining the 180 degree spread, turn trunk all the way to one side. Then turn trunk and arms together 180 degrees in the opposite direction with palms perpendicular to the water, thumbs up and just under the surface. Using paddles or mitts will greatly increase the resistance against the water.

- **Scull and Hug:** Review the scull and hug on page 40. Wearing the paddles and mitts, feel the exercise strengthen both the pectoral and tricep muscles, as well as the shoulders.

- **Bicep/Tricep Press:** Stand with hand paddles or mitts in chest-deep water and with elbows at side. Start with forearm and hand at a 90-degree angle to body. Then press the forearm and hand straight down to the thigh. Return to starting position by bringing forearm and hand back up to 90 degrees, moving against the resistance of the water.

- **Frog Jump:** In chest-deep water or in deep water (using a flotation belt or buoyancy vest), wearing mitts and/or paddles, start in vertical position, with hands at sides. Forcefully press both hands in front of body and at the same time, bring knees up in straddle position. Then return to starting position.

  This exercise is similar to a Nautilus® as paddles are pulling inward and outward.

Aqua Step

The aquatic exercise step is a state-of-the-art aquatic fitness product. Similar to the popular land-based step but designed for the water, the aqua step is often used in aquatic exercise programs for conditioning as well as for rehabilitation and walking programs. It is advisable to wear aqua shoes for safety, resistance, and comfort.

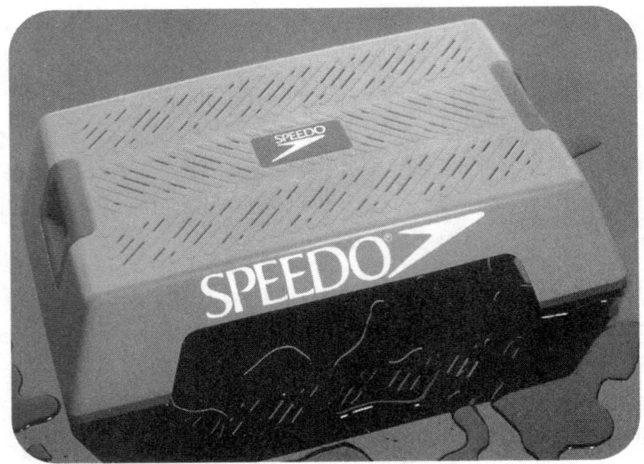

Courtesy of Speedo®/Authentic Fitness

Speedo Aqua Step

Exercises for the Aqua Step

- **Rocking Horse:** Step on to the aquatic step with one leg and kick backward with the other. Reverse legs and repeat.
- **Skateboard:** From a standing position on top of the aquatic step, kick one leg forward. Swing leg front to back while bending the opposite knee. Reverse sides and repeat.

Water Exercise Equipment for the Advanced Exerciser

As the popularity of water exercise has increased, so have the variety and range of equipment. Buoyancy and resistance devices have proliferated, offering a variety of options for new and competitive swimmers for balance and strengthening. An example for the advanced water exerciser are the Hydro-tone® boots.

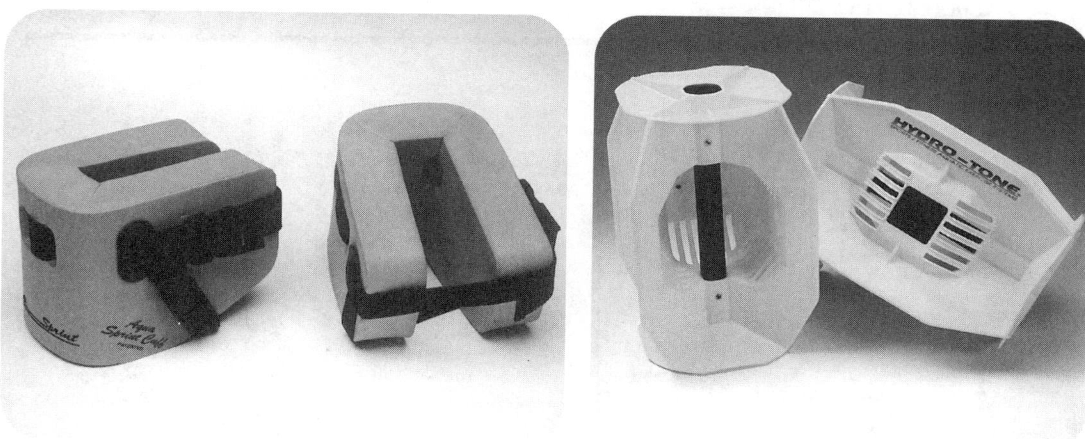

Courtesy of Sprint Aqua Cuffs

Buoyancy Resistance Cuffs

Courtesy of Hydro-Tone®

Hydro-Tone® Boots

Aqua Circuit

The aqua circuit is another method of training with WETs. Classes vary depending on facility, needs, and equipment. Here, you can mix and match WETs at different equipment stations for a set period of time.

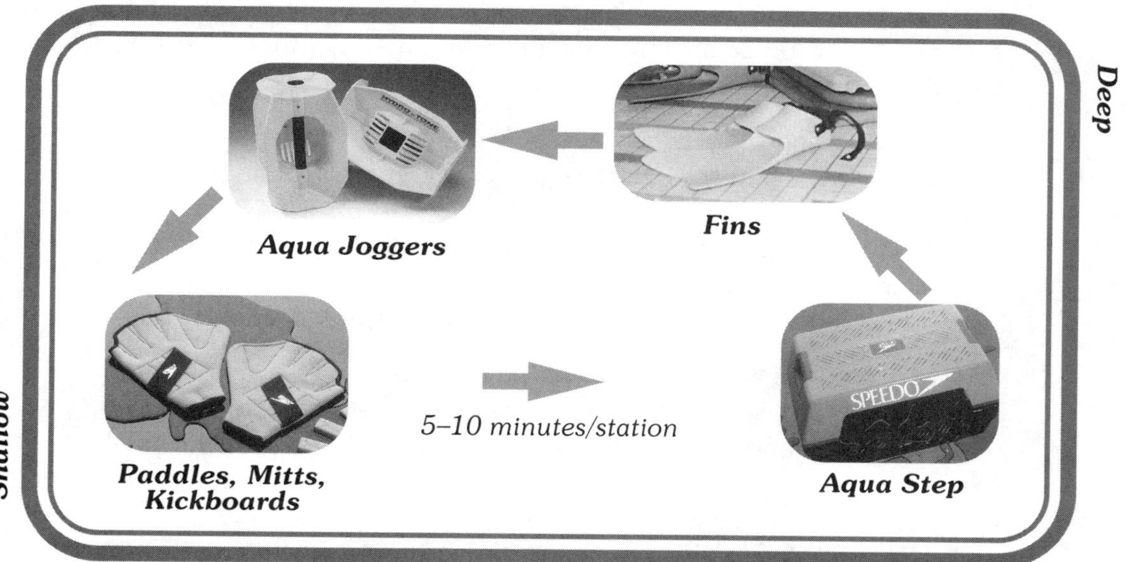

Aquatic Training Stations

Chapter 15

Courtesy of © 1993 IBM Corp.

Sport WETs

Throughout this book, learning to swim has been the primary focus. However, water is an ideal environment for athletes who participate in other sports, whether for recreation, fitness, or competition. Simulating the motions of other sports using the resistance of water and WET techniques has many benefits, such as:

- Conditioning year-round
- Strengthening specific muscle groups in a more soothing environment to avoid overuse or injury
- Increasing range of motion as part of conditioning
- Maintaining skill-specific training while recovering from injury
- Stretching out and relaxing after performing land workouts

Almost every sport and exercise can be practiced by following a simulated WET. Many sports can also be performed in the water, such as water volleyball and water polo. Jumping off the bottom of the pool (plyometrics) can strengthen muscles and provide practice for starts, turns, and push-offs as well as for diving.

The following WETs are exercises for cross training, track and field, and plyometrics.

Deep-Water Exercises for Cross Training

- **Stroke Punch:** This exercise is especially good for race walking, cross-country skiing, speed skating, a boxer's punch, and a fencer's parry. Stand in chest-deep water with feet shoulder width apart. Make fists and alternately punch arms forward underwater, allowing the shoulders to follow the full extension of the arm. For greater effect, pump arms vigorously.
- **Sport Swings:** This exercise is beneficial for racquet sports, especially tennis, as well as for golf, baseball, bowling, and fencing. Stand in chest-deep water with arms out at sides. Move one arm forward, as if swinging a racquet. Follow through and recover out of the water, then swing arm backward, as in a backhand in tennis, into the starting position. Repeat with the other arm.

  Use hand paddles or a pull-buoy for greater resistance. Be sure to follow through completely with each swing.

Deep-Water Running for Track and Field

Deep-water running is an excellent way to improve running. The runner gains flexibility and strengthens leg muscles by skill-specific movements, such as hurdling, while maintaining cardiovascular fitness. The runner is also less likely to sustain overuse or impact injuries that might occur doing comparable training workouts on land.

Aquatic exercise can be so effective in the rehabilitation of sports injuries that many varsity teams feature a hydrotherapy tank. Warm water and jets can also enhance the athlete's exercise regimen.

Many marathon runners do part of their training in deep water either on their own or in classes. Water training gives injured runners an opportunity to put in sufficient mileage to prepare for a big race. There have been runners who did not run on land until the day of the marathon. Other runners report excellent results by combining training with deep-water running and mileage on the roads.

Deep-water running covers the physical needs of a total running program including hip and ankle flexibility, and balances the ratio between quadricep and hamstring strength, upper body strength, and cardiovascular endurance training (especially for long events). An especially good aspect of deep-water running is the opportunity to vary the workout: to be creative, combine activities, and invent new workouts.

See Chapter 13 for deep-water running exercises.

Plyometrics

Plyometrics refers to the use of the leg muscles to create an extra "spring" in a movement. Plyometrics can be a simple activity, such as jumping up and down in the pool. Instead of only bobbing in the water, a plyometric movement bounds off the pool bottom and forcefully and quickly moves in streamlined form as high as possible. Plyometrics are especially good for developing the large leg muscles, such as the quadriceps. Employing plyometrics is helpful in improving swimming starts and turns.

The following exercises are plyometric WETs. Remember to maintain streamlined body form.

Sample Plyometric WETs

- **Plyometric Jump:** Jump up and down "ballistically" from pool bottom. Then use hands to push downward, creating a lift in the water. For an added lift, try this exercise using hand paddles.
- **Streamlined Jump:** Jump up from the pool bottom and bring arms overhead as if pushing off from the pool wall into a streamlined body position. Arms should cover ears and hands are crossed, one in front of the other.
- **Jump with Turn:** Jump off pool bottom as high as possible, making a quarter of a turn. Then make a half turn. This is similar to what the swimmer does underwater when doing a flip turn.
- **Shake-Out:** At the end of a workout set, jump off pool bottom, making a half turn, then a whole turn. Jump as high as possible at each turn. Then reverse directions.

Unit V

© Jeff Goldberg/Esto

Additional Aquatic Activities

One goal of aquatic fitness is to open up new ways of enjoying the water. Unit V presents popular water activities for enjoyment, physical conditioning, personal improvement, and safety. As aquatic skills improve from practice, the following activities make water fitness more interesting and challenging.

Chapter 16 explains the basics of diving—from the elementary sitting dive to competitive springboard and platform diving. Chapter 17 introduces the graceful sport of synchronized swimming, and Chapter

18 focuses on water games including water polo. Chapter 19 details the world of competitive swimming and triathlons. Chapter 20 covers safety and how to protect the swimmer in water environments.

The following chapters highlight the aquatic Olympic sports. These sports are governed by FINA (Féderation Internacionale Natacion Amateur) which includes competitive swimming, diving, synchronized swimming, and water polo. Long distance swimming is also governed by FINA. See Appendix C for each sports' United States governing body.

Chapter 16

Diving

Watching Olympic divers gracefully enter the water from tremendous heights is a thrill. Their skill and daring amaze us. And even though most of us will never dive competitively, these divers follow the basic steps that are true for all dives.

For the swimmer, a dive is an out-of-the-water start—it begins on land and ends in the water; it uses the resistance of a stationary object (such as the pool deck or starting block) to help the diver travel forward.

To begin learning the basic dives, review the prone (front) glide and recovery. Be particularly conscious of the push-off from the wall and of keeping a streamlined body position. Glide with arms overhead.

Diving Basics

In diving, an essential aspect of entering the water head first is to keep the arms always stretched out in front of the body during entry so that fingertips enter the water first for safety and streamlining. It is important to learn diving in steps; the components of the step-by-step progression of one dive become the foundation for the components of the next dive.

SAFE DIVING TIPS

- Always dive into water that is deep enough for the particular dive being practiced. For dives from the pool deck, the water should be at least 9 feet deep. Check the pool markers and check with the lifeguard to determine the depth of the pool.
- Extend arms overhead during every dive to streamline the body and for safe entry. Keep arms overhead until the dive is finished.
- When wearing goggles, make the strap a bit tighter than usual to withstand the impact of the water.

Five Basic Components of Diving

1. **Stance:** The diver starts from either a sitting, kneeling, or standing position, with toes curled around the edge of the pool or starting block. Body is balanced, poised, and ready for the take-off.
2. **Take-Off:** The body pushes off forcefully with the thrust or energy coming from the legs. Head is forward; the eyes look diagonally forward and downward.
3. **Flight:** The body is taut and streamlined and extends. It arcs smoothly through the air with arms overhead.
4. **Entry:** The arms are extended, with head tucked down between them and ears covered, with fingertips entering the water first.
5. **Recovery:** The diver returns to the surface of the water in a smooth arc by lifting the chin and angling hands and arms upward.

Diving Progression

For most new divers, dives begin where the body is close to the water's surface and progress to where body is far from the water's surface (i.e., the high board). The skills learned in each dive help the diver to achieve the next level in the progression.

The shallow surface dive is a variation of the basic push-off, (or an in-the-water start). The first out-of-the-water entry is from a sitting position. It is followed by the kneeling and semi-standing dives, and then the standing dives. The most efficient dives are the racing dives, often used by competitive swimmers from a starting block. After that, the diver learns to enter the water from higher elevations of springboards and platforms.

Sitting Dive

Sit on edge of the pool with feet flat against the pool wall. Extend arms in front of body covering ears with hands, which are pointed downward toward water's surface.Push off from the side of pool with legs straightened into a prone glide. Tuck the chin tightly to the chest and angle the arms down about 30 degrees to propel the body just beneath the surface. To recover, arch back slightly and lift the chin a little in order to return to the surface of the water in a prone glide. Arms remain overhead, angling upward, for streamlining and safety until recovering to a standing position.

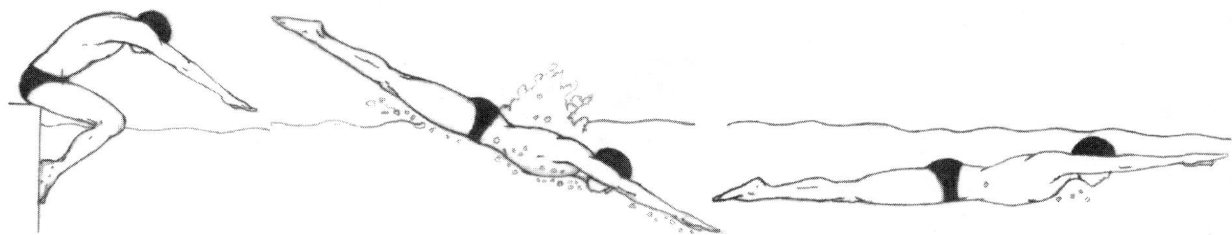

Sitting Dive

> *A porpoise dive can be practiced in the water by pushing off the bottom. Imagine diving over a barrel floating on the surface of the water but without touching the barrel.*

Kneeling Dive

Kneel at the edge of the pool, with weight on one knee and the toes of the other foot curled securely around the edge for traction. (Optional: raise the weight-bearing knee off the ground slightly for greater comfort.) Tuck chin to chest, and extend arms overhead with upper arm muscles tight against ears. To keep arm straight and hands together, hook thumbs, pointing fingers downward toward water.

To begin the takeoff, lean forward so that hands almost touch the water. Keep leaning farther and farther, gradually shifting almost all of the body weight onto the forward foot.

Next bring hips up, and extend the back leg behind to begin to streamline body for the flight. Continue to shift weight forward until the rear foot lifts off the deck and the body begins to fall toward the surface. Bring legs together and straighten while entering the water. Push off with the forward leg, so that instead of falling into the water, the body springs forward. Point hands downward at a 45-degree angle on entry, with chin remaining tucked down toward chest; point toes, and tighten leg muscles to obtain a streamlined position.

Begin to exhale a moment before breaking the surface of the water. Once in the water, continue to exhale slowly, and stretch and streamline the body as it glides through the water in a downward arc.

To recover, point fingers upward. Arch back slightly, lifting the chin and raising the head and arms toward the surface. Begin to kick, or simply remain in a streamlined float position, arms overhead, prior to recovering to a stand.

Kneeling Dive

Semi-Standing Dive

Once comfortable with the kneeling dive, progress diving from a slightly higher stance. Stand with one foot in back of the other (with the toes of the forward foot curled securely around the edge for traction to prevent slipping). **Pike** (bend) at the waist with head tucked down, eyes looking forward and toward the water's surface, and extend arms overhead, covering or hugging ears. Then press head and arms downward, while the back leg presses upward. Lean forward, lifting the back foot off the deck and shifting all the body weight onto the front leg, until moving forward toward the surface. Enter the water with fingertips leading. Straighten legs and bring them together, toes pointed. Make an arc underwater, as with the kneeling dive, and remember to keep head tucked down and arms close to ears until it is time to recover to the surface of the water by angling hands upward and recovering.

Semi-Standing Dive

Standing Dive

Stand in a piked position with knees bent slightly, both feet together, toes curled around the pool edge. Again, arms are extended straight in front of body at a 45-degree angle to the water, head is down, and upper arms are covering ears. Think of the body as a see-saw with the hips as the fulcrum. Bend knees more, then straighten them during take-off to give the dive a spring and, therefore, height. At the push-off, lift hips, extend legs up and straight behind the body, pointing toes.

Standing Dive

As the standing dive is refined, gradually straighten the body out of the piked position during flight. Keep head down and arms extended as the body stretches and springs up and travels over the surface of the water in a smooth, graceful arc before entering the water. Since the higher stance of the standing dive equals greater distance from the water, entering will be faster and deeper than with the kneeling or semi-standing dives. This may result in a longer recovery, so remember to exhale slowly until reaching the surface of the water by angling hands upward.

Racing Dives/Starts

There are three basic competition starts: the conventional arm swing, the grab start, and the track start. Starts and entries vary according to ability and needs.

Arm-Swing Dive

The conventional racing dive has been used for many years for all strokes swum in the prone position. Even a fitness swimmer may prefer to enter the water for a workout using this clean and fairly shallow dive.

In competition, the dive takes place off a starting block usually thirty inches above the water's surface. The object is to create as much *horizontal* forward propulsion and as little resistance as possible. In order to do this, a "hole" is created in the water by the hands entering first for the body to follow. This is also called a nonresistance entry because the body enters the water cleanly, through a space that it has created for itself.

Before learning the dive, get the feel of creating the hole by practicing in waist-deep water. Push off forcefully from the bottom of the pool as if diving over the surface of the water (a porpoise dive). During the over-the-water arc, extend arms overhead, arch back, and lift head. Then, enter the water, with dropped head and rounded shoulders, so the rest of the body passes through the hole created by the shoulders and the arms.

To begin the racing dive out of the water, step forward to the edge of the pool or onto the starting block. Stand straight with toes curled tightly over the edge, feet about hip width apart. Bend knees and let arms position themselves where comfortable and balanced. Body weight is forward, on the balls of the feet, and eyes are looking ahead.

To take off, swing arms down and around to the front in a semicircle. Begin to extend legs to initiate the flight. Straighten legs and lift head to look forward. By the time feet lift off, the arms have completed the swing and are straight ahead, pointed forward and downward at a shallow angle. The legs are as stretched and streamlined as possible. Once the body is completely extended over the water, drop head downward to enable the body to pass through the hole made by the hands. Entry should be relatively flat, at approximately a 20-degree angle to the water's surface.

Once in the water, glide, holding a streamlined position, until losing momentum, then start kicking, followed by the arm motion.

Arm-Swing Racing Dive

Grab Start

This is a more efficient variation of the racing dive. Although it is similar to the arm-swing start, it gets the swimmer into the water faster.

Stand at the end of the pool or on the starting block, feet hip width apart and with toes of one or both feet curled around the edge. Bend forward at the waist and grasp the platform or bar of the starting block. Hands are usually between the feet at this point, but hands can also be outside the feet. The grab position allows the swimmer to balance weight forward over the starting block. At the starting signal, overbalance the body by stretching it forward and pulling shoulders and head down. Then release hands from the platform grab bar as the torso goes forward. This levels off the trajectory when leaving the starting block in much the same way that the arm swing of the conventional racing dive does. The grab start, however, takes less time.

Track Start

This is a variation of the grab start, with the body weight on the back foot. This allows the racer a propulsive take-off and explosive start.

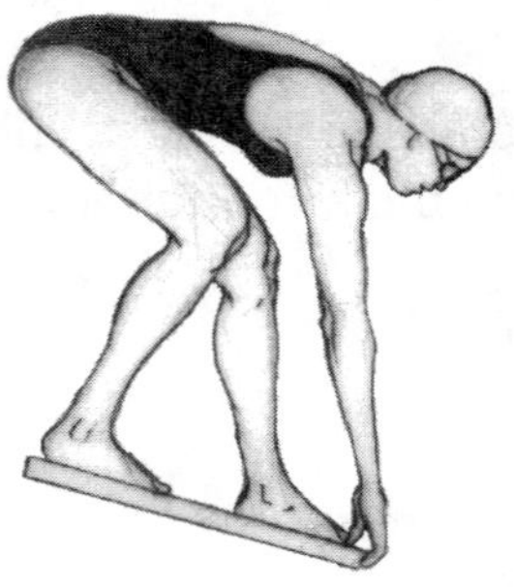

Grab Start

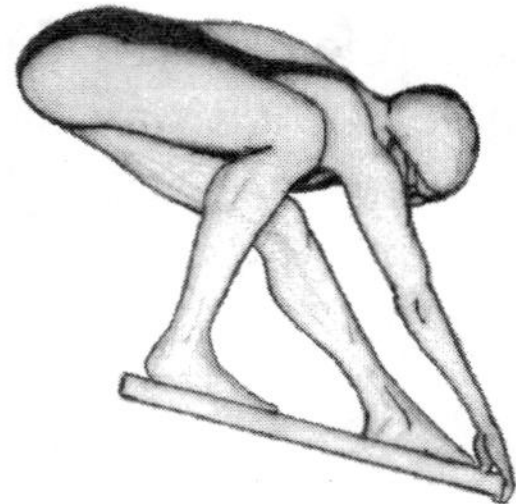

Track Start

Springboard Diving

The next step in the progression is the springboard dive, usually from a 1-meter or 3-meter (approximately 10 feet) board. One meter may not seem high, but diving at this height gives the feeling of flying, if only for a moment.

First, it is necessary to get accustomed to the height and springiness of the board. When ready to use the board, remember to maintain the habit of checking to see that no one is swimming near or under the board.

Springboard Diving Safety Tips

- Springboard diving requires special attention to safety.
- Learn to dive with a qualified instructor.
- Before diving, swimmers should be comfortable in deep-water.
- Be sure entry area is clear before beginning a dive.
- Swim away from entry area to nearest exit to clear area for next diver immediately after surfacing.
- Never dive while someone else is on the board.
- Make sure the diving facility conforms to current regulations.
- Do not dive if:
  —The diving area is unsupervised.
  —The diving area appears unsafe.
  —The depth demarcations are not clear.
  —The bottom of the pool is not visible, or the water is cloudy.
  —The board is too close to the pool edge or is too slippery.
  —The fulcrum of the springboard is not stable.

Hurdle

TAKE THE HURDLE TO SPRINGBOARD DIVING

*The **hurdle** is the skill that gives springboard divers the height they need to perform their dives. Height is obtained through the take-off; the hurdle changes the energy of the take-off into vertical distance, i.e., height. The fulcrum of the diving board allows "play" or **spring** in the movement of the board. The greater the height, the greater the* spring. *However, controlling the* spring *requires skill and practice. Even the famous "cannonball" dive uses the* spring *of the board!*

The Hurdle and the Take-Off

The take-off is preceded by three steps and a hurdle. To determine where to begin take-off, walk to the end of the board, turn around and line up heels with the edge of the board. To begin, take three steps forward; on the fourth step, jump and land with both feet on the board (hurdle). The point on the board where the hurdle is completed is the starting point of the take-off for the dive. Start the dive by walking forward three steps; hurdle and land with both feet on the board, jumping on the end of the board. The dive is then executed in the air at the height reached from springing up.

Practice this pattern first by jumping off the edge of the springboard. At the entry, the body should be streamlined in a vertical position with hands at sides or hands overhead.

For the underwater recovery, tuck body and return to the water's surface.

Go with the natural movement of the board. After jumping upward, land softly on the board, pushing it down. Do not jump away from the board. Let the board's springiness propel the body off and up.

Platform Diving

For competitive and experienced divers, there are diving platforms which are 5 meters, 7 meters, and 10 meters high. Many people may want to experience jumping off these high platforms. Before the first platform dive, practice jumping in a vertical position from the edge of the pool, then from a 1-meter springboard, and then, a 3-meter springboard. Then start with a jump from the 5-meter platform. (A 6-foot swimmer who jumps or dives from the 10-meter platform will be looking down almost 40 feet to the water.) At some diving facilities, there may be a 7.5-meter platform available.

Diving is an exciting aquatic activity but entails inherent risks. Learn diving skills under the supervision of a qualified instructor.

Springboards and Diving Platforms

Competitive Diving

Competitive diving is done from a 3-meter springboard or 10-meter platform. Competitive divers, such as 4-time Olympic gold medalist Greg Louganis, exhibit grace, power, and strength. This is the result of a lifetime of discipline and practice.

Some people, especially those who have gymnastic aptitude, enjoy the challenge of diving. Divers need physical coordination, keen perception of their body in space (kinesthetic awareness), strength, and a willingness to take risks.

In competitive diving, there are six groups of dives. The forward group is performed as the diver faces the front of the board. This group includes everything from a basic front dive to forward somersaults. In the backward group of dives, the diver has back to the water. For the reverse group, the diver faces forward on the board and dives rotating toward the board. In the inward group, the diver stands with back to the water and dives rotating toward the board. (These dives were once called cutaways.) Another group of dives are those that include a twist. The last group is the arm-stand group, which are platform dives. The diver begins in a handstand position at the end of the platform.

In competition, each dive is required to be performed in one of three body positions: straight, allowing no bend at the waist or knees. In some cases, the diver's back is arched. In the *pike* position, the legs are straight and the body is bent at the waist. For the tuck position, the diver is bent at the waist and knees, with thighs brought close to the chest and heels kept close to the buttocks. There is also a position category in competitive diving called the free position in which divers can choose the position for executing a dive.

What the Judges Look For

Each dive is rated from 0 to 10, using one-tenth or half point increments. A score of 0 is given to a dive that completely fails, 5 to 6 are for satisfactory dives, and 8.5 to 10 are for very good to excellent dives. Each dive is also assigned a difficulty rating from 1.2 for the simplest dive to 3.2 for the most complicated dives.

Each part of the dive is evaluated. Divers are judged on approach, take-off from the board, and elevation during the flight of the dive. The amount of lift which the diver attains affects the appearance of the dive and gives the diver more time to execute the dive smoothly and accurately. Finally, the judges note entry into the water—the amount of splash produced. The judges note proper mechanical performance, technique, as well as style, a subjective rating that is difficult to assess by an absolute standard. It is added to the overall score.

Greg Louganis won a record five World diving titles as well as four Olympic gold medals (1984 and 1992).

COMMON DIVING ERRORS AND WHAT TO DO ABOUT THEM

If You Are Doing This	Then Try This	Comments
Stance:		
Body is falling forward; off balance.	Grasp edge firmly with toes for support while maintaining your balance with your arms; hips serve as center of gravity.	____
Take-off:		
Legs hit edge of deck.	Push off aggressively, pointing toes at takeoff; be certain to curl toes over edge during stance.	____
Flight		
Body collapses.	Lift legs up while arms direct downward motion; keep body extended. Stretch and maintain streamlined body position; keep arms and legs together.	____
Entry		
Doing the belly flop, head and chest enter the water first.	Keep hips up; use arms to protect head and for streamlining; enter hands first.	____
Body crumples on entry.	Keep arms extended overhead until hips and feet have entered the "hole" made by hands.	____
Water enters the nose and/or mouth.	Begin exhaling a moment before head enters water, this pressure prevents water from entering.	____
Recovery		
Water enters the nose and/or mouth.	Continue to exhale to counteract water pressure.	____
Body pops up to surface too soon.	Delay recovery until forward and downward momentum have slowed; then start kicking.	____

DIVING EVALUATION CHART

Name ______________________________ Class ______________

Dates	Name of Dive	Common Errors	How to Correct Them

General Comments: Always follow safe diving guidelines.

____

____

____

Chapter 17

Synchronized Swimming

In Europe, where synchronized swimming began, it was called "ornamental swimming." In Hollywood during the Esther Williams film era, it was called "water ballet." Today, synchronized swimming has achieved Olympics status as a competitive sport that is judged, like diving, on a rigorous performance scale of required and optional figures and aesthetic routines.

A synchronized swimming routine is a performance to music as a solo, a duet, a trio, or a team of four to eight swimmers using various combinations of figures and swimming skills. The basic requirement to learn synchronized swimming is to be comfortable in deep water with basic swimming skills.

Body positions and figures give synchronized swimming its grace and visual balance in the water. Developed with consistent training, the positions and figures are combined with stroke variations, sculling, and treading. Practicing these routines helps to increase stamina and breath regulation; the entire body is toned and strengthened, especially the shoulder, leg, and abdominal muscles.

Is "synchro," as it is sometimes referred to, a sport or an art? It is both. As a sport, it is similar to other sports and requires rigorous training, endurance, strength, breath control, and responsive muscle coordination. In addition, the swimmer learns to synchronize movement to music by counting beats. The art is in making it all seem effortless, graceful, and choreographically interesting. The basic arm and leg components, body positions, and figures are described below.

Arm and Leg Components

Sculling

The main arm component in synchronized swimming is sculling. There are many sculling variations. The basic one for propulsion and support is head first sculling. The hands and forearms follow a figure 8 pattern (the infinity sign), pushing water toward the feet with the body moving head first. In a back float position, the hands are at the sides, close to and behind the hips, with fingertips pointed upward.

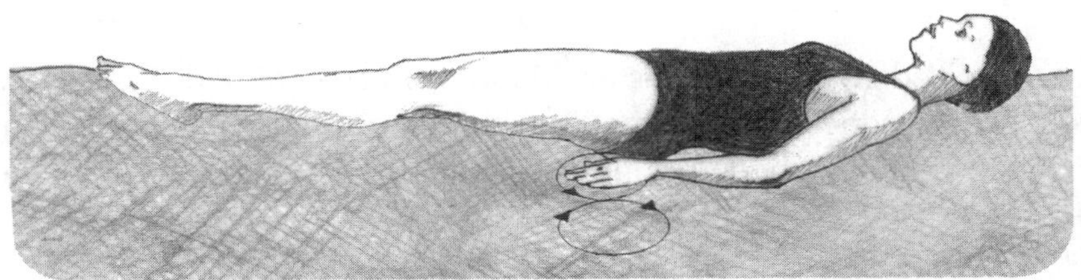

Sculling in Back Layout Position

Treading

The basic leg component for movement and support is treading. In a vertical position, practice a bicycle leg motion, scissors kick, or frog kick. Then try an "egg beater" kick by circling the legs inward one after the other. For a tug-of-war (with yourself), combine a leg tread with a support scull (figure-8 movement with palms facing upward). For variation, add mitts to sculling practice. The leg tread pushes body upward, while the support arm scull pushes body downward.

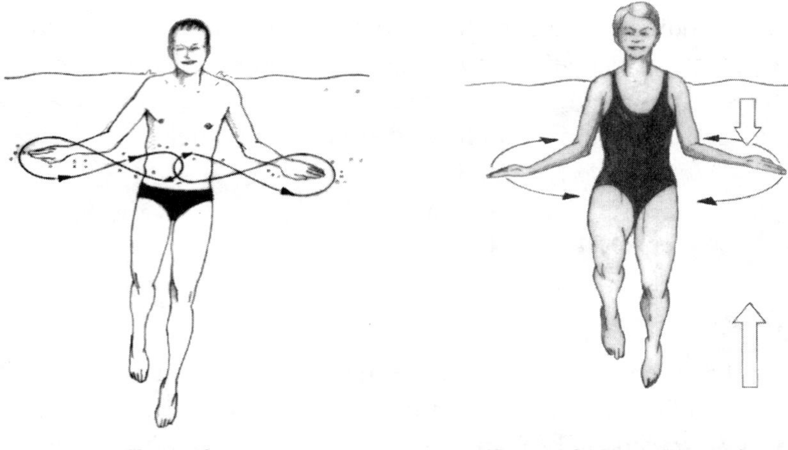

Treading ***Tug-of-War Treading***

Body Positions

Synchronized swimming skills are done from several body positions. A sequence or series of movements within a position is called a figure. The following basic body positions each include an example of a figure.

Back Layout

Begin in back float posiiton with face, hips, thighs, and feet close to the water's surface with toes pointed, with the body in good alignment, hands close to hips.

- **Corkscrew:** This figure begins in a back layout position. Rotate the body to the right side while at the same time extending the right arm overhead to help body roll (like a log). Press the head against the extended right arm until returning to back layout position. To help the roll, add a small flutter kick.
- **Marlin Turn:** The marlin turn figure is similar to the corkscrew in that it begins and ends in a back layout position. However, in the marlin turn, the arms are extended straight from the shoulders at a

90-degree angle to the body (T position). The body rotates to the right as in the corkscrew, with the right arm extended overhead as the body moves to a prone position, the left arm sweeps down to the thigh, and legs travel 45 degrees to the left.

To complete the marlin turn, continue pulling arms back to the T position, returning to the back layout position, with legs traveling another 45 degrees to finish the 90-degree turn.

A complete marlin sequence consists of four turns of 90 degrees, returning the body back to the original starting position and direction.

Marlin Turn

Tuck

The tuck position begins from a back layout position. The body is brought together in a compact tuck with the lower back slightly rounded, knees bent and brought toward chest to a 90-degree angle.

- **Tub Turn:** The tub turn figure begins in the back layout position. Bend knees bringing them toward chest, keeping shins close to the water's surface. Remaining in the tuck position, turn in a complete circle (360 degrees) to the right, pushing the water with a flat sculling motion by turning palms sideways in the opposite direction (to the left), keeping the face above the water.

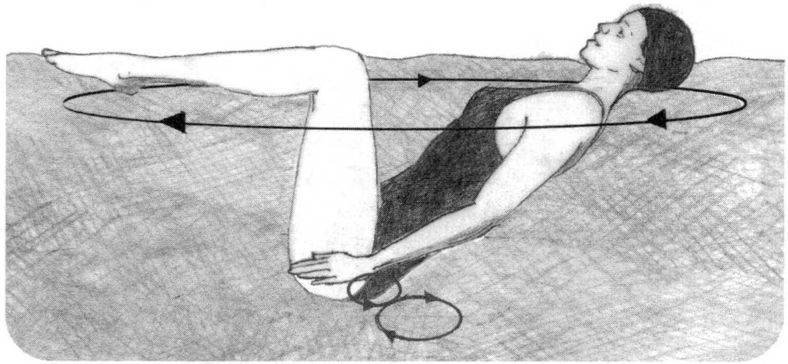

Tub Turn

Pike

From a back layout position, the body is bent inward at the hips at an acute angle, keeping legs straight. With extended legs raised toward the head, the upper part of the body rises to meet the legs, creating a hinged effect like a clam shell.

- **Clam:** The clam figure begins in a back layout position. With arms at sides, create a downward, outward, and overhead circular movement (like a butterfly arm stroke) as the hips pike. The hands

Clam Figure

then move out of the water to touch pointed toes, keeping legs straight before submerging. Since many synchronized swimming skills require submerging, it is advisable to use nose clips.

Arched

The body is arched so that the head, buttocks, and feet follow the arc of the circumference of an imaginary circle, keeping the body streamlined.

- **Shark Circle:** The shark circle begins in a back layout position. Turn to either side to assume a side layout with the top arm extended overhead. The arm should be next to the ear, just under and close to the water's surface. Then scull with lower arm just under the water and near hip to move body in a complete circle on the surface. Complete shark circle by resuming the back layout position. Practicing figures in the arched position should be done cautiously for people with lower back problems.

Shark Circle

Bent Knee and Ballet Leg

The body begins in a back layout position with toes pointed. One leg bends at the knee at 90 degrees toward the chest and then extends from the knee towards the ceiling. The other leg remains on the surface of the water. Rapid sculling close to and under the hips is used to maintain body at water's surface. While practicing, use the edge of the pool for the horizontal leg or a kickboard under one arm for support.

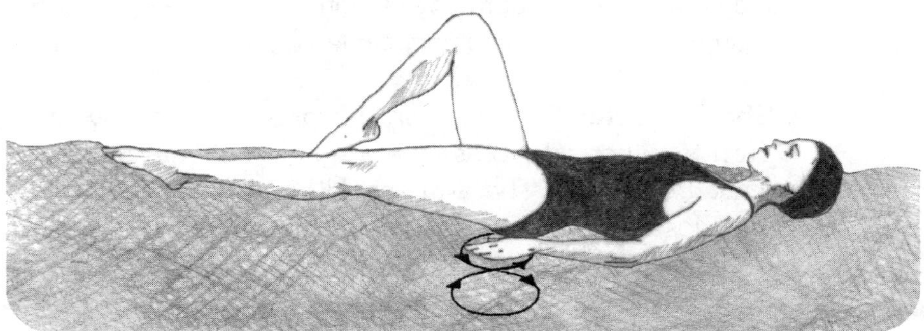

Bent Knee Position

Ballet Leg

A Synchronized Swimming Workout

Whether a synchronized swimmer's objective is improved fitness, expanded aquatic virtuosity, or competition, the magic formula is training and practice. A synchronized swimming workout has components similar to those of any fitness workout: a *warm-up, a main set,* and a *cool-down*. The synchro workout should last between 30 and 45 minutes. Ideally, work out three times per week on alternate days. Begin slowly and work progressively for safety, comfort, and the best results.

- ***Warm-Up* (5–10 minutes)**

  50 yards of easy crawl

  50 yards of backstroke

  Treading in place

  Underwater swimming using breaststroke

- ***Main Swim* (20–30 minutes)**

  Rest when needed

  - **Sculling**

    Scull 50 yards, head first (fingers upward) in back layout position

  - **Figures**

    Tuck turns: 2 times each to the right, 2 times to the left

    Ballet legs: From a back layout position with toes on the lip of the pool, scull rapidly as alternately bend and then lift one leg to the extended ballet leg position, then change, 2 times each

  - **Strokes**

    Swim 25 yards using the crawlstroke and the backstroke

    Swim 25 yards using the breaststroke and the sidestroke

    Swim 25 yards creating own stroke variations

  - **Combinations**

    Repeat the following sequence for 25 yards:

    3 crawlstrokes with head up, corkscrew, 3 backstrokes, and clam until reaching the wall; at the wall, turn with a half shark circle

- ***Cool-Down* (5 minutes)**

  Swim breaststroke for 25 yards with a full glide

  Easy crawlstroke for 25 yards

  Easy treading

Swimming Stroke Variations

Standard swimming strokes are varied to suit the theme of a synchronized swimming routine. Examples of swim stroke variations are highlighted below.

TABLE 17.1 ***Synchronized Swimming Stroke Variations***

Stroke	Head Position	Arm Motion	Leg Movement
Crawlstroke	Head remains forward and out of water.	Straight arm recovery	Bent knee flutter kick underwater
Breaststroke	Head remains out of water. Head turns at the catch of each stroke.	Hands splash on extension	Flutter kick underwater
Backstroke	Chin is up. Head remains still.	Backstroke or salute stroke	Slow bent knee flutter kick underwater
Sidestroke	Head remains still and/or alternates moving forward and back.	Alternate overarm with regular arm pull.	Alternate scissors with flutter kicks on glide.

Partner and Group Figures

The beginning synchronized swimmer can practice figures and strokes with partners or in groups of three or more people. Many figures begin in a back layout position with each person placing the toes, which are slightly turned in, under the chin of the swimmer in front. Be certain to review the safety signal for releasing the connection before attempting any figure that requires going underwater, such as a chain back dolphin.

SAFETY SIGNAL: *A safety signal between two or more synchronized swimmers can be any agreed upon sign, such as two taps to indicate that a swimmer will not be able to complete the figure without stopping for air, rest, or a change of position.*

Planking

Partners are connected in the back layout position. The swimmer in front grasps the ankles of the other swimmer and pulls the body forward over the surface of the water, while submerging slightly and moving backward under the other swimmer. The person in front must keep the feet of the partner together while pulling. As the plank is executed, the swimmers reverse positions.

Chain Back Dolphin

Partners connect in the back layout position. As the person leading the chain arches the back and begins to submerge underwater, the other partner sculls backward. Both partners use their arms to scull the dolphin around. When the leading partner surfaces, he or she continues sculling backward to help his or her partner surface.

Formations

Synchronized swimming formations or patterns can be symmetrical or asymmetrical, with movements performed either in unison, sequence, alternately, in contrast, or a combination of these.

Accordion Pattern

Swimmers begin a back float position alternating feet and head positions. The swimmers in this formation place their hands under the ankles of the floater with palms upward and elbows bent. The swimmers slowly extend and straighten their arms and legs—that is, open the accordion.

Circle Formation

Swimmers (four or more) begin in a back layout position. Each swimmer's inside arm is extended overhead and must be touching the ear. The elbow remains straight to create a circle. The hand is placed under the foot of the inside leg of the person behind. The outside leg is bent, with the sole of the foot pressing against the side of the other knee. This knee remains under the surface of the water. The outside arm sculls to propel the circle.

Costumes

When synchronized swimmers are wearing costumes relevant to their routine, the visual effects are intensified.

Inexpensive costumes can be made by trimming a standard fitness or competitive suit in a variety of ways. For instance, a basic fitness suit can be enhanced with ribbon, sequins, bangles, or metallic material.

Where Synchro Is Going

Just as gymnast Mary Lou Retton burst upon the Olympics scene in the 1980s and stirred American youth to become involved in a sport/art form—in training and competition—synchronized swimming has developed into an exciting athletic form for competitive women who are physically active. Synchronized swimming knows no age or gender barrier as a recreational sport. The spectacular success of the new event in the 1984 Olympics indicates that synchronized swimming is an appealing spectator sport as well as a participatory one.

There are classes for synchronized swimming as well as clinics, groups, competitions, and Masters programs at YWCAs, YMCAs, community centers, health clubs, and schools throughout the country. For information about programs, contact U.S. Synchronized Swimming, Inc.

Synchro Circle Formation

Chapter **18**

Water Games

© Shane Newmark

Many games and sports can be adapted to the water. Popular ones include water polo, water volleyball, as shown above, and water relays.

Water Polo

A century ago in the United States, water polo players were high-profile athletes. Water polo was introduced to the United States in 1888, and by 1898, ten years later, a national tour sponsored by the National Sportsmen's Association featured water polo matches that attracted up to 14,000 spectators. Water polo players were depicted in their own series of trading cards, similar to the professional football and baseball trading cards that young people trade today.

The histories of water polo and competitive swimming are intertwined. In fact, from the 1890s to 1930, every Amateur Athletic Union (AAU) swim champion was also an outstanding water polo player. The first American Olympic gold medalists in swimming, Charlie Daniels and Johnny Weissmuller (also known as Tarzan), initially established their reputations with water polo.

In the 1930s, water polo decreased in popularity perhaps because there were few rules and playing became too rough. However, in the 1950s, it was reintroduced in California high schools in its modern form and has been gaining in popularity ever since. As in earlier times, many top swimmers have also competed in water polo. These include Mark Spitz (a seven-gold medal winner in 1972), Matt Biondi, and Pablo Morales.

Aside from a high level of aerobic conditioning, water polo requires and develops strong swimming skills, and a feel for the water. It also develops agility, mental toughness, and promotes an atmosphere of interaction, interdependence, and comraderie among team members, similar to soccer and football. Water polo lends variety to seasonal swim training as well as exciting action during competition.

Although water polo is played by strong male swimmers who are willing to engage in intense competition, the introduction of protective headgear and smaller balls has increased water polo's appeal and safety for young men and women in a wide range of ages, levels, and abilities.

The men's record of 36 national swimming titles was set by Johnny Weissmuller between 1921 and 1928, who made his aquatic debut with water polo.

Rules of the Game

Water polo is played by two teams of up to 11 players each, with 7 players in the water at any given time. There are four 5-minute periods of play, with each team switching sides between each period. The playing area of the pool is divided with a half-distance line, a goal line, a 2-meter line, and a 4-meter line. Only the goalkeeper is permitted to stand on the bottom (within the 4-meter line); all other players are required to tread water and avoid touching the pool bottom during the game.

The aim is to score by throwing the ball into the other team's goal. This is a difficult skill because it is much harder to control a ball while treading in deep water rather than standing. After a goal, the defending goalkeeper takes a goal throw from the goal line. A free throw is taken by an opposing player nearest the place where the ball goes out of the pool or hits the side and bounces back in. However, another player must touch the ball before the goal can be scored. A corner is taken when a defender sends the ball over their goal line. The opposing players nearest to where the ball went out takes the corner from the 2-meter line.

Using both hands to throw or catch the ball, or pushing the ball underwater, count as ordinary fouls and allow the opposing team a free throw. Physically obstructing an opponent is a major foul; the player must leave the water for 45 seconds or until a goal is scored.

In a regulation competition water polo game, the minimum water depth is 2 meters (approximately 6.6 feet). A nonslip rubber ball is used, which is slightly smaller than a volleyball, weighing 15 ounces. If you have ever seen or played regulation water polo, you have seen players usually identified by blue and white numbered caps (with built-in plastic cups protecting the ears); goalies wear a red cap with #1. Rectangular goals are set at water level at the ends of a 20 × 30-meter pool. However, the game varies as needs, skills, level, and facilities permit. Contact U.S. Water Polo for more information.

Water Volleyball

Water volleyball is often played as a recreational activity and can be a fairly unstructured sport. It requires less swimming skill than water polo because it can be played in waist-to-shoulder deep water. Water volley-

Water Volleyball

ball is sometimes used as open practice at the conclusion of aquatic classes and can be easily organized during recreational swim times.

Similar to land-based volleyball, evenly divided teams (up to 11 players on each side at a time) take turns hitting a lightweight waterproof ball (an average size beach ball) over a net. The net can be an informal arrangement, such as the backstroke flags at the shallow end of the pool or a portable floating net. Some well-equipped pools have a net stored on the pool ceiling which can be lowered close to the water for a game.

Water volleyball can also be used as part of intramural competition, but also on an informal basis. Teams are formed either randomly or on some other basis, such as departments within the college or, perhaps, students versus faculty and staff. Beginning swimmers and water exercisers particularly enjoy water volleyball, and become more comfortable in the aquatic environment by just having fun.

Water Relays

Water relays work very well with swimmers of varying abilities. Shallow water swimmers and water exercisers can water walk (holding kickboards) while swimmers can do a medley of strokes.

- **Treasure Hunts:** Submerge rubber rings into shallow end of the pool, which correspond to an aquatic gift (cap, goggles, etc.) for the person who collects the most. This is especially appropriate for pool parties.

Team Games

Adapt a team game, such as soccer or football, to water. Use the shallow end of the pool with kickboards as goals. Create rules depending on the size of the class and time available.

Water Basketball

Many facilities have water basketball hoops available.

Water Basketball

There are many, many other games and relays that can be played in the water. Underwater hockey is one that is approved by the Underwater Society of America. See Appendix B for more sources for water games.

Chapter 19

© Aroldo Macedo

Competitive Swimming and Triathlons

Competitive swimming can be as simple as informal races organized by the instructor or lifeguard in a swimming class. However, if swimmers are interested in testing their swimming skills and endurance against other swimmers, in college, there are two main types of competition: intramural and intercollegiate. For adults from 19 to 99, there is the Masters Swimming program. For swimmers who want to combine swimming performance with running and cycling, there are triathlon competitions.

The closest result in the Olympic Summer Games occurred in Los Angeles in 1984 when Nancy Hogshead and Carrie Steinseifer, both from the USA, tied for the gold in the Women's 100-meter Freestyle with a time of 59.92.

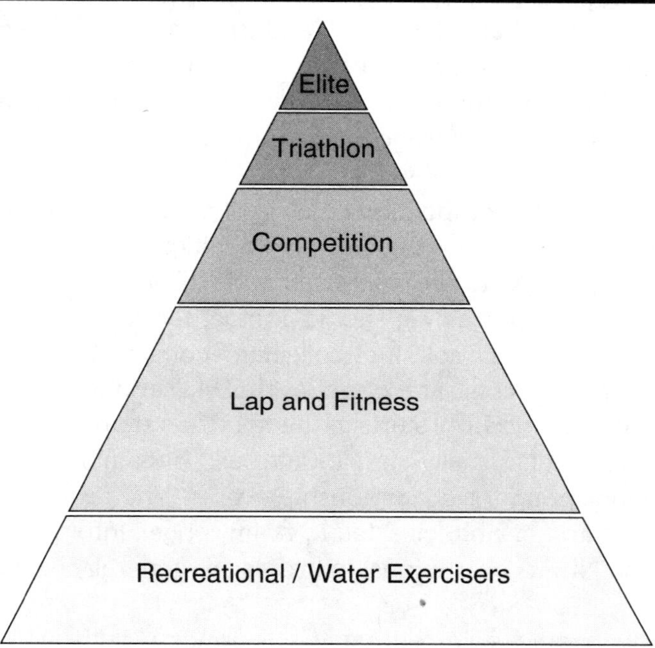

Intramurals

Some people are competitive and they want to perform their best skills with others. Even swimming students who know that their skills are still new enjoy racing against other swimmers. An appropriate entry can be an intramural event. These events are usually informal competitions with students from swim classes; they include swim races, water games (such as volley ball), and other aquatic activities. An intramural event is often held when students throughout the college use a given period of time during the week for club and recreational activities.

Intercollegiate

Swim competition between schools is organized similarly to other sports. Division or leagues in colleges and universities of comparable student body size and comparable budget size or rank are usually determined by the National Collegiate Athletic Association Board (NCAA). As with other sports, many schools recruit elite athletes. Schools with a given division (e.g., Divisions 1, 2, and 3) compete with each other for the division title. The intercollegiate competition is at a much higher level than the intramural competition and is often with nationally or internationally ranked college swimmers in the highest division, Division 1.

Intercollegiate competition involves structured team training with a coach, specific workout schedules, and additional conditioning requirements. Swimmers who are interested and willing to make the commitment to this type of training should contact the physical education department of their school. Intercollegiate competition often includes team tryouts with "cuts" at a given level of skill and ability. Most tryouts are held right after school starts in the fall when training begins. The intercollegiate meets usually start in late fall, November-December, and go into early spring for championship events. The faster swimmers, an individual swimmer and/or a team, swim longer into the season. The final season NCAA championship events are generally held in March or April.

Some people swim during the summer monthswith an outside team. Private and/or local teams may use the same swim facility or have the same coach as the local college. There are usually many additional choices for swimming during the summer. Again, a good place to seek information is a college's physical education department or an aquatics magazine.

Tracy Caulkins won a record of 48 United States swimming titles and set 60 United States records in a career that spanned the years 1977 through 1984.

United States Swimming, Inc., headquartered in Colorado Springs, Colorado, is the organizing body for swimming competition in this country. This organization establishes the guidelines for competitive swimming as well as conducting meets at national, regional, and local sites. There are also open meets and invitationals.

At the first modern Olympics in Athens in 1886, the swimming competition was held in the open water of the dangerous Bay of Zea. In 1904, swimmers jumped from rafts and swam in a canal. By 1908, the first Olympic swimming pool was constructed for the games in London—a simple hole dug in the grassy field of the central athletic stadium. Today, many aquatic facilities are technologically advanced, often featuring state-of-the-art electronic timekeeping systems.

OLYMPIC SWIMMING

An Olympic medal is the top international achievement for which an elite swimmer, diver, synchronized swimmer, or water polo player can aim.

The first recorded Olympic Games were held in 776 B.C., the time of the Ancient Greeks. The Greeks used sports to keep fit for warfare. The games took place every four years until 393 A.D.

In 1896, the first modern Olympic Games that included swimming were held in Athens, Greece. In 1904, diving was recognized as an Olympic sport, and finally in 1984, synchronized swimming was recognized. The international organizing body for swimming, the Féderation Internationale de Natation Amateur (FINA) was founded in 1908 and composed the rules for Olympic swimming events. FINA continues to be the international organizing body for swimming and aquatic sports.

Olympic Swimming Events

Freestyle: 50m, 100m, 200m, 400m, 800m (women only), 1500m (men only)

Backstroke: 100m, 200m

Breaststroke and Butterfly: 100m, 200m

Individual Medley: 200m, 400m

Freestyle Relay: 4 x 100m, 4 x 200m

Medley Relay: 4 x 100m

RECORD BREAKER: Mark Spitz of the United States won a record seven gold medals in the 1972 Olympics.

1996 CENTENNIAL OLYMPIC GAMES
Atlanta Games Organizing Committee
(404) 224-1996

Heats and Finals

In many competitive swimming events, there are more competitors than lanes in the pool. When this occurs, the swimmers are divided into heats. The number of heats depend on the number of swimmers entered in the event and the number of lanes in the pool. Each heat is usually arranged to place swimmers of comparable age together; in this way all swimmers have the advantage of competing against closely seeded competitors. The swimmers are arranged in a spearhead pattern (based on the time submitted on the entry form); the swimmer with the fastest time is assigned the lane right of center, and the other swimmers are alternately placed to the left and right of that swimmer, with the slowest swimmer in the heat using the outside lanes.

In the finals, the competition is more challenging because swimmers with the fastest times repeat the race against one another. The number of swimmers selected for the finals during a given competition depends on the number of lanes in the pool. The fastest swimmers in the finals will receive a trophy, medal or ribbon, or other award. Some competitions also offer a consolation final for the second fastest heat of swimmers.

Some competitions are swum as timed finals in which the finish is determined from the times of the swimmers who swim only once in a given heat.

Veteran Olympians, such as Janet Evans, Sumner Sanders, Erika Hansen, Mel Stewart, and Alexander Popov are continually being challenged by younger elite athletes, such as Fransizka van Almsick, Brooke Bennett, Tom Dolan, and Denis Pankratov.

Masters Swimming

There is more to swimming than doing laps. It is not necessary to be an Olympic swimmer to enjoy challenging one's abilities to the limit. Swimmers compete as well by swimming against their own times per distance, by racing, or by swimming in organized competition, either in the Masters swim program, or in a triathlon event.

From a modest beginning in 1970 of less than 50 participants, the program has grown to a meet of 30,000 Masters swimmers who compete nationwide. United States Masters Swimming, Inc., continues to sponsor adult fitness activities. In addition, there are international FINA-sponsored Masters meets where people compete and socialize worldwide.

The program's primary purpose is to promote physical fitness through training and competitive swimming. Events are held in a variety of distances and strokes. Most meets are organized by male and female competitors, divided by age within a five-year age bracket (19–24, 25–29, 30–34, etc.)

The Masters Swimming program provides recreational and social activities that can be enjoyed throughout a lifetime. Many sports programs become too strenuous later in life; the competition with stronger and younger athletes becomes too frustrating. However, in Masters Swimming, there are swimmers competing into their eighties and nineties. See Masters Swimming for further information.

Triathlon Competition

The triathlon event emerged in the 1980s. Aerobic activities of running, cycling, and swimming are performed in a dynamic trio. The only thing more difficult than competing in a triathlon is training for one. Most athletes know how to prepare for the running and biking portions of the event. However, many athletes may wish to learn how to train more effectively for the swimming portion. Indeed, when it comes to the aquatic component of this test of endurance, it is truly "sink or swim."

There have been many variations of triathlons, but an official competitive triathlon today is a combined event of swimming, cycling, and

Triathlon Swim

running. In the Ironman, a triathlon that is held every year in Hawaii and is the most challenging of all of them, the swim segment is 2.4 miles in open water; the cycling is 112 miles over rough terrain; the running portion is 26.2 miles, an official marathon length.

Most local triathlons are shorter in distance and less difficult. Although the ratio of the three sports is usually not weighted in favor of the stronger swimmers, swimming can still be an important factor for a successful triathlon. It is difficult to fake an open-water mile swim.

MINI-TRIATHLONS. *Although most triathlons are held in open water and natural terrain, a great way to start triathlon competition is to compete by time and/or distance in a protected environment, e.g., regulation length swimming pool, regulation track, running treadmill, or stationary bicycle. The Tinman triathlon is one-half the distance of the Ironman.*

Triathletes often vary routines and double up workouts. Even good swimmers train progressively, lap by lap. For intermediate swimmers who have not built up a lot of endurance, start with 10 laps. Then progress to 1/4 mile, lap by lap. Pacing, which is very important in a triathlon, is improved with interval training. Instead of swimming 1 lap at a time with 30 seconds of rest in between, swim 4 laps with 20 seconds of rest and build from there.

The distance that swimmers train depends on the length of the swim portion of the triathlon. In a triathlon, the swimming distances can range from as short as 1/4 mile to nearly 2-1/2 miles. Depending on the distance, a good length to train for is progressing from 1 to 2 miles. Preparing for an event with a 1-mile swim, train in excess of the distance. By overloading the body—that is, by making demands on it that are a little more than it can handle comfortably—the body is forced to adapt.

Triathlon Training Tips

The following tips are suggested for open-water triathlon training.

Before the swim:

- Study water currents, waves, and movements. Check tide charts when applicable.
- Note landmarks—flags, boats, rocks, marshes, lighthouses, mountains, shoreline to be able to judge progress while swimming.
- Listen carefully to directions for the swim—that is, the time of the starting signal, swim destination, landmarks, finish point.

During the swim:

- Breathe! Incorporate bilateral (alternate) breathing.
- Avoid overkicking. Allow body to roll to effect crossover kick.
- Keep arm stroke long and streamlined. Use the "S-pull."
- Keep a comfortable pace. Begin by relaxing and stretching out in the water; then slowly pick up pace to a comfortable level.

WHAT IS A FAST POOL?

What makes a "fast" pool? A fast pool provides optimum conditions for swimming competitors to achieve their fastest times. A turbulent pool is usually a slow pool. Optimum conditions are:

1. Minimum water depth—preferred is 6-foot deep moveable pool floor in shallow end. Acceptable is four feet.
2. Surface racing lane lines—preferred 9 feet apart, installed perfectly level with water surface the full length of the pool. Minimum additional outside lane width 1.5 feet (space between lane and pool wall). Acceptable lane width is 7 feet wide.
3. A filtered water system design that does not affect competitive swimmers but evenly distributes water to the pool during competition.
4. The ability to maintain the pool's actual water level exactly at the gutter lip after it is disturbed by water motion.

Competitive Training Equipment

Serious fitness swimmers, competitive swimmers, and triathletes also train by doing strength training. One example of strength training is tethered swimming. Tethered swimming is done by the swimmer attaching a strong cord to himself or herself and to a stationary point on the pool deck or a ladder.

One advantage of tethered swimming training is that it can be done in any size pool. It also enables the swimmer to isolate stroke components, to strengthen key muscles, and to concentrate on stroke techniques. Unlike dry land drills tethered swimming drills give the swimmer the water's resistance during strengthening exercises. Use the tether also for deep-water running or walking.

In competitive swimming as training progresses, it becomes more rigorous and more specific. Over the past few decades, swimmers have used particular kinds of equipment in workouts to build endurance and to help strengthen important muscles. Some equipment relies on working against the water's resistance. Other devices use technological advances to measure the body's progress. Some examples are highlighted below.

- **Swim Chute and Tether:** A water resistance device that resembles a mini-parachute. It is designed to be dragged through water. It provides a more energetic workout because the swimmer needs to work harder against the water in order to move forward. A tether can also be placed on a swimmer to stroke in place against resistance.
- **Heart-Rate Monitor:** Worn on the hand or body to enable the swimmer to measure heart rate during workouts. Learning to compare perceived energy exertion (subjective) with a heart rate (objective) is used in training to attain a target heart rate.
- **Swim Bench:** One of several devices designed for swimmers to move their arms through the whole range of stroke arm motions. This equipment has a digital gauge to measure the force of the arm pull.
- **Strength Training Equipment:** A variety of equipment utilizing weights, stretch cords, and other equipment that are swim-stroke specific.

Use timed swims and goal charts to log progress.

TIMED SWIMS PROGRESS CHART

Place/ Date	Distance	Time	Pulse Check	Comments
	1 lap/ 25 yds			
	1 lap/ 25 yds			
	1 lap/ 25 yds			
	2 laps/ 50 yds			
	2 laps/ 50 yds			
	2 laps/ 50 yds			
	3 laps/ 75 yds			
	3 laps/ 75 yds			
	3 laps/ 75 yds			
	4 laps/ 100 yds			

BEST TIMES AND GOALS

Stroke	Distance	Goal	Best Time	Date	Location	Comments
Crawlstroke	50 yds/m	:	:			
	100 yds/m	:	:			
	200 yds/m	:	:			
	500 yds/ 400 m	:	:			
	1000 yds/ 800 m	:	:			
	1650 yds/ 1500 m	:	:			
Backstroke	50 yds/m	:	:			
	100 yds/m	:	:			
	200 yds/m	:	:			
Breaststroke	50 yds/m	:	:			
	100 yds/m	:	:			
	200 yds/m	:	:			
Butterfly	50 yds/m	:	:			
	100 yds/m	:	:			
	200 yds/m	:	:			
IM	100 yds/m	:	:			
	200 yds/m	:	:			
	400 yds/m	:	:			

Chapter 20

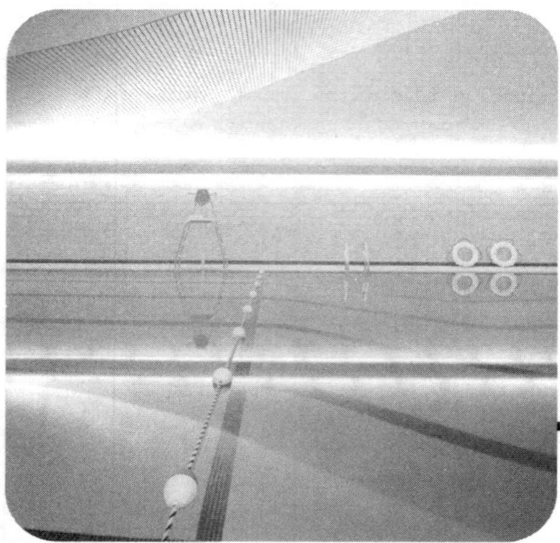
© Paul Warchol

Aquatic Safety

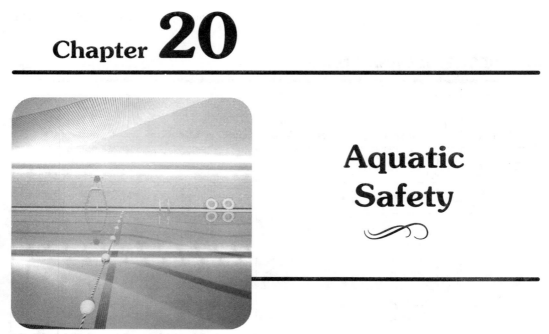

When swimmers make a realistic assessment of their abilities and limitations, they are better able to be safe and to remain safe in and near the water. Knowing how to swim safely is the first line of defense against swimming accidents. It is very important to know basic safety precautions for aquatic activities.

For the competent swimmer who is interested in becoming certified as an aquatic safety specialist, contact a local aquatic facility, instructor, director and/or organizations for additional information.

Basic Safety Guidelines for Water Fitness Activities

- Never swim alone.
- Swim only in supervised areas.
- Never swim under the influence of alcohol or drugs.

- Always check depth before entering the water.
- Always enter a pool or swimming area feet first if the depth of water is not known.
- Do not swim in a pool if the bottom at the deep end is not visible, or if the water is cloudy.
- Lifelines separate water depths. Do not hang on them. They are there for safety.
- Assess swimming capability and stay within your limitations.
- Watch out for the "dangerous too's"—too tired, too cold, too far from safety, too much sun, and so forth.
- Stay out of the water if overheated or overtired.
- Do not chew gum while swimming.
- Learn the proper way to dive and the safe depths for each type of dive.
- Use common sense about swimming after eating. The age-old adage to wait an hour after eating before safely swimming is not completely true. However, after a large meal, it is wise to let digestion get started before strenuous swimming.

Perhaps one of the most important safety courses to take is emergency First Aid and CPR (cardiopulmonary resuscitation). The American Red Cross, the American Heart Association, the National Safety Council, the Y's, as well as other organizations offer these courses throughout the country.

To stay afloat in one place using a minimum of energy, tread water using the figure-8 sculling arm motion and bicycle or frog kick. Keep movements smooth and slow with the body in a vertical position. Try to relax until help comes. If several people are waiting for help, the group should create a "huddle" formation in order to sustain body heat.

Treading Water

Huddling

Rescuing Someone in Trouble in the Water

When in a situation where another swimmer is in need of help, keep in mind that the swimmer who needs help is very frightened. The rescuer should keep talking to the swimmer and explain exactly what he or she is doing and intends to do. The rescuer should avoid entering the water or being in direct contact with the person in trouble because the person may panic and drag the rescuer in or under the water and then both lives would be seriously at risk.

Rescues from Land:

Nearby:

1. Lie on the pool deck, dock, or shore with feet slightly apart. Hold on to a fixed object if possible, or if someone else is available to help, have them hold on to your feet.
2. Reach out with a life preserver, pole, stick, or an article of clothing, holding body weight back. Have the person in trouble in the water hold on to one end of the object and pull the person to the edge of the pool or dock or standing area.
3. If necessary to grab on to the person in trouble, it is advisable for the victim who is conscious to swim behind the rescuer and grasp the rescuer's armpit(s). For an unconscious victim, the rescuer grasps underneath the victim's wrists and tows victim to safety.

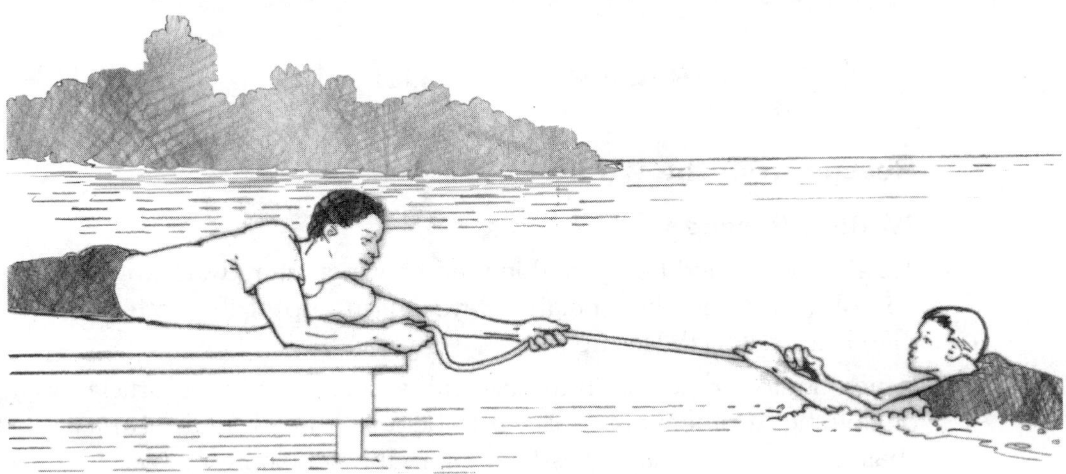

Rescue—Nearby

Further Out:

1. If the person is too far away to reach by the above methods, throw something that will help the swimmer in trouble to float, such as a floating ball, life preserver, personal flotation device (life jacket), or flotation belt.
2. Try to aim the object so it lands just in front of the person in trouble. While it is easier to aim with an underarm throw, an overarm throw can travel a longer distance.
3. Once the swimmer in trouble grabs on to the floating object, encourage the swimmer to kick to safety.

Rescue—Further Out

Rescue from the Water:

Wading Rescue

1. Take off shoes and heavy clothing, and having entered the water, do not go beyond chest height. Have a firm grip of the bottom, then lean back with legs apart.
2. Reach out to the person in trouble with a pole, stick, or an article of clothing. If others are available to help, link hands and form a chain for leverage and, if possible, out to the person in trouble.
3. Bring person to safety.

Wading Rescue

Swimming Rescue

1. Do not undertake a swimming rescue without training. The rescuer's life is in immediate danger. Locate someone trained in water rescue.
2. If there is no one trained in water rescue, avoid coming in direct contact with the person in trouble. Always reach out with a life preserver, pole, stick, or an article of clothing.
3. Make sure the person being rescued holds on to the object. The rescuer should swim the sidestroke, towing the other person back to safety.

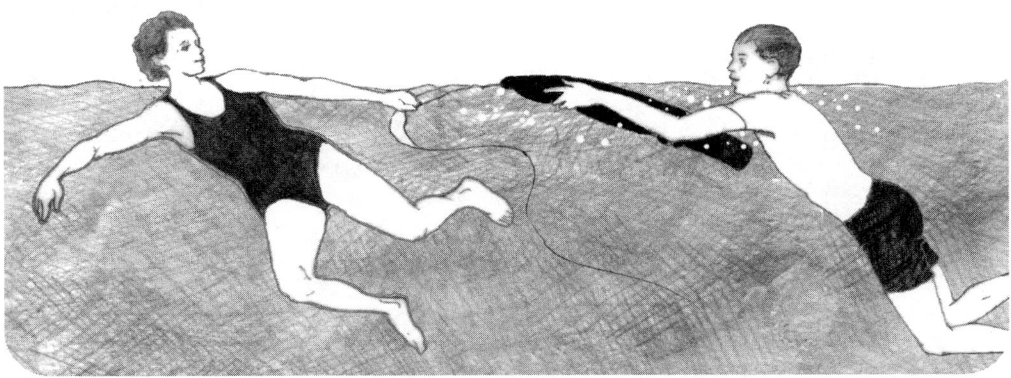

Swimming Rescue

These guidelines offer examples of lifesaving knowledge. As mentioned earlier, all swimmers need to go to the next step and take a lifeguard training course.

AN OUNCE OF PREVENTION

The saying, "an ounce of prevention is worth a pound of cure," is the first swimming rule. The most important lifesaving measures are learning to swim well, avoiding potentially dangerous situations, and using common sense. Below are some situations, mainly in an open-water environment, that can be prevented using forethought and caution.

Problem	***Prevention***
Finding oneself in deep water and being unable to get out.	Listen to the body before swimming. Do not overestimate swim skills, fatigue, or body heat from sunburn.
Encountering strong current, under- and high tides.	Check with lifeguard about tow, currents and time of tides. Do not overestimate ability.
Encountering a storm, rain, or darkness.	Always check weather and time of day before planning to swim.
Unable to continue swimming because water is unexpectedly cold.	Swimmers tire more easily in colder water. Open water is 10 degrees colder than a swimming pool, even in summer.

Open-Water Safety Review

- Have an emergency action plan in case of a water emergency, regardless of swimming ability.
- Choose a safe place for water recreation.
- Use common sense as well as specific precautions in planning any aquatic activity.
- Swim parallel to shoreline when distance swimming in open water.
- Use only U.S. Coast Guard approved Personal Flotation Devices (PFDs) as well as approved rescue tubes for emergency situations.
- Check local weather forecast before open-water swimming or boating.
- Know how to recognize and treat hypothermia, heat exhaustion, and heat stroke. (This can be reviewed in American Red Cross standard community and emergency First Aid courses.)

Unit VI

Special Topics

Unit VI completes this handbook on aquatic fitness and covers topics that relate water fitness to people's daily lives.

Chapter 21 discusses special water environments, including open-water swimming. Chapter 22 is an overview of aquatic fitness for all members of the family, covering the complete life span including the benefits of prenatal water exercise. Chapter 23 presents aquatic fitness for people with medical and physical problems. One of the features of aquatic fitness is that it can be an open door for recreation and fitness for many people whose disabilities prevent them from fully participating in other physical activities.

Chapter 24 discusses nutrition from both a health and fitness point of view. Grooming, beauty, and health cues will be answered in a conversational question-and-answer format in Chapter 25.

Chapter 21

Other Water Environments

© N. Y. Daily News

Whether one is on, in, or near open water, it presents unique enjoyment and challenges. The more skills a swimmer has mastered, the greater the opportunity in open water for using them.

Open water includes natural bodies of water—lakes, ponds, quarries, and rivers. Man-made lakes also share some characteristics with natural open water; the walls, the tile or cement pool bottom, and lane lines are not present. But open water also includes the biggest pool of all—the ocean. Note that salt water feels different than fresh water, mainly because the salt in the water increases buoyancy.

Safety is important in open-water swimming whether swimming for recreation or for aerobic training. Listed below are some important tips:

- Wear a bright colored cap for visibility, e.g., neon orange or yellow.
- Choose from a variety of wet suits when swimming in cold water to maintain body heat.
- Never swim alone. Swim with a buddy, with the supervision of a boat, and/or in a supervised area.
- Swim parallel to the shoreline whenever possible. Note fixed points on land to use as landmarks when swimming.

- Use alternate breathing, raise head every 10 or so strokes for navigation.
- Use common sense:
  —Check the water conditions (often this information is posted at the lifeguard's station) and the tides. Pay attention to beach rules.
  —Check water depth; know where the water drops off in a shelf formation and where there are sandbars.
  —Be aware of hazards, hidden objects, and so forth.
  —Be certain that turbulent weather is not forecast.
  —Complete swim during daylight hours.

Knowing one's limitations in the water as far as speed, strength, and endurance is necessary because swimming in open water often requires more energy. There are no pool walls or pool bottom for pushing off or resting. In addition, swimming in waves and/or currents requires extra work, and open water is sometimes cooler, which also burns up energy. Once a swimmer has left land, enough energy needs to be reserved to return to the shore or some other stationary point.

STRATEGIC TIP: *When swimming an open-water course, take a break to rest by turning onto back for a few strokes of the backstroke. Crawlstroke navigation and a raised head may cause the lower back to tire. (The backstroke is also a handy strategy to use when turning around a buoy marker in competition.)*

Many people like to swim laps in a lake or beach setting; that is, swim between rope markers or docks several times for a given distance. Check with the lifeguard first as to the distance between the two points.

For example, a swimmer who wants to swim approximately one mile on a 100-meter course, needs to swim 16 laps or 8 double laps.

An enclosed crib is often found at beaches and lakes where the lengths are comparable to a long course distance, e.g., 50 meters or a part or multiple. Plan to swim within the limitations of one's competency and fitness level. Be careful of docks as they can be slippery from organic matter and water and often are not quite stationary. When tired, rest by floating on back or swim to chest-deep water and stand.

SUNSCREENS

Open water by definition means outdoors. And outdoors means swimming in the sun. It is possible to become sunburned on cloudy days. And being in the water does not mean that the skin is not exposed to the sun; in the water, awareness of the sun's rays is diminished.

- Use waterproof sunblock appropriate to exposure time and skin type. Try to purchase one with broad spectrum protection.
- Do not become complacent because a sunblock has been applied. Continue to monitor exposure. Reapply after swimming.

Skin Diving and SCUBA Diving Training

SCUBA stands for Self-Contained Breathing Apparatus. SCUBA diving is generally done in the ocean and sometimes in lakes or quarries. Before undertaking SCUBA diving, a swimmer should be completely comfortable in deep water and take a certified SCUBA course of instruction.

Skin Diving

The use of fins, mask, and a snorkel for underwater sightseeing is easily learned. The fins are used for forward propulsion. The mask, which covers the nose and the mouth, is for greater underwater vision and the snorkel is for uninterrupted breathing. Breathing through the snorkel needs to be slow and deliberate; breathing with a snorkel will feel different while swimming.

TIP: *For skin divers and swimmers with neck problems, it is suggested to use the mask and snorkel without turning the head to either side, and to breathe continuously.*

The following organizations certify and train for SCUBA diving.

PADI
Professional Association of Diving Instructors
1251 East Dyer Road #100
Santa Ana, CA 92705-5605
714-540-7234

SSI
SCUBA Schools International
2619 Canton Ct.
Fort Collins, CO 80525-4498
1-800-892-2702

NAUI
National Association of Underwater Instructors
PO Box 14650
Montclair, CA 91763
1-800-553-6284, x232

Shoreline Exercises

For swimmers who also enjoy the beach, there are exercises that can be done at the shoreline of a lake or at the beach.

- **Sand Jog:** Walk or jog at the shoreline in ankle-, knee-, or thigh-deep water. The deeper the water, the more energetic the workout.
- **Sandy Sit-Ups:** At the water's edge, lying on back with knees bent, bury feet in the sand. Sit up and touch one elbow to the opposite knee. Repeat with the other elbow.
- **Leg Sand Sweeps:** Sitting at the water's edge with legs extended, create sand circles by bringing feet together and separating them.

Spas and Whirlpools

Bathing in natural warm springs was once a fashionable pastime of those who could afford to travel to lavish resorts and benefit from natural mineral baths and a period of rest. Later, warm baths were used in hydrotherapy—specific exercise programs to promote healing to injured or diseased limbs. Now spas and whirlpools are popular in health clubs and private homes, offering the opportunity not only for general well-being, but also to help relieve tension and fatigue and to improve the range of motion in joints which are stiff because of injury or disease.

The total amount of time in a spa or whirlpool should be no longer than 15 minutes. Hold each stretch for 30 seconds; rest for 30 seconds so as not to overheat. Use the water jets for intensified water-massaging action on various body parts, such as ankle, knee, shoulder and wrist joints, and back.

TIP: *Pregnant swimmers should not use a spa. A fetus depends on the mother's body for "air conditioning"; if the mother's body overheats, serious problems may result.*

- **Spa Footies:** Sit on the edge of the spa with feet at the water's surface. Rotate the lower legs so that the feet circle inward, then outward, then move forward, backward (up and down), and from side to side. Mix and match these rotations.
- **Spa Sit and Kick:** Sit at the edge of the spa. Begin with a slow rhythmic flutter kick. Then alternate kicks—easy dolphin, breaststroke (flex feet as much as possible), as well as flutter. To add variety, change the intensity and speed of the kicks: 30 seconds of moderate kicking; 30 seconds of rest.
- **Cross Leg Sit and Stretch:** Sit in the bent-knee position, soles of the feet together. Press knees toward the bottom, stretching the inner thighs. Then rock from side to side.
- **Victory Stretch:** Sit in the corner of the spa with back against the wall and legs in a V position, knees straight. Separate legs as far as possible, trying to touch a corner wall with each leg. Keep legs straight and bring legs together slowly, alternately crossing one leg over the other.

WATER PARKS WORLDWIDE

Seagaia Ocean Dome—Miyazaki, Japan

The Seagaia Ocean Dome is a 3-story, 1-million square-foot, enclosed, man-made beach on the island of Kyushu, 930 miles south of Tokyo. A quarter of a mile away from the Pacific Ocean, Seagaia can accommodate 10,000 people on its 280-foot shoreline and temperature-controlled water, which is chlorinated and salt free.

The name Seagaia is a combination of the English word, *sea,* and the Greek word, *earth.* The ocean dome provides vacationers with simulated tropical surroundings under a 660-foot retractable roof (the world's largest). Ten vacuum pumps create computer-generated waves several times a day. The indoor temperature is maintained at 82 to 86 degrees. The pool contains 3.6 million gallons of water and includes a 243-foot water slide as well as other attractions.

The beach at the Seagaia complex is composed of 600 tons of artificial white sand made from crushed, polished pebbles. There is an amusement theater where vacationers can ride the rapids in a raft that pitches and rolls—and they get wet with splashes of water as the world's most famous rapids are projected on a wide screen. The facilities are open every day, with the dome opening in especially good weather.

Public Aquatic Facility in Japan (1973)

Duke Kahanomoku, a native of Hawaii, is considered by the aquatic world as the pioneer of modern surfing. A competitor in three Olympic Games, Kahanomoku also helped popularize the 6-beat flutter kick (6 kicks to one arm stroke). When he missed a place on the United States swim team at the age of 42, he qualified as an alternate on the water polo team. Duke Kahanomoku was honored in 1995 by Speedo® Authentic Fitness™ as the pioneer of modern surfing.

The Swimming Treadmill—The Flume

The International Center for Aquatic Research at the United States Olympics Training Center in Colorado Springs, Colorado, houses one of the few state-of-the-art swimming treadmills. This fully controlled swimming environment is used to evaluate all swimming techniques under all conditions. The steel flume is 25 meters long and has a 265-horsepower pump that can move water at the rate of 3 meters per second. Swim coaches and scientists evaluate swimmers' stroke techniques, using high-tech video imaging. By closely scrutinizing stroke mechanics, coaches can improve a swimmer's stroke efficiency for better performance.

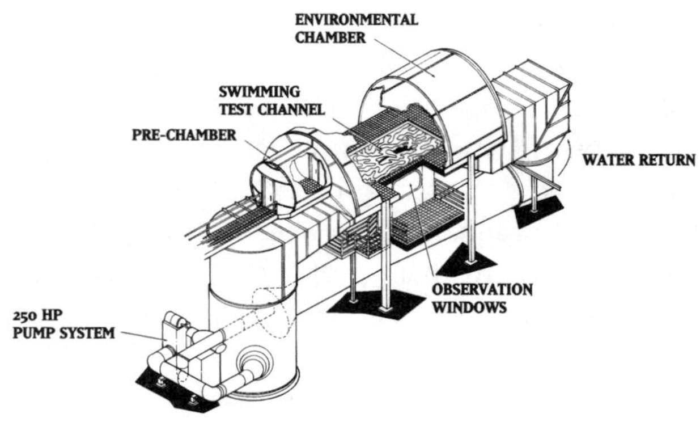

U.S. Olympic Training Center
Colorado Springs, Colorado

Chapter 22

Family Fitness

The family swim and family fitness cover the ages from before birth through the elderly years—the eighties, nineties, and beyond. Everyone can participate in water enjoyment.

The Prenatal Period

Today, most obstetricians encourage their patients to engage in some form of physical conditioning, believing that a woman whose body is in good physical condition may be less likely to have difficulty during labor and childbirth. Women who have not been physically active prior to pregnancy now are being urged to participate in physical conditioning programs throughout pregnancy, but always with a physician's advice.

For the pregnant woman, appropriate exercise will improve cardio-aerobic fitness and make for a strong heart and lungs, efficient circulation, and efficient oxygen utilization. These are all important components for a comfortable pregnancy and an uneventful labor and delivery. A healthy system is important for the baby because blood must be efficiently transported from the mother's body to the placenta, the baby's source for oxygen and nourishment. And an improved fitness level is an asset throughout pregnancy because it helps minimize the fatigue most women experience.

Exercise during pregnancy also strengthens and tones the muscles used during the birth process. At the end of the pregnancy, a mother who is in good condition is better prepared for the physical demands of childbirth.

The known benefits of exercising during pregnancy refute the ideas held by previous generations that exercise harms a woman's reproductive organs, and that exercise during pregnancy is dangerous to the unborn child. The uterus is a well-protected organ, guarded by strong ligaments and surrounded by pelvic bone. The unborn child is cushioned from injury by the abdominal wall, the strong uterine muscle, as well as by the amniotic fluid and amniotic sac.

There are other definite advantages to water exercise for the pregnant woman. Activity in water puts a minimum of stress, strain, and pounding on the pregnant woman and water itself is soothing and relaxing. There are also benefits of weight control. A mother-to-be gains from 20 to 30 pounds during a normal pregnancy; swimming and water exercise helps keep off excess pounds. Being in water has a diuretic and natriuretic effect; that is, it causes the body to naturally rid itself of excess water and salt which often cause edema, discomfort and high blood pressure during pregnancy. Water exercise may also reduce the stiffness at the ankles and wrists caused by water retention that some women experience.

Because the uterus changes dramatically in both size and shape during pregnancy, it requires other muscles to maintain it in its proper position. Giant elastic bands known as the broad ligaments keep the uterus safely suspended in the middle of the pelvis. Surrounding the uterus are abdominal and pelvic floor muscles. Good abdominal muscle tone improves this support and also helps to maintain the integrity and function of other organs as they are displaced by the growing uterus.

Strong back and abdominal muscles are also better able to accommodate weight changes, lessening the stress on the back, hips, and thighs. Swimming and water exercise help the pregnant woman to strengthen the abdomen and back and shoulder muscles and thus helps to carry the added weight more easily and also maintain good posture, which is essential to a comfortable pregnancy. Aquatic exercise can also provide relief from back discomfort often experienced during pregnancy.

Another consideration is that the mother's blood supply increases 25 to 50 percent during pregnancy. A sensible fitness program enables the heart to handle this and other demands with greater ease. As mentioned before, improved cardiac efficiency minimizes edema in the extremities and prevents varicose veins. A routine of water fitness during pregnancy can also have benefits after the birth of the baby; many women report that their postpartum recovery is fast and without complications.

To be buoyant and horizontal, the main characteristics of swimming, immediately relieves a pregnant woman's breathing. In a horizontal, buoyant position, the weight of the uterus is not resting on the diaphragm. The pressure exerted on the bladder and pelvic organs is decreased. Swimming and water exercise also means that weight is off the feet. Exercising in cool water reduces the risk of overheating and the baby is kept cool at the same time.

> ***TIP:*** *A pregnant woman should not begin an aquatic fitness or any other exercise program without the approval of her doctor.*

Childhood

Swimming is the ideal family activity. One of the best gifts a parent can give a child is to teach him or her swimming and water play. It is a gift a child will keep for life and it will be a pleasure to give.

An infant can be introduced to the joys of water almost immediately after birth. A water environment is already familiar to the infant, who has just spent nine months in amniotic fluid. An infant in water will instinctively paddle and hold his or her breath if submerged (although babies lack the strength to get their faces above the water to breathe).

It is very important to project a positive attitude when introducing a baby to water. A baby will enjoy the water only if the teacher and/or parent are comfortable and confident in and around the water. Babies are very receptive to the emotions of people around them, and if an infant senses fear or discomfort, then the experience of the water may be unpleasant.

Bringing an infant to the water and using the proper approach will start a child right away on the road of safety, fun, and fitness. A parent can aid very directly in the development of a baby's muscular strength, coordination, and balance. There are even some indications that children who engage in water play and swimming at an early age are healthier, more intelligent, and more sociable than those who do not. And teaching a baby how to stay afloat will provide an important safety skill. In addition, working with a baby in water can enhance the bonding process and the parent/child relationship.

Safety Comes First

When working with a baby in the water, remember that the baby has no control over any environment. Be careful to avoid shocks of temperature change, sudden immersions, or rough water. Keep a close watch on the baby's health and the hygiene of the swimming facility. *Never, ever, leave a baby alone in or around water, or divert attention from a baby even for a moment.* Keep expectations reasonable—no two-year-old is ready to swim the length of a pool. You may have seen television or magazine reports of the seemingly astounding capabilities of so-called "water babies," but be aware that movies of babies swimming for long periods are usually staged and edited, and that few if any infants can swim alone for more than several seconds. A child usually is physically capable of sustained independent swimming only after reaching the age of three.

Following are examples of what children experience in the water at each stage of growth.

Newborns

It is never too early to start teaching an infant to love the water. The best way is to try to make a newborn's baths as pleasant as possible.

A newborn will be ready for the first bath at about two weeks after birth (when the navel has healed). Time the first bath to take place when the baby is in a happy mood, and where the baby will be most comfortable. Do not start the bath when the baby is hungry, tired, or crying.

Never under any circumstances divert attention from an infant even for a second during the bath. Let the telephone and door go unanswered, if necessary.

Make sure the water in the bathtub or sink is approximately body temperature. Check the temperature with a thermometer, since a temperature that feels comfortable to an adult may be extremely unpleasant to a baby. The sink, basin, or tub should be about half filled with water.

When the baby is placed in the sink or tub, support the head and neck with one hand, and gently lower the baby into the water while maintaining eye contact, smiling, and speaking soothingly. Submerge the baby slowly, feet first; only one-half to two-thirds of a baby's body should be below the water's surface. Put the baby on his or her back in a semi-upright position and never lying flat. Always elevate the baby's head higher than the hips.

When playing with a baby in the bath, try to include love pats and tickling, as well as gentle rocking. Also stretch the baby's arms across the chest, to the sides, and overhead. Bend and flex hands and feet and move the legs in a bicycling motion; these motions will help a newborn develop motor control and strength.

Infants

Between six months and approximately a year and a half, a baby can learn basic water skills. Rarely will a child younger than two years old be able to master conventional swimming techniques. However, babies enjoy playing in the water, and both adult and baby benefit from the bonding time.

Always make sure that the pool is clean, the air is warm, the water temperature is comfortable, and there is a secure part of the pool where the parent or adult and baby will not be bothered by other swimmers or exposed to pool turbulence. Always stay in standing depth only. Keep the baby in the water for a maximum of one-half hour at a time, and try to use the pool one to three times per week. Inform the baby's pediatrician of the baby's pool activities.

Some courses on infant swimming claim that babies can be taught to kick, breathe, float, and turn over in the water as well as to paddle a few feet to the edge of the pool for safety. Consider enrolling in a course, but do not expect the claims stated above. What is most important is for babies to acquire a love for water, a sense of security, and basic water skills. Lessons will also help strengthen muscles, help to develop balance and coordination, and perhaps teach a young swimmer how to relax and play in the water.

To make sure that a child benefits as much as possible from this water experience, create a happy, pleasant, and secure water environment. Remember to maintain eye contact with a baby in the water; smile, talk, cuddle, kiss, pat, and even try singing! If the parent/teacher is confident in the water, the baby will respond to this enthusiasm.

Try the following exercises to teach a baby basic water skills.

Start by simply cuddling a baby in the water, with the body partly submerged to get the feel of the water. Walk across the width of the pool. Pay close attention to the baby at all times, being careful to support the face out of the water. Since a baby's head is proportionately heavier at this stage of growth, remember to keep the hips lower than the shoulders. Use hands to gently wet the baby's face with water so that the baby is comfortable with the feeling of water gently coming over the head. The baby may be startled at first, so be reassuring verbally throughout.

Next, try bobbing with the baby. Hold the baby upright, gently lifting and lowering to shoulder level in the water. As the baby learns to enjoy this, increase the depth until the baby is submerged to the neck.

Next, combine bobbing with breath control. In a face-to-face position, the baby's mouth and the adult's mouth are lowered to the surface of the water. If the baby responds positively, then the baby is lowered to cover more face in the water. Eventually the baby is lowered to eyebrow level. Make sure the baby is underwater only for a moment. Smile, compliment, kiss, and soothe the baby when bringing the baby out of the water. Eventually, babies learn to hold their breath for a few seconds and enjoy the feeling of submerging.

Hold the baby around the chest, thumbs at nipple level, facing the parent/adult, so that the face is out of the water with head higher than hips. Slowly walk backward so that the baby is drawn through the water. Do not forget the positive reinforcements—smiling, cuddling, and talking.

Give the baby a feeling of floating by holding the baby on the back and swirl, making sure that the baby's face is out of the water. Support the head and neck with both hands and walk backward, maintaining eye contact. The baby's legs may begin a crawling, kicking motion. Extend the swirling on the baby's back by holding the baby's hands and extending the arms overhead.

Toddlers and children are affected by loss of heat more quickly than adults. Be alert for signs of coldness.

Babies can learn to hang on to the edge of the pool with their head up. This is an important safety skill. Hold the baby at the pool wall with head up and body in the water. Place baby's hands on the edge, holding the baby's hands there as the parent's arm supports the baby's body. Gradually, the support is transferred from the baby's body to the arms so that baby is supported by the arms as he or she grasps the pool edge. Be sure to smile and talk during this process.

An additional skill a baby can learn is how to make a safe entry and exit to and from the pool deck. Babies can enter from the edge of the pool by falling forward into an adult's arms. Bring the baby back to the edge of pool after entry and repeat.

Toddlers

During the toddler stage, approximately one and a half to three years of age, a baby goes through one of the most important phases of development. A child is extraordinarily receptive during this period of life, very curious and adventurous. In fact, some experts contend that a child experiences approximately 60 percent of personality and attitudinal development during the toddler stage.

One of the ways to teach children during the toddler stage is repetition. If a variety of games and exercises are taught during water play, it is very important to repeat the games and exercises so that the child develops familiarity and facility with the water skills involved in the games. You'll probably find that the toddler enjoys playing games that are familiar rather than continually being exposed to new games.

The toddler is able to learn to move through the water, prone and supine, perhaps with a push; to bob in the water to a limited extent, to breathe after emerging; to enter the water by jumping in and surfacing; and perhaps to do a simple stroking motion, based on the movements used in crawling. In fact, some classes for toddlers teach them to swim through underwater hoops.

The toddler stage is the time to blow bubbles underwater. Begin by teaching how to blow bubbles on the surface. Make analogies to blowing through a straw or blowing out birthday candles. Next do the "submarine"; walk backward while holding toddler face to face, giving the feeling of movement. At the count of 3, gently lower the child underwater for a moment. Be sure to kiss, praise, and cuddle after each submarine.

Improvise a "magic slide" by setting a kickboard or inflatable plastic raft over the edge of the pool. Gently place the child on the slide so that the child enters head first, wide-eyed, and into the open arms of an adult.

It is very important to make the toddler's swim time as much fun as possible. Use water toys, such as balls and inflatable animals. Combine play with the development of skills, strength, and coordination. For instance, have a toddler swim or paddle a few feet to retrieve a toy, or teach the toddler breath control by making a game of reaching underwater for colorful objects. When ready push a toddler in a front float, upon a signal, to the pool's edge.

During the toddler stage, consider obtaining a small outdoor wading pool. *Never leave the toddler unattended in the pool, and empty the pool when not in use.* (It is recommended to buy a pool that can easily be emptied by one adult. Even a small pool will be very heavy when full of water.) Fill the pool with several inches of water only, and keep a supply of toys such as balls and other floating objects available.

Preschoolers

Between three and five years of age, a preschool child will be able to master some more of the basic swimming skills and participate in a swimming program that will help develop a fit and healthy body as well as a love of the water.

Often the facilities used in organized swim programs and classes have a raised platform placed in the pool that adjusts the pool depth to about two feet. Look for a preschool program run by experienced staff that places priority on water safety. Swimming programs for children three to five, if well designed, should be progressive in nature.

What swimming skills can a preschool child learn? Most children will be able to learn water adjustment skills, breathing techniques, prone and supine floats, a basic crawlstroke, and how to change positions in the water from back to front and front to back.

Although the adult may not be involved in water instruction at this stage, encouragement from the adult makes a big difference in how well a child participates and enjoys the program. Make a point of swimming with the child outside the regular program, keeping abreast of accomplishments, helping the child master skills, and providing plenty of encouragement.

Youngsters from Six to Sixteen

Review swim skills already learned and those a child may now be learning in class.

Use the "train and engineer" position to practice skills in prone position. The child faces the parent/teacher and places hands on the adult's shoulders, which should be submerged at water's surface. The adult supports the child in the prone position by placing hands under the child's hips to enable the child to practice breathing techniques and flutter kicking. The engineer (adult) walks backward as the child kicks and locomotes forward (train).

The child may practice these skills if one kickboard is placed under each arm for support. Arms rest on the boards at the surface, with elbows bent, so that the kickboards are not below the surface of the water. The adult stands in front of the child and guides the child by lightly holding on to the front end of the boards.

Tossing pennies to the pool bottom for children to find and retrieve is a great activity, encouraging holding the breath and opening eyes underwater.

A favorite game is the whale ride in which a child holds an adult's shoulders piggyback style for a ride around the shallow area, and on the child's oral command "whale," the adult dips under the water for a moment.

At age six a child should be capable of learning all the basic swimming skills and strokes. This is an excellent age for a child to acquire more formal aquatic training. A child of this age may even prepare for participation in a competitive swimming program. Competitive programs are usually open to children between the ages of 8 and 18 years. Competitive programs will vary in what they require—how much instruction and coaching the child will receive, and how important competition is in the program. Adults should compare these factors with what is known about a child's maturity, prior experiences, and motivation to determine what kind of competition the child should enter.
Competitive programs are available at Y's, boys and girls clubs, community recreation and school facilities, and private swim clubs.

Reducing Risk of Water Accidents

Drowning is a leading cause of injury-related deaths in children. The American Academy of Pediatrics in Elk Grove Village, Illinois, recommends the following guidelines to reduce the possibility of childhood drowning.

Small Children (Under 4 years of age)

- **Never leave children alone in bathtubs, spas, wading pools, or any other body of water.**
- Remember that swimming lessons do not automatically drownproof small children.
- For private pools, fence the entire pool so that it is separated from the house. A pool cover should not be relied upon as a substitute for a fence.
- Be sure emergency equipment, such as a safety pole, is available at poolside.
- Adults should learn cardiopulmonary resuscitation (CPR).

Older Children (5 to 12 years)

- Be sure that they have an opportunity to learn how to swim.
- Be sure that children never swim alone or without adult supervision.
- Be sure that children wear an approved flotation device (life jacket) while they are swimming in or near deep water.
- Be sure children learn to check the water for any hazards before entering.
- Be sure children are aware of the dangers of skating or playing on frozen lakes, ponds, or streams.

Seniors

Americans are living longer. Since 1960, the number of people in the United States 85 years and older has increased by 232 percent compared to 39 percent for the overall population. During the 1980s, about 15,000 people were over 100; by 1990, that number had jumped to 36,000. By the year 2000, it is expected to continue to increase to 77,000.

Many seniors believe that years should not interfere from activity and exercise. They are living proof that it is never too late to take up new interests and make new commitments. Below are reasons for seniors to participate in water exercises:

- Fulfills the need for exercise
- Makes up for limitations in other physical activities
- Increases feeling of well-being
- Eases the pain of arthritis and increases the range of motion in affected joints
- Offers a safe and enjoyable lifetime activity

Seniors need an active physical and mental lifestyle to maintain health. Many physical conditions that older adults experience dictate the need for low-impact exercise. Among these conditions are: high blood pressure; decrease in synovial fluid in the joints; less acuity in eyesight and hearing, and increased reaction time. When movement is limited because of injury, accident, or illness, unaffected parts of the body can still benefit from exercise to maintain as much fitness as possible.

Water exercises such as ankle circles, opening and closing hands, wrist circles, and arm and leg circles in tepid water are all helpful.

Safety always comes first. Here are some extra tips.

- Ideally the water temperature should be 82 to 85 degrees F, preferably with a support bar along the side (or a lower gutter to grasp).
- A pool depth of 3-1/2 to 4-1/2 feet is best, but as long as the swimmer feels safe and sure-footed on the deck and in the pool, what is available will be fine. Use water shoes for comfort and safety.
- Safety is especially important on entry and exit from the pool. Arrange for someone to be available to assist with entry and exits, if needed.
- Swim and exercise at a comfortable pace.

Older adults who exercise know about their body, its condition, and its potential. A water aerobics class is a chance to have fun and "work out the kinks," a time to be personal—touch, exercise with partners, tell stories, socialize, and laugh.

The American Heart Association has concluded that *no exercise* is a risk factor all by itself. Because of the many benefits of water exercise, it makes good sense for seniors to include water fitness activities in their lifestyle.

Chapter 23

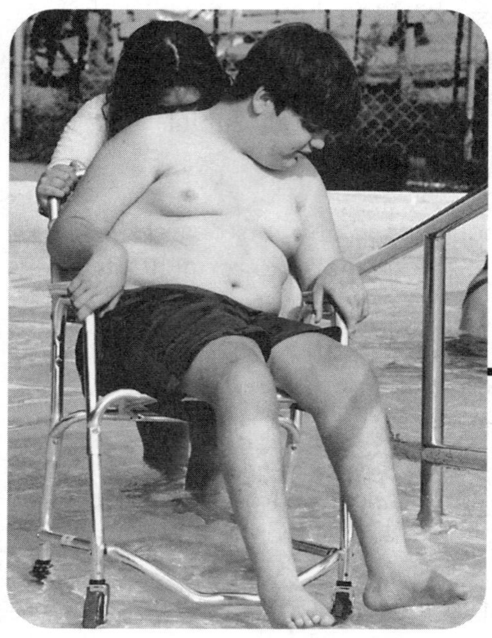

© Will Faller

Aquatic Fitness and Special Needs

One aspect of water is that it is a great equalizer. Many people who are limited in their ability to exercise on land can benefit greatly from the buoyancy, freedom of movement, and safety of exercising in water. Some health concerns that are helped by water fitness are:

- Obesity
- Arthritis
- Osteoporosis
- Mood Disorders
- Asthma
- Epilepsy
- Visual Impairment

For those with special needs, it is particularly important to exercise in water with the approval and guidance of a physician.

Obesity

There are many reasons for obesity. Some of them are:

- Genetics
- Lifestyle (The current North American lifestyle is relatively sedentary, and family time is often built around eating.)
- Eating Patterns

For the obese not only does water represent comfort and safety, and a relatively easy avenue for exercise. In water, body weight is only one-tenth of actual body weight. It is easier to exert energy in the water and water exercise causes low impact on the body joints. For people who are self-conscious about body weight, water is a psychological cover and safety net for legitimately participating in the fitness world.

Arthritis

Some physicians feel that most people over 40 have a touch of arthritis. It is a condition that appears to engender more questions than answers or antidotes.

Arthritis is a gradual, progressive degeneration of the joints. Its symptoms include pain with movement, heat, redness, stiffness (especially in the morning), swelling, loss of movement, and often functional deformity.

Research indicates that exercise makes it possible for those with arthritis to manage their lives with more independence and less pain. Water, with its cushioning effect, is the ideal medium for exercise. A water exercise program for persons with arthritis provides an opportunity to participate in a recreational group activity that specifically improves health and a sense of well-being. Warm water, buoyancy, and the movement against the resistive property of water make swimming and water exercise effective in decreasing pain and stiffness, and in improving joint flexibility for people with arthritis. Some people also experience increased muscle strength and improved coordination, endurance, and ability to perform daily tasks.

Several modifications can be made to a program for those who have arthritis.

1. Increase the amount of time spent on the warm-ups.
2. Move steadily and gradually through the water, so that the water's resistance can be safely used to improve strength and coordination.
3. Decrease the already reduced impact by keeping one foot on the ground at all times. Replace water jogging and hops with rocking and stretching of toes.
4. Reduce stress on the joints by reducing the number of repetitions.
5. Do not use weights.
6. Swim only in water temperature that is at least 85 degrees or higher (with appropriate warm air temperature).
7. Do not work through pain. A person in pain with a "hot joint" should be advised to swim only easy repetitions. A basic rule regarding pain and exercise says that pain after two hours (known as residual pain) indicates the activity has extended too long and the next session should be shorter.

Programs

Several water exercise programs have been developed for people with arthritis including the Arthritis Foundation, which has also published a pamphlet outlining water exercises ideal for arthritis patients.

The two broad categories of exercise for people with arthritis include therapeutic and recreational exercises.

Therapeutic exercises are activities prescribed by a doctor, physical therapist, or occupational therapist. These exercises are based on a person's exact needs and are designed to reach a certain goal (for example, increase muscle strength) and range of motion.

Recreational exercise includes any form of movement or relaxation that refreshes the body and mind. It can be done alone or in groups. Recreational exercises or activities can maintain or improve joint mobility, range of motion, and muscle strength. They can also increase endurance. They add to a therapeutic program, but do not replace it.

Exercise in both swimming pools and spas is often an excellent adjunct to the therapeutic regimen prescribed by the physician for a person with arthritis. Doctors often advise that people with arthritis soak in warm water in the morning before beginning their daily activities. This is a time when many people with arthritis find that pain and stiffness are at their worst.

Osteoporosis

Osteoporosis is a condition caused by the reabsorption of calcium by the body, leaving the bones brittle and prone to fracture. It occurs mainly in women and often after menopause.

Weight bearing exercise is generally prescribed to prevent, retard, or reverse osteoporosis, along with a special diet. Water exercise in shallow water is partially weight bearing, and the safety aspects of exercising in water recommend it to those with osteoporosis.

Mood Disorders

Sheppard Pratt Health System in Baltimore, Maryland, has developed programs in the water for patients with emotional disabilities and have obtained encouraging results. The relaxation that comes from water, the sense of freedom, and the increased self-esteem that comes from learning new skills have been helpful. Therapists report easier communication after water exercise.

Asthma

Asthma is a disorder of the respiratory system affecting people of all ages. Spasms of the bronchial tubes result in attacks of coughing, wheezing, labored breathing, and shortness of breath. Frequently, asthma is a result of allergic reaction from dust, animal hair, or some foods. In many cases, asthma can be controlled by medication or an inhaler.

Since allergies are the most common cause of asthma, swimming is actually helpful because allergens are usually less prevalent at the water's surface. The warm, moist air of swimming pools provide an ideal environment, then, for those people with asthma that is caused by allergens.

In cases, though, where energetic exercise of five to eight minutes in length brings on an asthma attack, the condition is known as exercise induced asthma (EIA). Humidity and temperature changes are important factors in inducing asthma during strenuous exercise. However, where the exerciser has improved physical fitness, coping with asthma becomes easier.

The basic elements of swimming—combining muscular activity with rhythmic breathing—have benefited persons with asthma. However, certain precautions should be maintained:

1. An inhaler or medication should be brought poolside.
2. Instructors and/or lifeguards should be told about swimmers with asthma.
3. Those with exercise induced asthma (EIA) should have a ten- to fifteen-minute warm-up before strenuous activity.
4. Swimmers with EIA are advised to alternate five minutes of vigorous activity with five minutes of rest to avoid attacks. The fitness level of the swimmer determines what level of activity is considered vigorous.
5. If an asthma attack occurs in the water, the swimmer must stop immediately and be given appropriate care.
6. Certain ventilation systems in indoor pools retain a high level of chlorine and other and other air pollutants. These may make asthmatic individuals prone to attack.

Epilepsy

Epilepsy, a disease which has been known about for centuries, is caused by an abnormal discharge of electricity in the brain. It is defined as recurrent loss of, or impairment of, consciousness accompanied by muscular movement. It is more prevalent in persons who have brain dysfunction or injury, such as cerebral palsy.

The cause of epilepsy has been understood only in the last few decades. Historically, there has been considerable prejudice against people with epilepsy; it was feared because it was thought to be contagious. However, now, 75 percent of epilepsy cases can be controlled by anticonvulsant drugs.

Sometimes epileptics can feel a seizure coming on. A sensation of anxiety or depression, known as an aura, precedes the seizure.

In some cases, seizures are brought on by sudden changes in environment (e.g., entering the swimming pool). Also the flickering of light reflecting off the water's surface may bring on a seizure in a few individuals.

Other triggers might be allergies and fatigue.

A person whose epilepsy is controlled by drugs or other means can participate in a swimming class with these safety guides taken into consideration:

- Class instructors and lifeguards on duty should be made aware of a person with this condition.
- In the event of a seizure, tilt the person's head back so the airway is clear, making sure that the head is above water. Keep the person away from the sides of the pool to avoid hitting the sides, and tow the person to shallow water if possible. Get qualified help.
- Once the person has recovered, the person should not reenter the water for the remainder of the session.

TIPS FOR VISUALLY IMPAIRED SWIMMERS

I swim several days a week for 30 to 45 minutes as part of my cross-training for cross-country skiing, tandem cycling, racewalking, and rowing, I participate in all of these sports at a fairly high level—and have competed in all of them at one time or another, with varied success.

Competition History:

US Disabled Ski Team—1983–1989
- Olympic Silver Medalist, 1984
- National Champion, six years

US Disabled Cycling Team—1989–1991
- 7th in World, 1990
- National Champion, 1989, 1991

continued

I swim at a health club but I also belonged to a Y at one time as well. I actually found the Y personnel to be the most accommodating in terms of orienting me to the facilities. They are a community facility and feel their obligation to serve the diversity of the community. I have actually had a health club blatantly discriminate against me by saying I could not join the club. They tried to tell me that it is a private club and they do not have to let in everyone who desires membership.

What is even more astounding is that their main concern was my safety in the swimming pool. They wanted to know how I would determine when it was time to turn around at the end of the lane. Even though I pointed out that a substantial number of swimmers with correctable vision took their glasses off to swim and that the club was not concerned about them, it took the threat of a lawsuit to get the establishment to take my $1,100. I now use the facility often and have a good relationship with many of the staff.

Here are some tips for people with little or no vision:

- When learning a new stroke or improving a technique, a hands-on approach is best. I like the instructor to take my arms and legs and to actually go through the motions so that I can feel how it is to be done.
- Become familiar with the locker room, shower area, and pool area. It may be helpful to bring a friend or ask a staff member to tour the facility.
- Develop a pattern and follow it. For instance, use a locker in the same area each time, put a towel in the same place, use the same shower, and so forth. This helps with orientation and independent movement.
- Identify the towel in a special way to distinguish it from everyone else's towel since all facility towels are usually the same. I hang my towel close to where I get into the pool and leave my white cane there as well.
- Become familiar with the swimming patterns followed at the pool. For instance, when lanes are marked slow, medium, and fast, swim the lane that is most appropriate. Progress to circle swimming when there are several people swimming in a lane.
- To check distance from the swimmer in front, check the degree of turbulence in the water. When the water becomes more turbulent, I know I am gaining on the person and I then slow down.
- After a few laps, the length of a pool is clear. Keep an arm out in front to avoid crashing into the wall. I sometimes count strokes from one end to another—this is a good training exercise.

—Laura Oftedahl
Boston, MA

Americans with Disabilities Act

Since the Americans with Disabilities Act (ADA) became law in 1990, water fitness is even more accessible, available, and valuable to people with special needs. Today those with special needs can find equipment to assist them in and around the water. For example, there are:

- ***Lifts***—motor and mechanically powered
- ***Collars***—for neck support
- ***Movable pool floors***—adjustable height for wheelchair/ stretcher transfer
- ***Poolside mats***
- ***Special ladders***
- ***Stools/benches/chairs***—for pool and locker room comfort
- ***Flotation devices***—for added support, safety and comfort, e.g., ankle/wrist floats, kickboards, mask, fin and snorkel

Flotation devices can be extremely helpful for people with physical impairments. For instance, an *amputee* may have unequal densities on each side of the body causing the side with higher density to sink. This imbalance causes a swimmer to be less stable in the water and less likely to float. This is also a consideration for those affected by paralysis. In some cases, flotation devices are used to relocate the center of buoyancy and provide reliable stability in the water, making swim skills achievable.

In 1961, during John F. Kennedy's presidency, the Kennedy family chose to disclose that one of their siblings was mentally disabled. Until this time, people with a mental disability were often purposely not discussed. With this announcement and a rise in national awareness, disabled people began to be viewed according to their ability rather than their disability. One of the first programs which emerged for people with special needs was the Special Olympics. President Kennedy's sister, Eunice Shriver, was the innovator of the Special Olympics which gives people of varying abilities the opportunity to gain new experiences and confidence through athletic achievement. The

Special Olympics has grown into an international event of great size where people with special abilities compete with each other, such as the event in New Haven, Connecticut, in July 1995.

There is also the Paralympics, which takes place after the regular Olympics every four years, as well as local, national, and international chapters that sponsor competitions throughout the year.

Chapter **24**

Nutrition

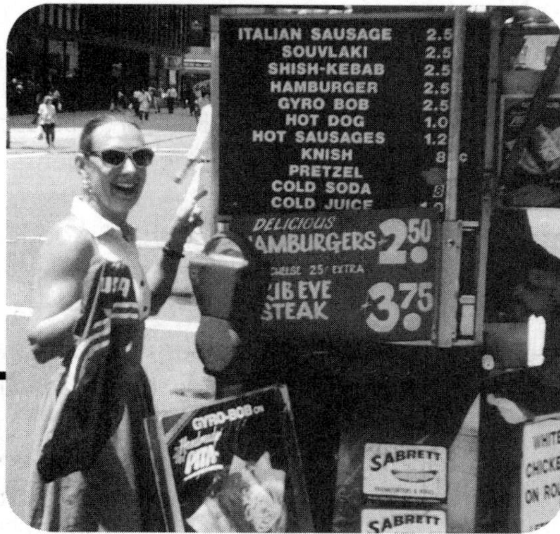

There is a complementary relationship between good nutrition and exercise; they are the health twins. This chapter explores nutrition from the point of view of health—how it contributes to freedom from disease and how "smart eating" contributes to fitness performance. Fitness students have an excellent opportunity to gain an understanding of the why's and how's of everyday living. An understanding of food is basic not only to a fitness program but to every phase of life.

Nutrition is defined by Webster's dictionary as the science or study of a proper, balanced diet to promote health, especially in human beings. The purpose of this chapter is to discuss the scientific basis of good nutrition, and to describe a smart nutritional lifestyle.

Guidelines for eating smart have been distributed by many government and private organizations. Among them:

The United States Department of Agriculture (USDA)
The American Dietetic Association
The American Heart Association
The National Cancer Society

It is not surprising that a good nutritional lifestyle recommended by these organizations is almost identical. This chapter explores this consensus, but *not* as a set of rules that must be followed.

First, it is necessary to understand the nutritional needs of human beings and then study the foods that fulfill those needs. Since both human bodies and the foods that nourish them are made of atoms and molecules, it is necessary to discuss some very elementary chemistry.

Students and people "on the run" do not always have the opportunity to eat smart. This chapter will, therefore, concentrate on how to make wise food choices, order from available menus, read food labels, and shop wisely in a supermarket and not rely on special diets.

The New Nutrition

The United States Department of Agriculture (USDA) in 1957 devised the Basic Four food plan as a guide to better nutrition. In these guidelines the USDA advised adults to eat four servings daily from a combined fruit and vegetable category. In 1992 after considerable research the USDA issued new guidelines and present them as the Food Guide Pyramid. This program recommends that the vegetable group contribute three to five servings and the fruit group two to four servings, increasing the recommendations to five to nine servings for the two groups combined. Sadly, few Americans follow even the old recommendations. Two servings daily is typical, and many people rarely eat fruits and vegetables at all.

Rather than duplicating the information in the *Food Guide Pyramid* booklet, this chapter discusses the six food groups in the *Food Guide Pyramid* from the point of view of nutritional needs and shows how the number of servings was arrived at.

Why We Need Food

1. We need food to supply *fuel* for muscles so that they can move arms and legs for external activity, as well as for internal motions of the organs and body fluids.
2. We need food to supply material to replenish cells after they wear out so that the body can keep its integrity.

The Foods We Eat

The organic compounds that make up food are divided into two major groups. The first group makes up the bulk of food that is ingested and is called the **macronutrients.** The major function of the macronutrients is to supply the energy compounds that fuel muscles and maintain body temperatures. This group is also called energy nutrients. The three energy nutrients are **carbohydrates, proteins** and **fats.**

The second group of organic chemicals that food contains, but in small quantities, is the **micronutrients.** These are the **vitamins** and **minerals.**

While *water* is not chemically considered an organic compound, it does constitute about 50 percent of body weight and will be discussed separately.

Lastly, the importance to health of *fiber*, a form of non-digestible carbohydrate found in food, will be discussed.

Macronutrients

Carbohydrates

Carbohydrates trace their name from the fact that no matter what food source they come from, their structural formula (the number of different atoms in their make-up) is carbon, hydrogen, and oxygen in the same *proportion* as in water (H_2O), thus the term "carbo" for carbon and "hydrate" for the water. For example, the chemical formula for the important carbohydrate *glucose*, also known as blood sugar, is $C_6H_{12}O_6$. Although hydrogen and oxygen are in the same ratio as in water, a carbohydrate reverts to carbon, carbon dioxide, and water rapidly only after the food is "scorched" by overcooking and it has given up some of its stored chemical energy as heat. Glucose has the name blood sugar because it circulates in the blood and supplies energy (through the complex mechanisms of cell biology) to both the brain and muscles, after which it also reverts to carbon dioxide and water.

It may seem that glucose, which is found in fruits, vegetables, and honey, is the ideal food, particularly because it is absorbed directly into the blood stream. The body chemistry tries to keep the glucose level between narrow limits, however, because too much pure glucose all at once may be too much for the body to handle.

Glucose and several other sugars are called monosaccharides. Ordinary table sugar, called sucrose, is a molecule composed of the linking together of glucose and another monosaccharide called fructose. Sugars that are composed of two monosaccharides linked together are called disaccharides. The body has mechanisms for converting disaccharides to two glucose molecules.

When hundreds or even thousands of glucose molecules are linked together in a food to form one giant molecule, that large molecule is called a polysaccharide. The largest source of the polysaccharides are the starches; thus the term "starch" molecule is synonymous with polysaccharide molecule. The foods called the starches are the grains (the seeds of grasses), such as wheat, rice, oats, rye, barley, corn, and millet. Other sources of starch are potatoes, lentils, and beans.

These foods have provided 50 to 80 percent of the energy (calories) for human beings from the beginning of recorded history and on all parts of the earth (except the Arctic Circle) up to the present day. This long tradition has only been broken in modern times, with a shift in the affluent nations toward more flesh foods (this shift is only possible with affluence since it takes roughly five pounds of grain to support livestock that produces one pound of meat).

The shift in dietary distribution has, not surprisingly, been accompanied by an increase in the diseases of affluence, mainly heart disease and cancer. Therefore, the USDA's guidelines are correct to emphasize a return to the original human diet with a large portion of calories coming from starches.

The difference between the digestion of starches, which are also known as the *complex carbohydrates*, and that of the *simple carbo-*

hydrates known as sugars is that while the simple carbohydrates go into the blood stream almost immediately, the complex carbohydrates go into the blood stream gradually (something like a slow-release process), allowing stabilization of the blood sugar (glucose) level. In the Food Guide Pyramid, starches are the foundation of a healthy daily food choice, with 6 to 11 servings of bread, cereal, rice, or pasta as the advised daily goal.

One serving from the starches is roughly one ounce; for example, one slice of bread or one ounce of ready-to-eat cereal. When reading food labels given in grams, note that 28.4 grams equals one ounce. Food intake does not have to be measured to such precision, but keep in mind that 400 grams roughly equals 3-1/2 ounces. For calorie counters, carbohydrates (simple or complex) supply four calories of energy per gram.

Proteins

Protein is the "stuff" of which living things, both animal and vegetable, are made. In the animal kingdom this includes muscles, organs, nerves, and blood vessels. It does not mean that to produce muscle tissue one has to eat animal muscle.

Protein is composed of carbon, hydrogen, and oxygen, like carbohydrates (and fats), but it also has nitrogen in its composition. Nitrogen is a member of every group of chemicals known as *amino acids*. Protein, that is, all living tissue, is made from some combination of the 22 amino acids linked together. All but eight of the 22 amino acids can be made in the body, provided nitrogen is available. These eight are known as the *essential* amino acids. Not only must all eight essential amino acids be present to construct new tissue or replace broken down tissues, but they must be present in roughly the same proportion as the tissue being built in the body. The body breaks down an ingested protein food into its amino acids and then reassembles the amino acids into the living tissue that has to be built.

The USDA pyramid shows two separate groups of high protein foods. Group one is milk and milk products such as yogurt and cheese, clearly animal products. Group two consists of meat, poultry, fish, dry beans, eggs and nuts. How did dry beans and nuts get into this high protein group? Because they are rich in amino acids.

Animal protein sources generally provide a better balance of the eight essential amino acids than do the vegetable sources of beans and nuts. Despite this fact, many people around the earth obtain adequate protein nutrition (as centuries of their ancestors did) by a phenomenon known as *complementary protein*. This consists of combining vegetable sources of protein in such a way that each source supplies one or more essential amino acid(s) that the other sources are weak in, such as rice and beans or peanut butter and whole wheat bread.

The pyramid specifies two to three servings daily from each of these high protein groups. For the dairy group a serving is one cup of milk or yogurt or 1-1/2 to 2 ounces of cheese. For the flesh food, beans, eggs, and nuts group, a serving is 2–3 ounces of lean meat, poultry, or fish. One-half cup of dry cooked beans, or one egg, or two tablespoons of peanut butter count as one ounce of flesh food.

In calories, one gram of protein supplies four calories; however, protein is often found in foods containing a lot of fat which is 9 calories per gram.

Lipids (Fats)

The *lipids* include solid fat, liquid oil, triglycerides, and cholesterol. The lipids are compounds of carbon, hydrogen, and oxygen chained together, but the hydrogen and oxygen are *not* in the same proportion as in water.

The lipids serve important functions in the body. They participate in much of the body's internal chemistry, support the body organs, give the body heat insulation, and supply stored energy for emergency conditions when food is not immediately available. They are particularly suited for this last task, since they contain 9 calories per gram, more than twice the energy density of carbohydrates or protein.

Since the need for stored energy is not present when food is readily available and excess lipids are associated with many disease processes, the pyramid puts pure fats and oils into the *use sparingly* group.

The body also converts simple sugars that are not immediately used for energy into stored fat so that added sugar is also in the *use sparingly* group.

Micronutrients

Vitamins

Vitamins are not energy nutrients themselves but are essential constituents of body enzymes, which are compounds manufactured by the body, and required for the metabolism of the three energy nutrients. Vitamins are required in exceedingly small ("micro") quantities. There are two classes of vitamins, the water soluble (B and C) and the fat soluble (A, D, and E). Meats and meat substitutes, milk and dairy products, fruits and vegetables all provide vitamins; fruits and vegetables are especially good sources. The pyramid specifies three to five daily servings from the vegetable group, and two to four servings from the fruit group.

A serving from the fruit group could be one medium apple, banana, or orange, or 3/4 cup of fruit juice. A serving from the vegetable group could be one cup of raw leafy vegetables, 1/2 cup of cooked or raw chopped vegetables, or 3/4 cup vegetable juice.

Should everyone take vitamin supplements? The consensus among health professionals is that to be sure about reaching the necessary number of daily vitamins and minerals (including the "anti-oxidants"), taking multi-vitamin and mineral supplements with anti-oxidants daily can only be beneficial. It is advisable to check with a health professional if unsure about mineral and vitamin intake.

Minerals

Minerals are inorganic chemicals that either are constituents of body structures (bones, teeth, muscles, nerves, and blood) or are required in small amounts for chemical reactions in the body. Most foods contain some minerals, but certain foods are known to be especially good sources of certain essential minerals. For example, milk and milk products are known to be good sources of calcium. Sea foods are good sources of iodine, which although essential, is required only in small amounts. Fruits and vegetables are good sources of potassium. Red meats, liver, and legumes (beans) are good sources of iron.

Fiber

Fiber is a nondigestible carbohydrate that influences the speed with which other nutrients move through the digestive system. Control of this transit time is important for health; it must be slow enough to allow for the absorption of the nutrients in the food but not so slow that harmful disease processes can occur. Whole grains contain more fiber than refined grains (i.e., 100 percent in whole wheat bread compared to white bread). Therefore, eating whole grains will increase the amount of fiber in the diet. Fruits and vegetables are also good sources of fiber. High fiber diets help to protect against colon cancer.

Water

As mentioned earlier, about 50 percent of body weight is water. It is a component of both body fluids and tissue, and it is the medium in which most of the body's chemical reactions occur.

Water is actually more immediately essential to life than food. It is recommended that at least 64 ounces (eight 8-ounce glasses) be taken daily from tap water or beverages. Fruits and vegetables contain a considerable amount of water but should not be relied upon as the sole source of water.

Food Summary

The Food Guide Pyramid (Home and Garden Bulletin Number 252), prepared by the Human Nutrition Information Service for the United States Department of Agriculture, sets out the latest knowledge on nutrition (and thus the best performance in work or athletics). These guidelines are based on eating a variety of foods in as near to their natural state as possible. They stress limiting fat intake to no more than 30 percent of the total calorie intake. For people with a personal or famly history of heart disease, 20 percent is recommended. To do this, high fat and high cholesterol foods have to be used sparingly. This requires using skim milk and low-fat (1%) dairy products instead of whole-milk dairy products. Using lean cuts of meat instead of high-fat varieties, (such as sausages and hot dogs) and limiting egg yolks will also reduce fat intake.

The booklet may be obtained from:

U.S. Government Printing Office
Attention: R. Woods, Consumer Information Center-3C
P.O. Box 100
Pueblo, Colorado 81002
Ask for booklet 117Z

Nutritional Project

For one week keep a journal of all food selections. *Eat in the same places and at the same times as much as possible.*

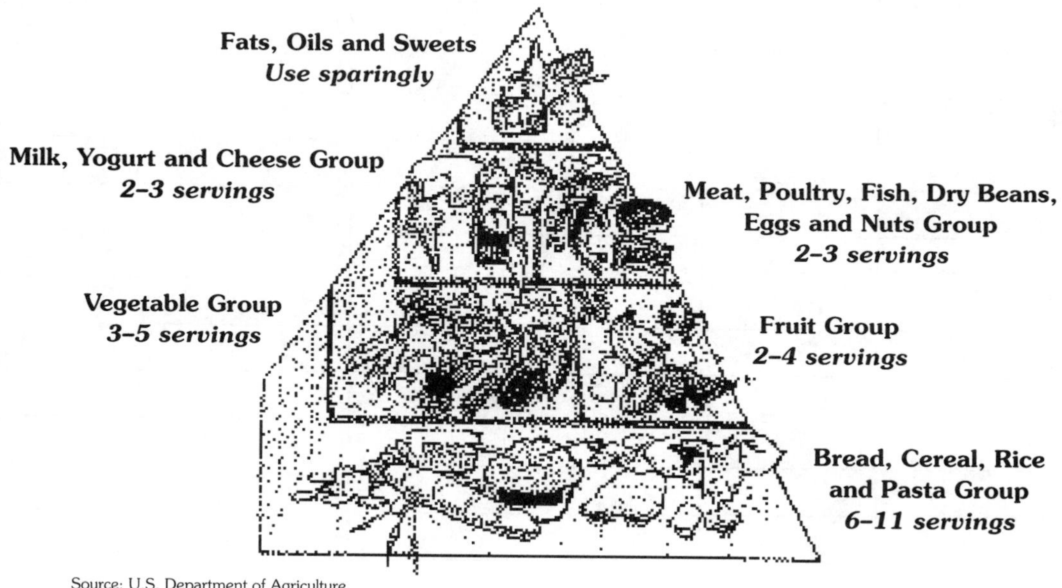

Source: U.S. Department of Agriculture

Food Guide Pyramid

Snacking is healthy. Many small meals throughout the day are healthier than a few big meals; it is *what* the snack is that makes the difference. Also write down:

1. What food choices changed after reading this chapter and what food choices were made. Indicate what previous food choices were.
2. What food choices did not change, and what foods were selected.

Use the nutrition journal below to record daily food intake.

NUTRITIONAL JOURNAL

Day/Date	Time	Food Intake	Comments

Exercise, Weight Loss, and Calories

Approximately 65 million Americans are on a diet at any one time. Yet dieting alone rarely results in significant or permanent weight loss. Many popular diets require cutting calories below a level that is safe or balanced nutritionally. Combining diet *and* exercise is a more successful way to lose and maintain desired weight.

Exercising can actually make dieting easier. Current research suggests that moderate exercise will temporarily raise metabolism so that calories are burned at a higher than normal rate following exercise.

Losing weight gradually—up to two pounds per week—is the safest and most effective way. To lose weight, calculate the number of calories to cut from daily intake. However, daily intake should never drop below 1,200 calories.

One pound of fat yields approximately 3,500 calories. To lose one pound of fat a week by dieting alone, it is necessary to eliminate 500 calories a day. By combining regular exercise with reduced caloric intake, more calories will be burned. For example, by burning 500 calories a day through exercise, another pound each week can be lost. For most people one to two pounds per week can be lost through diet and exercise.

Caloric expenditure during exercise depends on the intensity of the exercise and body weight. More calories are burned by exercising at higher intensities. Note that a moderate intensity is most effective for weight control and maintenance. This is true because primarily fat is burned during moderate exercise; also, it is possible to exercise longer at this pace. Carbohydrates are the primary energy source used at high work levels. The amount of exercise should be appropriate for one's age and health status.

Weight Loss Guidelines

1. Limit intake of total fat and cholesterol.
2. Limit sodium (salt) intake.
3. Avoid simple sugars; increase intake of complex carbohydrates and fiber.

The following lists provide suggestions for meeting weight loss goals, indicating which foods are permitted and which foods should be limited or avoided. Note that these lists are not exhaustive.

1. **Limit intake of total fat and cholesterol**

Foods to Eat	***Foods to Avoid or Limit***
Lean meats	Fried foods
Skim and low-fat milk and other dairy products	Cooking oil
Poultry (without skin)	Butter
Fish	Margarine
Fresh fruits	Salad dressings
Fresh vegetables	Mayonnaise
No-oil salad dressings	Fatty red meats
Breads prepared without oils or shortening	Cold cuts/lunch meats
Tuna fish in water	Hot dogs
Egg whites	Sausage
	Egg yolks
	Cookies
	Chicken skins
	Tuna fish in oil
	Heavy cream
	Half-and-half
	Whole milk
	Whole milk cheeses

2. **Limit sodium (salt) intake.** Dairy products and meats contain a significant amount of sodium naturally. These amounts are acceptable when consumed in moderate quantities and will provide enough sodium in the diet to meet most individuals' needs. It is possible to eliminate the use of table salt and still meet sodium requirements.

Foods to Eat	***Foods to Avoid or Limit***
Fresh fruits and vegetables	Salt—when cooking
Unsalted cheese	Potato chips, pretzels, salted crackers, salted nuts
Hot cereals prepared without salt	Canned foods (unless unsalted)
Breads (low salt)	Hot dogs
Natural/no-salt peanut butter	Bacon
Rice cakes	Ham, lunch meats
Unsalted crackers	Dry cereals (except no-salt varieties)
Low-fat unsalted cheese	Olives and pickles
	Cheese (no-salt varieties)
	Commercial peanut butter

3. Avoid simple sugars; increase intake of complex carbohydrates and fiber.

Foods to Eat	***Foods to Avoid or Limit***
Fruit juices without added sugar	Table sugar, corn syrup
Preserves prepared without sugar	Cookies
Fresh fruits and vegetables	Cakes and pastry
Frozen vegetables	Soda
Unsweetened canned and jarred fruits	Pancake syrup
Unsweetened frozen fruits	Candied fruits
Whole grain bread	Jelly, preserves, and jam
Brown rice	Candy
Whole grain cereals, oatmeal	Sweetened dry cereals
Wheat and rice cakes	Prepared cake mixes
Bran	White breads
Plain nonfat or low-fat yogurt	Canned fruits in heavy syrup
Beans, all types (unsalted)	Yogurts prepared with sugar or corn syrup
Dried fruits	

Tips

1. Prepare foods without added oils or fats. Foods cooked with added oil may taste good, but they do not wear well for heart and body.
2. Trim all meat, fish, and poultry of any visible fat or skin. Select lean cuts of meat.
3. Use fresh instead of processed foods.
4. Select skim or low-fat milk (1 percent fat) and dairy products.
5. Limit cholesterol by eating no more than three egg yolks per week. Egg whites contain no cholesterol and need not be limited.
6. Limit meats to about four ounces at any one meal and six ounces total per day.
7. Space meals regularly throughout the day to help avoid prolonged periods of low blood sugar levels.
8. Use herbs, spices, and lemon juice for food flavoring instead of salt.
9. Steam fresh or frozen vegetables instead of boiling to preserve vitamins. Avoid overcooking.
10. Save extra cooking time by preparing larger quantities, especially of main courses, which can be frozen or refrigerated for future use.
11. Prepare brown rice ahead of time so that it is always on hand.
12. Use bananas, berries, and raisins as sweeteners on cereal and in yogurt or for snacks.
13. Make beef or chicken stock for soups by simmering the beef or chicken and placing the broth in the refrigerator (not the freezer). The fat can then be easily removed. Store homemade stock in refrigerator or freezer for future use.
14. Read labels carefully. The major ingredient of prepared foods is listed first.
15. Drink coffee in moderation.
16. Always eat a breakfast that is high in complex carbohydrates, which supply the energy needed to face the day's activities. Oatmeal and shredded wheat are good sources of complex carbohydrates.

17. Drink alcohol in moderation. A glass of wine with lunch or dinner will not ruin everything!
18. Look for jams, jellies, preserves, and conserves that are prepared with fruit and fruit juices.
19. Limit or avoid regular sodas, which contain too much sugar. Also avoid club soda, which contains salt. Drink seltzer or water. Add seltzer to fruit juices to create natural sodas. Avoid beverages containing sodium.
20. Don't assume that the word *natural* on food packaging means proper nutrition. Read the ingredients carefully. Do not assume that low fat or low salt is substantially lower in fat or sodium.
21. Beware of other names for sugar: fructose (fruit sugar), corn syrup, and sucrose.
22. Prepare raw vegetables for snacks. Try carrots, celery, cherry tomatoes, and cucumbers.
23. Avoid food shopping when hungry. It is more difficult to resist the lure of chocolate chip cookies or cheesecake.
24. It is not necessary to shop always in a health food store. The ordinary supermarket provides some of the most healthful foods around.
25. When eating out, follow these additional guidelines:
    - Ask for sauces and salad dressing "on the side" so you can use them sparingly, or ask that they be left out altogether.
    - Order nonalcoholic drinks, particularly those with fruit juices and seltzer, and water.
    - Don't eat everything if no longer hungry. Don't be shy about asking for a doggie bag. Leftovers make quick meals the next day.
    - Order baked potatoes (without butter or sour cream) instead of french fries or home fries.
    - Ask that food be prepared without oils, sauces, salt, or MSG.
    - Avoid fast food chains unless eating from the salad bar.
    - Order poultry and fish instead of red meats. Keep the main portion small to medium (three to six ounces).

Chapter 25

Courtesy of International Hall of Fame, Fort Lauderdale, Florida

Questions and Answers

The question and answer format of this final chapter addresses concerns frequently raised about water exercising and swimming. The questions are divided into the general areas of programming, safety and courtesy, health and beauty, competitive sports, nutrition, medicine, and special considerations.

Doing the Program

Q: *If I cannot get to the pool, can I practice swim skills?*

A: Whether at home, at work, or traveling, take a few minutes to do the following Sweats to WETs—water exercises done on terra firma.

- **Lower Body:** While seated on a straight chair, on the edge of a sofa or a bed, find a comfortable way to practice:
  1. Flutter kick for the crawl and backstroke
  2. Modified whip kick for the elementary backstroke and breaststroke
  3. Dolphin kick for the butterfly

- **Upper Body:** While sitting at a desk or at a table, or while watching TV, practice the following upper body exercises:
  1. Overarm stretch
  2. Triceps stretch
  3. Head and shoulder roll

Be a self-critic by standing or sitting in front of a full-length mirror and simulating the arm movements for all the strokes. The feedback is immediate.

Practice rhythmic breathing without being in the pool. Fill a basin, a bowl, a pot, a wok, or the bathroom sink with enough lukewarm water to comfortably immerse the face up to the hairline. Exhale into the water through the nose and mouth, forming bubbles. Then turn head to breathing side to inhale, and once again exhale into the water. This is rhythmic breathing as in the crawlstroke.

For breaststroke and butterfly breathing, practice lifting and lowering your chin just above the water, exhale as lowering face into the water, forming bubbles, and inhaling as lifting up head.

Make a regular practice of doing those Sweats to WETs, especially on days between swims. You will be reinforcing swim skills while keeping toned, fit, and eager until the next swim workout.

Q: *This is the first time I've used water exercise in a structured way. Are there any guidelines you can give me?*

A: First, you should do WETs in warm water (low- to mid-80 degrees). Exercise in chin- to chest-deep water for the best water resistance. While exercising, breathe fully and continuously, and exercise to some favorite music. Add equipment for greater resistance against the water.

Q: *What is new in water fitness equipment?*

A: Aquatic exercise equipment continues to proliferate. Examples are plastic spa bells and styrofoam logs which are used for buoyant support, stretching, and exercising.

Safe and Courteous Swimming

Q: *How can I be prepared for a safe swim?*

A: Never swim alone. Be sure a lifeguard is present on deck. Listen to your body. Do warm-ups and cool-downs. Learn CPR (cardiopulmonary resuscitation). (Call the local American Heart Association or Red Cross chapter for courses.)

Q: *Sometimes I think swimming is a contact sport. What are the rules of the pool?*

A: The recent surge in fitness swimming has reinforced the need for observing pool courtesy, since pools and rules are not always created equal with regard to lap length, number of swimmers per lane, and allotted time per swim session.

Review the following swimming courtesy guidelines:

- Lanes in pools are often divided by speed. Start at your own pace. Speed is relative to the lane in which you are swimming, and those with whom you are swimming.
- Observe the posted swimming patterns in the facility. When there are two swimmers allowed in a lane, the lane is sometimes split, otherwise, circle swimming is usually in effect.
- During circle swimming, always swim on the right-hand side of the lane and move in a counterclockwise direction.
- To pass a slower swimmer, first tap the toes of the swimmer. Then, at the wall, turn and precede the slower swimmer.
- Use equipment carefully. Avoid hanging onto lane lines, blocking the pace clock, or interfering with lap swimmers by standing at the shallow end of the lane.

If there are differences of opinion between swimmers, the lifeguard should be consulted immediately.

Q: *What safety precautions should I be aware of in open water?*

A: In open water area, check for posted precautions including water temperature, currents, tides, submerged pilings, and so on. Never dive into unknown waters. Learn cardiopulmonary resuscitation (CPR) by taking a course offered by the local American Red Cross or American Heart Association chapter.

Health and Beauty Cues

Q: *What kind of bathing suit is best for doing my swim workouts?*

A: Choose a bathing suit that is comfortable, lightweight, and attractive. Be certain that there are no uncomfortable string or strap placements that can rise up or slip down and suit fits securely around buttocks and bust. There are various combinations of Lycra-based fabrics available on the market. Whatever a suit is made of, be sure to rinse it thoroughly after each use to prolong its life.

Q: *Is chlorine harmful?*

A: Chlorine is used in many pools to keep them free of harmful bacteria and viruses that might cause the spread of disease. It will not hurt the body. Chlorine also oxidizes and removes particles in the water—algae, ammonia, and organic waste products, products that bacteria feed upon. However, the combination of chlorine and water can dry skin and hair.

Q: *Why is it important to get rid of all the chlorine on my skin?*

A: Chlorine and salt water remove the oils that keep natural moisture in. Paradoxically, prolonged immersion in water of any kind can actually dry skin. Use a moisturizing soap when showering off after a swim. While still slightly damp, apply a moisturizing lotion; those containing urea or lactic acid are helpful.

Q: *Does tinted (or permed) hair require special care?*

A: Chlorine enters the hair shaft, causing hair to swell and stretch more than normal. Hair that has been chemically treated is more porous and delicate than "virgin" hair, and may be more prone to breakage, split ends, and discoloration. Make an extra effort to keep hair dry. Wear a lycra cap under a latex or silicone one. Lycra is not waterproof, but it is a smooth, absorbent lining that acts as a buffer.

Q: *How can ears be protected during swimming?*

A:

- **Ear Plugs:** Plugs seal the outer ear canal; they are reasonably priced and easily available.
- **Lamb's Wool** (available in drugstores): Place a small piece of lamb's wool into the outer ear canal and seal it with petroleum jelly.
- **Bathing Cap:** Use a snug-fitting bathing cap that covers the ears.

Q: *I seem to get a lot of water in my ears. What's "swimmer's ear?"*

A: Getting water in the ears is annoying and can lead to "swimmer's ear." During a swim, water sometimes travels up the eustachian tube, the connecting tube that stretches from behind the nose to behind the eardrum. An infection in the nasal passages can cause water to transfer the inflammation to the middle ear. This is known as "swimmer's ear."

Be a Sport with WETs!

Q: *How can WETs be applied to the skills of other sports?*

A: WETs can be used to cross-train for other sports as well as strengthen and condition muscles, especially during off-season. WETs allow the athlete/exerciser/swimmer to maintain and improve skills. For example, the aqua jog and stroke punch are good choices of WETs for cross-training. For arm skills that are used in tennis, baseball, and golf, use hand paddles or a pull-buoy for extra resistance in the water. For walking, jogging, cross-country skiing, and downhill skiing, which use alternating arm and leg movements, simulate the motions of these activities against the water's resistance.

Q: *I am interested in becoming a competitive swimmer and may also want to enter a triathlon. How can I prepare myself?*

A: If the smell of chlorine and the roar of the crowd whets your appetite, go for the swimmers' endorphin high. Check with a local swim facility as to swim clubs nearby that schedule workouts. Also consider Masters swimming. This is a competitive program for adults from ages 25 to 90 in five-year age groups. Meets are held locally, regionally, nationally, and internationally. For more information, contact United States Masters Swimming for a local affiliation. See Appendix B for information regarding competitive and other aquatic organizations.

Q: *I get to a certain point in my program and cannot make progress. What should I do?*

A: What you need is a pep talk, so here it is. View hitting a plateau as part of a bigger picture of swimming for fitness, with all the long-term benefits that were of interest initially. Dedication and self-discipline are needed with any long-term goal; time and energy are required to see progress. Maintain adequate sleep and proper nutrition.

Q: *Where can I find out more information about safety during SCUBA diving?*

A: Contact the Dive Alert Network, which is a source for the underwater diving industry. It provides medical research on concerns, such as avoiding decompression sickness and handling nitrogen absorption. Their address is 3100 Tower Boulevard, Suite 1300, Durham, NC 27707. Their phone number is 800-446-2671. They also have a phone specifically to give help in the event of a diving emergency: 919-684-1111.

Food for Thought—Eat to Swim

Q: *How many calories need to be consumed to lose weight or maintain a desired weight?*

A: This depends on several factors—age, activity level, health, individual metabolism. However, if over 21, approximate the required caloric intake by multiplying the desired weight by 15. For example, to maintain body weight of 120 pounds, daily caloric intake would be about 1,800 calories (120 × 15 = 1,800). Keep in mind that for a physically active person, the daily caloric intake should not drop below 1,200. Remember that exercise and dieting go hand in hand in weight reduction.

Q: *How can I calculate weight loss?*

A: There are 3,500 calories per pound of body weight. Weight loss can be obtained by eating 500 fewer calories a day and maintaining the same activity level. Eliminating 3,500 calories per week, the net weight loss for a year would be about 50 pounds. After doing WETs, metabolism is increased, which helps to burn more calories.

Q: *Why do I always drink a lot of water after swimming?*

A: Even though swimming feels like a "no sweat" activity, perspiration and dehydrating occur. Drink water before and after swimming. Even during the swim, drink water!

Q: *How should I adapt my eating schedule to the time of day I swim?*

A: **Sunrise Swimmer:** For an early-bird workout, have a light breakfast, perhaps consisting of two portions of carbohydrates, before swimming.

Liquid Luncher: If swimming during lunch but no chance to snack, have a substantial breakfast, say, two or three portions from starch foods, one protein, and one fruit.

Pre-Dinner Swimmer: Swimming before dinner but with no opportunity for an after-lunch snack, have both a substantial breakfast and lunch, with at least two starches and one protein for both breakfast and lunch.

Post-Dinner Swimmer: Swimming after the evening meal, have a substantial breakfast, lunch, and snacks so that supper can be reasonably light.

Rx

Q: *I have a back problem. What swim skills and strokes are best?*

A: The backstroke is most effective for helping to alleviate back concerns. It allows a comfortable position to be maintained for back support. Also try the sidestroke. Avoid the butterfly stroke entirely. Check with a physician.

Q: *I am a senior with a cardiac condition. How can I safely follow an aquatic fitness program?*

A: After checking with a doctor, slowly begin with Sweats to WETs—especially water walking. Then gradually increase the workout to include laps. Stop immediately if you are dizzy, short of breath, or cold.

Q: *I occasionally have shoulder and/or leg problems. How can I continue a water fitness program?*

A: If the upper body area, the shoulders, for instance, is causing difficulty, concentrate on lower body skills and WETs exercises—kicking while sitting on the edge of the pool, or use a kickboard on which to rest the arms and shoulders while kicking laps.

If the lower body (the knees, for instance) is causing difficulty, practice upper body arm skills and WETs using a pull-buoy to support the legs.

Q: *How can I choose and fit the perfect goggle?*

A: Goggles come in many shapes, sizes, materials, price ranges, as well as various colors, nosepieces, strap styles, and placements. They are also made with corrective lens of 1 to 9 diopters to correct near-sighted vision (Speedo®/Authentic Fitness). Swimmers may find particular seal materials (e.g., rubber, silicone, plastic) are most effective. When goggles are pressed to eyes and a slight suction effect occurs, they are probably a good fit. Place strap high on the crown of the head for most secure fit, wearing a cap underneath.

Q: *Sometimes I get a cramp. How can it be avoided?*

A: Most often a cramp occurs when kicking too hard, or swimming before doing warm-ups. A leg cramp occurs most often in the calf muscle. If you feel a cramp coming on, stop at once and release the contracting fibers by applying direct pressure with a fist to the affected area, and quickly release pressure. Repeat until the cramp has subsided.

Q: *I know I'm not in shape, but I get winded very fast when I swim. Am I doing something wrong?*

A: First, warm up for at least five minutes. Also, a lot of people who are just beginning to swim seriously tend to overkick, that is, they try to get more propulsion from their leg movement than proper swimming is designed to provide. If overkicking, the large muscles in the legs are consuming a lot of oxygen; therefore, a person tires quickly. Since most swim strokes are done from the upper body, concentrate on getting speed from the arms and shoulders and train the legs to do less, especially with crawlstroke.

Q: *My timing in the rhythmic breathing of the crawlstroke seems to be off. What can I do?*

A: Concentrate on exhaling underwater by turning the head past the midline of the body. This also gives more time to exhale and helps to even out the body roll, balancing the stroke.

Special Concerns

Q: *Is it possible to alter the proportions of my body using this program?*

A: It is very difficult to change one's body proportions; they are a birthright. What you can do is work toward a redistribution of body weight. Understand, too, that exercise may increase body weight at the same time it decreases the amount of fat carried in the body, because muscle weighs more than fat. You will look trimmer even though there may not be an appreciable difference in weight. This swim program, done consistently and in conjunction with a sensible eating regimen, will help burn up fat, build muscle tone, and achieve weight loss.

Q: *I do a swim workout regularly, but I am planning to become pregnant soon. Should I continue to swim during my pregnancy?*

A: After obtaining a doctor's approval, continue swimming regularly but avoid overexertion. This program, which combines laps and water exercises, will help make pregnancy more comfortable and enjoyable. It will keep muscles supple and strong, helping prepare for labor and delivery.

Q: *I have arthritis. Should I follow this program?*

A: Yes, but first, see a doctor before beginning. With a physician's approval, slowly start with the Sweats to WETs warm-up/cool-down exercises. Gently stretch muscles and increase circulation to joints. In the water there is almost no impact on stressed areas of body. Move on to laps.

Q: *Many sports have a hall of fame to honor their notable achievers and accomplishments. Is there one for aquatics?*

A: Yes. The International Swimming Hall of Fame (ISHOF) in Fort Lauderdale, Florida, includes men and women from all branches of aquatics. The complex contains the Henning Aquatic Library with swimming archives and a complete bookstore and swim shop. The hall of fame also runs swim training camps at its Olympic pool.

The International Swimming Hall of Fame has branched out into Asia and Europe. Its goal by the twenty-first century is to have an ISHOF satellite on five continents.

Q: *Is rest important in training?*

A: Yes, rest is definitely important in training, whether learning to swim or as an Olympic hopeful. An instructor or coach will help create a workable program around rest and relaxation and training.

Q: *What is the future of aquatics?*

A: In 1995, the National Aquatic Summit conferred, bringing together over 60 organizations representing 100 million Americans involved in aquatic sports. It endorsed the goal of "Every American a Swimmer for Life."

Appendix A

Personal Record

Skill Progression Checklist

Week	Dates/Days	Skills	Pages	Comments
1	______	Introduction		______
2	______	______	______	______
3	______	______	______	______
4	______	______	______	______
5	______	______	______	______
6	______	______	______	______
7	______	______	______	______
8	______	______	______	______
9	______	______	______	______
10	______	______	______	______
11	______	______	______	______
12	______	______	______	______
13	______	______	______	______
14	______	______	______	______
15	______	______	______	______

Pool Data

Equipment Checklist

_____ Swimsuit

_____ Goggles

_____ Cap

_____ Towel

_____ Aquatic shoes

_____ Plastic bag

_____ Shower amenities

Additional Information

Pool location: ______________________________

Locker # ______________________________

Key # ______________________________

Emergency contact # ______________________________

Pool Hours: ______________________________

Pool Fees: ______________________________

Swim Calendar

Month	Monday	Tuesday	Wednesday	Thursday	Friday	Saturday

Heart Rate Record Chart

Week	Date(s)	Warm-Up	Aquatic Main Set	Cool-Down	Comments (e.g., Distance, Time)
1					
2					
3					
4					
5					
6					
7					
8					
9					
10					
11					
12					
13					
14					
15					

Create Your Own Workout Chart

Warm-Up (Sweats to WETs) ______________________________

Main Set

WET Drills ______________________________

Distance/(in laps/time) ______________________________

Optional:

Timed swim/pulse check ______________________________

Cool-Down (Sweats to WETs) ______________________________

Aquatic Completion Certificate

Congratulations to

____

name

Has Completed

____

class/level

At

____

facility/college

____________________ ____________________

Date Instructor's Signature

Appendix B

Sources of Aquatic Information

Supplier/ Manufacturers

AARDVARK SWIM AND SPORT
14101 Sullyfield Cr. #220
Chantilly, VA 22021
(800) 729-1577

AFA, INC.
aquarobics™
Box 5752
Greenville, SC 29606
(Specialists in Water Fitness and Recreational Therapy Flotation Products)
(803) 877-8428

AQUA-JOGGER
Excel Sports Science, Inc.
Suite 100
450 West 5th Avenue
Eugene, OR 97401
(800) 922-9544

AQUASOURCE INTERNATIONAL
5509 North Rockwell
Bethany, OK 73008-2051
(800) 728-4157

ARENA, N.A.
6900 South Peoria Street
Englewood, CO 80112
(800) 685-6988

BARRACUDA SPORTS PRODUCTS
Skyline N.W. Inc.
0224 S. W. Hamilton Street
Portland, OR 97201
(800) 547-8664

BIOENERGETICS
WET VEST
5074 Shelby Drive
Birmingham, AL 35243
(800) 433-2627

COMPETITIVE AQUATIC SUPPLY
15131 Triton Lane
Suite 110
Huntington Beach, CA 92649
(800) 421-5192

COMPETITOR SWIM PRODUCTS
910 Lake Road
Medina, OH 44256
(216) 725-4997

DACOR
(Diving and Snorkeling equipment)
161 Northfield Road
Northfield, IL 60093
(708) 446-9555

DOLPHIN INT'L CORP.
P.O. Box 98
Shillington, PA 19607
(800) 441-0818

FINALS SWIMWEAR
1466 Bwy. #500
N.Y., N.Y. 10036
(800) 345-3485

FORCE FINS
28 Anacapa Street
Santa Barbara, CA 93101
1-800-FIN-SWIM

GULBENKIAN SWIM, INC.
70 Memorial Plaza
Pleasantville, NY 10570
(800) 431-2586

HIND CORPORATION
3765 South Higuera
San Luis Obispo, CA 93401
(800) 235-4150

HYDRO-FIT AQUATIC FITNESS GEAR
440 Charnelton Street
Eugene, OR 97401
(800) 346-7295

HYDRO-TONE FITNESS SYSTEMS
16691 Gothard Street, Suite M
Huntington Beach, CA 92647
(800) 622-8663

INT'L SWIMMING HALL OF FAME MAIL ORDER COMPANY
5755 Powerline Road
Ft. Lauderdale, FL 33309-2074
(800) 431-9111

J & B FOAM FABRICATORS, INC.
(Water Exercise Equipment)
P.O. Box 144
Ludington, MI 49431
(800) 621-3626

JD PENCE AQUATIC SUPPLY
3139 Pacific Avenue
Forest Grove, OR 97116
(800) 547 2520

KAST-A-WAY SWIMWEAR
9356 Cincinnati/Columbus Road
Route 42
Cincinnati, OH 45241
(800) 543-2763

KIEFER INC.
1700 Kiefer Drive
Zion, IL 60099
(800) 323-4071

LESLIE'S SWIM & POOL SUPPLIES
20222 Plummer Street
Chatsworth, CA 91311
800 233-8063

LINCOLN EQUIPMENT, INC.
2051 Commerce Avenue
Concord, CA 94520
(510) 687-9500

METRO SWIM SHOP
1221 Valley Road
Stirling, NJ 07980
(800) 526 8788

NIKE SWIMWEAR
(Jantzen, Inc., Authorized Licensee of Nike Swimwear)
P.O. Box 5959
Portland, OR 97228
(800) 828 2393

NORCAL SWIM SHOP
2449 2nd Street
Napa, CA 94559
1-800-752-SWIM

NZ MANUFACTURING
Stretch cords for swim training
7405 S. 212th Street #125
Kent, WA 98032
(206) 872-9779

RECREONICS, INC.
4200 Schmitt Avenue
Louisville, KY 40213
(800) 428-3254

SPEEDO® AUTHENTIC FITNESS CORP
6040 Bandini Blvd.
Los Angeles, CA 90040
(800) 547-8770
(800) 5-SPEEDO

SPRINT-ROTHHAMMER INT'L, INC.
P.O. Box 5579
Santa Maria, CA 93456
(800) 235-2156

SPORTWIDE, INC.
P.O. Box 16134
San Luis Obispo, CA 93406-6134
(805) 544-9350

SWIMSKIN
675 Forest Avenue
Portland, ME 04103
(800) 341-0246

SWIM ZONE
918 4th Street North
St. Petersburg, FL 33701
(800) 329-0013

TURBO, INC.
216 Oxford Hills Drive
Chapel Hill, NC 27514
(919) 967-6715

TYR SPORT
P.O. Box 1930
Huntington Beach, CA 92649
(714) 897-0799

THE VICTOR
P.O. Box 4400
Miami Lakes, FL 33014
(800) 356-5132

WATERMARK TRAINING EQUIPMENT, INC.
2810 "A" Academy Drive
Auburn, WA 98092
(800) 939-5510

WATERWEAR
P.O. Box 687
Wilton, NH 03086
(603) 654-9885

WORLD WIDE AQUATICS
10500 University Center Drive
Suite 250
Tampa, FL 33612
(800) 726-1530

ZOOMERS
(Fins for swim training)
926 Washington Street
San Carlos, CA 94070
(415) 591-4097

ZURA SPORTS
975 Eastwind Drive, Suite 150
Westerville, OH 43081
(800) 890-3009

Publications/Aquatic Magazines

AQUATICS INTERNATIONAL MAGAZINE
Argus Publications
6151 Powers Ferry Road
Atlanta, GA 30339
(770) 955-2500

FITNESS SWIMMER MAGAZINE
P.O. Box 7420
Red Oak, IA 51591-2420
(800) 846-0086

INSIDE TRIATHLON
1830 North 55th Street
Boulder, CO 80301
(303) 440-0601

MASTERSSPORTS MAGAZINE
400 East 85th Street
New York, NY 10028
(212) 535-7550

POOL AND SPA NEWS
Leisure Publications
3923 West 6th Street
Los Angeles, CA 90020
(213) 385-3926

SCUBA DIVING
33 E. Minor Street
Emmaus, PA
(800) 666-0016

SPORTS PUBLICATIONS, INC.
(Publishers of: SWIM MAGAZINE, SWIMMING WORLD MAGAZINE, and SWIM TECHNIQUE MAGAZINE)
228 Nevada Street
El Segundo, CA 90245
(310) 607-9956

TAPER AND SHAVE
(Elite and NCAA Swimming Newsletter)
(916) 272-4662

TRIATHLETE
121 Second Street
San Francisco, CA 94105
(800) 441-1666

TRIATHLON FEDERATION/USA
P.O. Box 15820
Colorado Springs, CO 80935-5820
(719) 597-9090

WORLD AQUATIC NEWS AND TRAVEL
P.O. Box 70366
Pasadena, CA 91117
(818) 793-2582

Swimming/Aquatic Organizations

AAHPERD
American Alliance for Health, Physical Education, Recreation and Dance—Aquatic Council
1900 Association Drive
Reston, VA 22091
(703) 476-3400

AMATEUR ATHLETIC UNION OF THE U.S.
3400 West 86th Street
Indianapolis, IN 46268
(317) 872-8680

AMERICAN NATIONAL RED CROSS
8111 Gatehouse Road
Falls Church, VA 22042
(800) 667-2968
or your local ARC chapter

AMERICAN SWIMMING COACHES ASSOCIATION
304 S. E. 20th Street
Fort Lauderdale, FL 33316
(305) 462-6267
(800) 356-2722

ARTHRITIS FOUNDATION, NATIONAL OFFICE
1330 West Peachtree Street
Atlanta, GA 30309
(800) 283-7800

AQUATIC EXERCISE ASSOCIATION
902 Albee Road, #2
Nokomis, FL 34275
(813) 486-8600

AQUATIC THERAPY AND REHABILITATION INSTITUTE
1032 So. Spring Street
Port Washington, WI 53074
(414) 284-3663

COUNCIL FOR NATIONAL COOPERATION IN AQUATICS
P.O. Box 26268
Indianapolis, IN 46226
(317) 546-5108

F.I.N.A. FÉDERATION INTERNATIONALE DE NATATION AMATEUR
U.S. Address
425 Walnut Street
Suite 1610
Cincinnati, OH 45202
(513) 381-2793

FÉDERATION INTERNATIONALE DE NATATION AMATEUR
International Address
c/o FINA
9 ave de Beaumont
Lausanne, Switzerland
41-21-312-6610

INTERNATIONAL SWIMMING HALL OF FAME WORLD HEADQUARTERS
1 Hall of Fame Drive
Fort Lauderdale, FL 33316
(305) 462-6536

JEWISH COMMUNITY CENTER ASSOCIATION OF NORTH AMERICA
15 East 26th Street
New York, NY 10010
(212) 532-4949

NATIONAL ASSOCIATION OF UNDERWATER INSTRUCTORS
4650 Arrow Highway
Suite F-1
Montclair, CA 91763-1150
(800) 553-6284

NATIONAL COLLEGIATE ATHLETIC ASSOCIATION
6201 College Blvd.
Overland Park, KS 66211
(913) 339-1906

NATIONAL RECREATION AND PARK ASSOCIATION
Aquatics Section
650 West Higgins Road
Hoffman Estates, IL 60195
(800) 677-2236

NATIONAL SAFETY COUNCIL, AQUATICS
Ellis and Associates
1121 Spring Lake Drive
Itasca, IL 60143
(800) 621-6244

NATIONAL SPA AND POOL INSTITUTE
2111 Eisenhower Avenue
Alexandria, VA 22314
(703) 838-0083

NATIONAL SWIM SCHOOL ASSOCIATION
776 21st Avenue North
St. Petersburg, FL 33704-3348
(813) 896-7946

POLAR BEAR CLUB-U.S.A.
376 Naughton Avenue
Staten Island, NY 10305
(718) 979-8370

PROFESSIONAL ASSOCIATION OF DIVING INSTRUCTORS (PADI)
1251 East Dyer Road, #100
Santa Ana, CA 92705
(714) 540-7234

PRESIDENT'S COUNCIL ON PHYSICAL FITNESS AND SPORTS
701 Pennsylvania Avenue
Suite 250
Washington, DC 20004
(202) 272-3421

SCUBA SCHOOLS INTERNATIONAL/SSI
2619 Canton Ct.
Fort Collins, CO 80525-4498
(303) 482-0883

SPECIAL OLYMPICS
1325 G Street N.W.
Washington, DC 20005
(202) 628-3630

UNDERWATER SOCIETY OF AMERICA
Fin Swimming
P.O. Box 628
Daly City, CA 94017
(415) 583-8492

U.S. DIVING, INC.
201 S. Capitol Avenue
Suite 430
Indianapolis, IN 46225
(317) 237-5252

U.S. MASTERS SWIMMING, INC.
2 Peters Avenue
Rutland, MA 01549
(508) 886-6631

U.S. SWIMMING, INC.
One Olympic Plaza
Colorado Springs, CO 80909
(719) 578-4578

UNITED STATES SYNCHRONIZED SWIMMING, INC.
Pan Am Plaza
Suite 510
201 South Capitol Street
Indianapolis, IN 46225
(317) 237-5700

UNITED STATES WATER POLO, INC.
Pan Am Plaza
Suite 520
201 South Capitol Street
Indianapolis, IN 46225
(317) 237-5599

UNITED STATES WATER FITNESS ASSOCIATION
P.O. Box 3601333
Boynton Beach, FL 33436
(407) 732-9908

WORLD WATERPARK ASSOCIATION
P.O. Box 14826
Lanexa, KS 66285-4826
(903) 599-0300

YMCA OF THE U.S.A.
101 N. Wacker Drive
Chicago, IL 60606
(312) 977-0031
(800) USA-YMCA

YOUNG WOMEN'S CHRISTIAN ASSOCIATION OF THE U.S.A.
726 Broadway
New York, NY 10003
(212) 614-2700

Health and Nutrition Sources

AMERICAN COLLEGE OF SPORTS MEDICINE
P.O. Box 1440
Indianapolis, IN 46206
(317) 637-9200

AMERICAN HEART ASSOCIATION
7320 Greenville Avenue
Dallas, TX 75231
(214) 750-5300

AMERICAN MEDICAL ASSOCIATION
535 North Dearborn Street
Chicago, IL 60610
(312) 464-5000

UNITED STATES FOOD AND DRUG ADMINISTRATION
5600 Fishers Lane
Rockville, MD 20852
(301) 443-3170

Canadian Aquatic Organizations

AQUATIC HALL OF FAME AND MUSEUM OF CANADA
Sub. of Aquatic Federation of Canada
600-330 Portage Avenue
Winnipeg, Manitoba
Canada R3C 0C4
(204) 956-0490

CANADIAN AMATEUR DIVING ASSOCIATION
1600 James Naismith Drive
Gloucester, Ontario
Canada K1B 5N4
(613) 748-5631

CANADIAN AMATEUR SYNCHRONIZED SWIMMING ASSOCIATION
1600 James Naismith Drive
Gloucester, Ontario
Canada K1B 5N4
(613) 748-5674

SWIMMING/NATATION CANADA
1600 James Naismith Drive
Gloucester, Ontario
Canada K1B 5N4
(613) 748-5615

Electronic Systems and Aquatic Software

AQUATICA
Aquatic InterNet Information
515 Seabreeze Blvd.,
Suite 1000
Fort Lauderdale,
FL 33316-1623
(305) 922-1899

COLORADO TIME SYSTEMS
1551 East 11th Street
Loveland, CO 80537
(800) 279-0111

DAKTRONICS, INC.
331 32nd Avenue
Brookings, SD 57006-5128
(605) 697-4300

HY-TEK SWIM SOFTWARE SYSTEM
P.O. Box 12789
New Bern, NC 28551
(919) 633-5111

INTERNATIONAL SPORTS TIMING
Swim scoreboard and software
3286 Kentland Ct. SE
Grand Rapids, MI 49548
(800) 835-2611

POLAR HEART MONITOR
99 Seaview Boulevard
Port Washington, NY 11058
(800) 743-9248

ULTRA COACH
9635 Monte Vista Avenue
Suite 201
Montclair, CA 91763
(800) 400-1390

Strength Training/ Special Needs— Lifts and Large Equipment

AQUACISER, INC.
Underwater treadmill
953 So. Frontage Road West
Suite 204
Vail, CO 81657
(800) 825-8798

AQUATIC ACCESS , INC.
Water power lifts, etc.
417 Dorsey Way
Louisville, KY 40223
800-325-LIFT

AQUATRENDS
Water Workout Station
649 U.S. Highway One,
Suite 14
North Palm Beach, FL 33408
(407) 844-3003

AQUATIC ADVANTAGE
Bench for swim stroke simulation
1434 Cola Drive
McLean, VA 22101
(800) 666-6997

ARJO, INC.
8130 Lehigh Avenue
Morton Grove, IL 60053
(800) 323-1245

DELPHIS SWIM PRODUCTS
Coach Scope—underwater video
P.O. Box 242
Carpinteria, CA 93014
(800) 762-6801

EXER-GENIE
Portable swim stroke simulator
680 Paseo Vista
Thousand Oaks, CA 91320
(805) 499-4861

FINIS MONOFINS
700 Beaver Court
Discovery Bay, CA 94514
(510) 516-1359

HORTON PRODUCTS COMPANY
Horton Safe-Lift: pool access machine for disabled or injured
P.O. Box 36277
Pensacola, FL 32516
1-800-SAF-LIFT

KDI PARAGON
Competition starting platforms
12 Paulding Street
Pleasantville, NY 10570
(914) 769-6221

MARINE RESCUE PRODUCTS, INC.
P.O. Box 3484
Newport, RI 02840
(800) 341 9500

REHAB SYSTEMS
Swim-Step™ Pool Access System
3481 South University Drive
Fargo, ND 58103
(800) 726-8620

SPECTRUM POOL ACCESS
Lifts and safety ladders, ramps
9600 Inspiration Drive
Missoula, MT 59802
(800) 776-5309

SUITMATE EXTRACTOR CORP.
705 Martin Drive
P.O. Box 99
South Elgin, IL 60177
(800) 553-3353

SUPER SWIM CORP.
Deck-based tethered swim system
10711 Deer Run Farms Road
Ft. Myers, FL 33912
(800) 848-1222

TRIAD TECHNOLOGIES, INC.
Deck storage for aquatic fitness products
219 Lamson Street
Syracuse, NY 13206
(315) 437-4089

VASA SWIM TRAINER
12 Winter Sport Lane
Williston, VT 05495
(800) 488-VASA

WATER SAFETY PRODUCTS, INC.
P.O. Box 510861
Melbourne, FL 32951
(800) 987-7238

Index

Notes

Notes